THEODORE DREISER

AND THE SOVIET UNION

1927-1945

A FIRST-HAND CHRONICLE

by Ruth Epperson Kennell

INTERNATIONAL PUBLISHERS
New York

ACKNOWLEDGMENTS

To my helpmate, Frank Risley Kennell, who revised, corrected and indexed the book, which he called "stoop labor." His firm hand kept me at this task when my cats, my garden and my social crusades called me.

To the reference desks at the Palo Alto Public Library, the Hoover Institution and the Stanford University Library.

For the use of extracts from copyright material to: Harold J. Dies, trustee for the Dreiser Trust, from *Dreiser Looks at Russia* and *Hoosier Holiday*, and from *My Life with Dreiser* by Helen Dreiser. World Publishing Co., from Dreiser's *Color of a Great City. The New Yorker* for 14 lines from the poem, "Greetings, Friends," by Frank Sullivan, Dec. 24, 1938, copr. c 1938, 1966 by The New Yorker Magazine, Inc. *The New Republic*, from John Dos Passos' report on the Harlan miners' strike, Dec. 2, 1931. Doubleday & Co., from *Scottsboro Boy* by Haywood Patterson, 1950. *Chattanooga News Free Press*, from editorial, Oct. 30, 1939. *The Saturday Review*, from reviews by Granville Hicks of *America Is Worth Saving*, February. 22, 1941, and of Swanberg's biography of Dreiser, Apr. 24, 1965, *Saturday Review of Literature;* and from John Barkman's review of *Part of the Truth* by Granville Hicks in 1965 Saturday Review Services for Newspapers. Monthly Review Press, from *American Radicals*, 1957, John Lydenberg's essay, "Ishmael in the Jungle." North American Newspaper Alliance, from a series of articles on his Russian tour by Theodore Dreiser, 1928.

To the Memory of

SERGEY DINAMOV

1901-1939

A beloved friend of Theodore Dreiser during his stay in Moscow, and thereafter, the young literary critic wrote many articles and scholarly essays on the works of the American novelist. He edited the first Soviet edition of Dreiser's collected works (1928-1930.)

Son of a working class mother, a Bolshevik, who was one of the first deputies to the Moscow Soviet, young Sergey served in the Red Army during the Civil War. Before his untimely death, he had become director of the Institute of Red Professors.

Sergey Dinamov occupied an important place in the period of Dreiser's life recorded in these pages. I am proud to dedicate what I have written to his memory, as Theodore Dreiser would have wished.

Author's Foreword

For twenty years after the death of Theodore Dreiser, the material in these pages which I had considered confidential during his lifetime, remained in my files. This, despite the suggestion of Helen Dreiser in a letter to me, October 9, 1946:

"I think it would be wonderful if you wrote something about your trip in Russia in '27-'28.... But I would like to talk to you at length about the whole thing." She died before plans for a meeting in New York could be realized.

We were well into the turbulent '60s when I finally resolved to prepare my material for publication. The country was still suffering from the consequences of the Cold War which had started a few weeks after Dreiser's death on December 28, 1945. Winston Churchill's speech at Fulton, Missouri, on February 3, 1946, had launched the nation on this disastrous path. Its immediate effect was to cool the warm feelings of the American people toward our Russian ally, and to stop all aid to Russia in rebuilding its shattered economy.

Churchill's double-dealing at Fulton would not have surprised Dreiser. He had noted, when he cabled his support to the Red Army after the invasion, "how England for her own preservation comes to the aid of Russia." He had denounced the "phony war," and later, the delay in opening a Second Front as devices to deceive public opinion and exhaust Soviet military and economic strength.

The political results of Churchill's speech were the Truman Doctrine and the "containment of communism" policy of John Foster Dulles. After Korea and other U. S. military adventures since 1946, it finally led us into the Vietnam quagmire.

In the longer view, two generations of students have been brainwashed. Their textbooks have been purged of meaningful facts about the Russian Revolution, the causes of World War II, and the decisive role of the Red Army in our common vic-

7

tory. Nevertheless, as our drafted armies sank deeper into the Vietnam morass, and mass protests spread, demonstrations on the campus and uprisings in the ghetto began. Students resisted the draft and rebelled against the irrelevance of the school curriculum and its acceptance of militarism and racism. A militant minority began to resort to direct action, feeling the urge to tear down our corrupted institutions without pausing to study the causes, and make plans for rebuilding them.

There may be a timely message for our rebellious youth and their troubled elders in these pages. My documented account of what Theodore Dreiser saw of the Bolshevik Revolution on its tenth anniversary, and his maturing understanding of its significance should be useful to serious readers. Fresh data, however controversial, about a man who became an important part of our era, are of value. Our young people are today custodians of the mounting revolt against the senseless savagery of U. S. military adventurism abroad and an emerging police state at home.

When Theodore Dreiser went to the Soviet Union in 1927 as a guest of the government, it was a critical period in the gigantic task of building a socialist society in a hostile capitalist world. The New Economic Policy had been adopted as a temporary measure to ease the transition process. It had to be terminated because private traders and the old kulak (rich peasant) class were becoming too strong.

A bitter controversy between two blocs, led by Trotsky and Stalin, threatened the very existence of the Soviet power. What should be the new party line, especially in agriculture?

Although this was confusing to Dreiser, in his interviews with political and industrial leaders he asked shrewd questions concerning the social and economic conditions of the country ten years after the revolution. His boastful loyalty to American capitalism — as the chronicler of its phenomenal industrial development — and his doubts about the new Soviet system met with good-natured and patient response. The guest's temperamental reactions gyrated between, "These dubs couldn't run a peanut stand," and extravagant praise, such as his impulsive declaration to Sergey Eisenstein, the famous film director:

"I predict that in thirty years Russia will lead the world." He did not live to see the Soviet Union orbit Sputnik I, in exactly thirty years, on October 4, 1957.

It was quite by accident that I became Theodore Dreiser's secretary. My husband and I had come to the Soviet Union in August 1922, with a group of technicians and skilled workers in the Industrial Colony Kuzbas which had undertaken the rehabilitation of the coal mines and completion of the chemical plant in Kuznetsk Basin in Siberia. After finishing our two-year contract, Frank went to Tomsk to teach in the Institute of Technology and I to Moscow to do library work on the recommendation of Kuzbas director, S. J. Rutgers. That summer Frank, who was recuperating from a serious injury in Tomsk, came to Moscow and took our six-year-old son with him to England. His mother had rented a seashore cottage and I planned to join them as soon as possible. My unexpected involvement in the Dreiser tour delayed our re-union.

I kept a diary on the 77-day tour for my employer, my own composition, and made a carbon for myself at his request, since he expected me to help him later with his material. This 50,000 word chronicle is my main source of data for Part One.

I am a story-teller, but the story of Dreiser's tour needs no artful embellishments. It has all the necessary elements — conflict, suspense, humor and pathos, hardships and danger, snowbound trains, wrecks, an earthquake and a brush with death. He was ill with bronchitis when he arrived in Moscow. A Berlin doctor had warned him that he might not survive a winter tour. Against the advice of his hosts, he insisted upon a private tour and his own secretary, and upon an itinerary which sometimes would take him away from the main rail lines and through regions recently ravaged by civil war, famine and pestilence.

Still under the spell of America's high industrial development and the prosperity of the Coolidge boom, he expressed his impatience at the low standard of living and low stage of industrial development. It annoyed him to be reminded of the causes for this by the two women who accompanied him — a "contentious" young secretary and an official guide. His compassionate nature was outraged by the sight of a homeless child, or "these huddled masses." Arriving in Odessa, after an uncomfortable voyage, he cried out with childish finality: "I'd rather die in America than live here!" In his first letter to me, he exulted over Paris, "warm and bright." Naturally, these were the immediate reactions of a highly impressionable man to passing discomforts, especially when ill. A creative writer needs to be thin-skinned, sensitive to his environment.

On the other hand, the "Father of American Realism" was sometimes warm in his praise. His dry humor delighted the Russians, whose sense of humor is so much like ours. I appreciated especially his sense of the ridiculous and admired his perseverance. In spite of physical hardships and outraged feelings, he insisted upon continuing the tour in order to see for himself "what these Russians are up to," and report his findings to a waiting homeland.

If illness had not prevented his accepting the government's invitation in 1936 to visit the Soviet Union again, to see what they had accomplished in the eight years since he was there, he would have been pleased to find living and travel conditions greatly improved.

In 1946, had he been alive, he might have been invited to come and see what the Germans had done to the places he had visited 15 years before. That would have been a quite different picture.

In Yasnaya Polyana, for example, the Nazi troops had occupied the whole area, had burned the new Tolstoy school, partially destroyed Tolstoy's home, and desecrated his grave.

In Leningrad, which he had admired above all cities, he would have found the heroic survivors of the 900-day siege, during which close to a million people had perished from starvation, shellings and bombings. Fine old buildings which had been damaged were being restored by the dedicated labors of the younger generation.

In Kiev, the ancient cultural center of the Ukraine, he would have been outraged at the destruction of historic places, and at Babi Yar, the ravine where the Nazis slaughtered 100,000 Jews.

In Kharkov where he had viewed the splendid new civic center under construction and had predicted that in ten years it would be a Ukrainian Chicago, what would he have found 15 years later? The skyscrapers burned out or mined by the retreating Germans; half the 900,000 population gone, 120,000 young deported to Germany for slave labor, 160,000 Jews killed.

In Stalino, coal mining center of the Donetz Basin, which he had found so "alive," he would have seen the wreckage of factories and coal mines left by the Germans as they fled. Their efforts to exploit the coal had failed because of the stubborn passive resistance of the population.

Today, a quarter century after this widespread devastation in all the places he had visited on his tour, Dreiser would have been delighted to find the ravaged places completely restored, and vast, new industrial and cultural development everywhere. There is still a shortage of housing, but it takes a long time to replace housing for 25 million homeless people. Forty years after Dreiser's tour, the USSR, surviving the most catastrophic destruction in human history, is recognized as one of the two greatest world powers. Their socialist society provides a standard of living for all the people approaching the level of an average American middle class family — with no extremes of wealth or poverty.

Part Two opens with the pilgrim's homecoming, in February 1928. At the pier in New York he spoke warmly to the swarm of reporters of the things he liked in Soviet Russia. Publishers were soon pressing him for articles and books. His syndicated NANA articles were already in print. Much too soon, he was pouring out his priceless, undigested material. In order to meet the publisher's deadline, he hastily put together the book, *Dreiser Looks at Russia*, the chapters arranged by subjects, with pretentious headings, but shallow, often uninformed content; for example, "Communism — Theory and Practice." In an effort to be objective, he contradicted himself repeatedly. Only a few quotes here and there indicated that he ever consulted the diary. He could have used its chronological order and expanded its contents to make a lively, informative travelogue.

It is obvious that I do not idealize the hero of my story. I have tried to present him exactly as I knew him. But his human frailties appear unimportant before his monumental works. His realistic novels and short stories of earlier years were followed during the last 17 years of his life by eloquent pamphleteering. He protested legal injustice, fought for the rights of labor, denounced British imperialism and exposed the "inequities" of the American Establishment. In his last years, he offered the Soviet system as an alternative: "Now no longer an experiment but a proved success, affecting the health, education and social welfare of 200 million people. . . working one for all and all for one."

American critics belittled Dreiser's social tracts, although the art of pamphleteering has an honored place in the works of great writers: for example, Milton's *Defense of a Free Press,* and Zola's *J'Accuse.* Dreiser's critics complained that he had "forsaken the novel for the soap box."

My source material for Part Two consists of scores of his handwritten letters to me during the years after the tour, up to a few days before his death, and carbon copies of some of my replies. He sent me press clippings, his published and unpublished articles, pamphlets and books. He welcomed my comments.

Since his death the writings of Theodore Dreiser, even the earlier novels on which his fame rests, have received scant attention. Not one American edition of his complete works has yet been published. On the other hand, in the Soviet Union, the editor of *Soviet Life*, Prokofy Begunov, wrote me (August 20, 1966):

"There is a great demand in our country for Theodore Dreiser's books. His works have appeared in the period of Soviet power in 15 languages (of the USSR) in 150 printings aggregating over 12 million copies. Eleven of these editions have been reprinted in English in the USSR. The last 12-volume edition of Dreiser's works came out in 200,000 copies."

In 1969, Theodore Dreiser was one of the three most widely read American authors in the Soviet Union: Mark Twain, Jack London, Theodore Dreiser. Young and old are familiar with his books. His wide popularity among this cultured, socially enlightened people afforded him deep comfort during the last years of his life.

Dreiser never regretted that he chose to be in the right with two or three — the minority who pass on the germs of ideas which ultimately prevail. I believe that the last eighteen years of his life gave him more spiritual satisfaction and more zest for living than he had ever known. Theodore Dreiser had found himself.

Palo Alto, California　　　　　RUTH EPPERSON KENNELL
April 19, 1969

NOTE: The documents upon which this book is based are deposited in the Dreiser Archives of the University of Pennsylvania Library. Facsimiles have been sent to the Institute of World Literature in Moscow.

Oct. 9, 1946.

Dear Ruth Krunnell:

Thank you very much
for your letter. It was very
interesting to me.

I think it would be
wonderful if you wrote something about your trip
in Russia — in 27. 28.
It is true that Mr. Dreiser
wrote very little about that
part of his journey, and it

~~~~~~~~~~~~~~~

With sincere Regards

Helen Dreiser

Excerpt from Helen Dreiser's letter to the Author, urging her to write a
book about Dreiser's journey.

Contents

APPENDIX 309

Stalino, Donetz Basin, Dec. 19, 1927. *Left to right:* l'Etienne, a Latvian, chief district agronomist; Dr. SophiaDavidovskaya; Dreiser, Ruth Kennell and local guide

PART ONE

The Russian Tour

November 1927-January 1928

(Top left) Sergey Dinamov, editor of Dreiser's works in Russian. *(Top right)* "A Soviet Bookman" — a friendly caricature of Khalatov, head of the State Publishing House, by Deni. *(Bottom right)* "Gaika" — Tiflis Councilman. *(Bottom left)* May O'Callaghan ("OC").

CHAPTER I

MOSCOW

1. Dreiser Resists a Conducted Tour

On an evening in early November, the young editor of the Anglo-American section of the State Publishing House was taking me to the Grand Hotel to meet one of the distinguished guests of the Soviet Government.

We walked briskly down the Tverskaya (now Gorky Street) from the Lux Hotel for foreign workers. Long red streamers on every building glowed through the falling flakes of winter's first snow. The crowds on the broad avenue which led into Red Square were smiling and hopeful. After the hard years of World War I, revolution, civil war, famine and pestilence, the Russian people were celebrating the tenth anniversary of their revolution.

Tall, gaunt Sergey Dinamov tapped on the door of a palatial suite. A soft, youthful voice called, "Come right in."

Theodore Dreiser sat at a carved table on a brocaded white satin sofa playing solitaire. Soft white hair above a lofty brow made him look older than his 56 years. His searching gray eyes, a slight cast in one, surveyed me with lively curiosity. He began to question me brusquely.

"Who's this? An American girl—from Oklahoma! You've been in Russia *five* years! What the devil are you doing here?"

Dinamov tried to explain in halting English that I was helping him edit anniversary editions of American writers. "And now she writes the prefaces for your books...."

But the Grand Old Man of American Realism continued to prod me relentlessly. I uneasily recalled lines in his foreword to *Color of a Great City:*

"I was never weary of spying out how the other fellow lived and how he made his way."

21

It was this insatiable curiosity which had brought him to the country which was building the first socialist economy.

As we were leaving, he confided dryly, "A Berlin doctor warned me that I might not survive a winter tour of Russia, but I'm going to find out what these Russians are up to if it kills me."

He put his arm around the thin shoulders of the somewhat crestfallen editor of his books. "We'll get together later, young man."

I hurried back to my room on the third floor of the Hotel Lux. A page of the first draft of my preface to Dreiser's volume of short stories, *Chains*, was in the typewriter. I had left it suddenly when Sergey Dinamov had burst in with the exciting news, "Drayzer een Moskva!"

Now that I had met the author, I reread what I had written about him: "a cosmic philosopher, brooding over a world of puny human beings from an impersonal height, he records their petty tragedies and everyday experiences with patient minuteness and merciless exactness."

So here I was, another puny human being for the great realist to analyze. "But first I'll analyze him," I vowed, sitting down at the Corona in the drab room. I worked till midnight finishing the six-page preface to *Chains,* which was being rushed to press. (Its colorful jacket was designed by Hugo Gellert, who was in Moscow for the tenth anniversary celebrations.)

In *Dreiser Looks at Russia* (Liveright, 1928), published later in Moscow with my preface, Theodore Dreiser explained why he had decided, reluctantly, to come to the Soviet Union:

"While it is known that I am an incorrigible individualist — therefore opposed to communism — the Soviet Government invited me to visit Russia to investigate conditions there, and I accepted on my own terms. . . . I spent 11 weeks there."

Alert to propaganda, he was suspicious of the Russians. On the following day, after my first meeting with him, Scott Nearing, one of the American delegation to the anniversary celebration, came to see me at the Lux Hotel. He said he had found Dreiser sitting in his suite drinking vodka and in a bad mood. "He threatened to leave," Professor Nearing announced.

I asked what in the world was wrong. It seemed that the celebrated individualist had balked at being entertained collectively. He wanted to explore on his own, see what he wanted to see, have his own secretary and interpreter who was "not a Russian lackey."

"I think he has you in mind," Professor Nearing concluded, with a quizzical glance.

Panic-stricken, I protested that I had prefaces to finish and library work besides. "I can't just walk out. I'd lose my job in the library."

He assured me that everything would be arranged for a leave of absence. The salary of 125 U. S. dollars and traveling expenses seemed fabulous to me.

"So hurry down and save him from another bottle of vodka!"

Again I found the irascible delegate playing solitaire. Often, in the weeks ahead, I was to see him like this, brooding over those enigmatical cards. Years later, he wrote in the *Rotarian* (August 1939):

"To me, solitaire has the merit of suggesting an invisible opponent far cleverer than myself."

He glanced up as I entered and his moody expression gave way to a crooked half-smile.

"So you did come! That Nearing's a fine fellow — I like him. Say, how do you go about getting a meal in this lousy hotel?"

He was pleasantly surprised, 20 minutes later, to have a savory dinner served in his sitting room by a competent waiter in formal attire. He remarked that he guessed I had an Aladdin's lamp hidden up my sleeve.

There was to me, also, some magic in that evening. By a happy chance, I had two tickets from "Kultotdel," the professional workers union to which I belonged, for a new play at the Arbat Studio. So when my employer inquired, "Well, what have you got up your sleeve for the evening?" I pulled out the tickets.

"I'm in your hands," he said contentedly.

We hired a little one-horse droshky equipped with runners for the winter. Dreiser crowded his bulky form in beside me, drew the fur robe about us and laughed like a delighted child as we skimmed over the snow-padded cobblestones.

The play was *Verineya,* a drama of the October Revolution, from the popular novel by Lidia Sifulina. During the intermissions, we strolled with the crowd through the rooms of the former mansion. They were munching apples, or drinking tea from a samovar in the dining hall, or drinking the popular mineral water Narzan.

Dreiser commented caustically that he didn't notice many workers. I retorted that while they were a privileged class, they didn't wear identification badges. This was the first skirmish of the tour—he was to jibe like this often, obviously to prod me into defending the new order.

He made no comments throughout the tragic drama. Before the final curtain, the young revolutionist Verineya was shot at the gate of her log hut by a tsarist spy, as she hurried home to nurse her baby. I was in tears but my employer thought the play was "not so hot."

Out in the crisp night air, his happy mood returned as he bargained with a bearded *izvozchik* in high fur hat and long sheepskin *shuba.* But when the shrewd old driver dropped me at the Lux Hotel and I told him I wouldn't see him until evening tomorrow, Dreiser looked crestfallen.

"How come, thou faithless one?"

I explained patiently that tomorrow was November 7, the tenth anniversary of the October Revolution, "which you should know, because that's the reason you're here."

"Say, why do you call it 'October Revolution'?"

"Because, by the old Orthodox calendar it's October 25th."

"Good. I'll try to remember that. But why do you have to take the day off?"

"I'll be marching with my union in the parade all day."

"Oh, all right," he agreed glumly. "I'll look up Junius Wood— the Chicago *Daily News* office is in the Grand Hotel."

We were marching for hours that day under a dove-gray sky. The soft snow turned to slush and mud beneath the tread of a million boots, for the temperature was still mild. On this day every town and village was having demonstrations like this. The workers and employees marched in their trade union groups, which included directors, technicians, professors, office employees, skilled and unskilled workers, and droshky drivers. Each factory and business and cooperative store was represented by its local union, identified by its own bright red banner. Political activity centered around one's place of work, where delegates were elected to the local soviets.

When our section reached the Tverskaya, there was a long wait to enter the mainstream, which was filled with columns of marchers carrying banners with slogans in white letters against flaming red: "Workers of the World Unite." "Down with British Imperialism!" "All hail the Soviet Power!" There were effigies of fat capitalists, speculators, kulaks, priests. The singing marchers kept step to the stirring band music. While waiting at the intersection, we cleared a circle to dance. Finally, our lines poured into the Tverskaya and became a part of the turbulent, colorful sea flowing into the Red Square. At long last we were passing the reviewing stand on top of the temporary wooden mausoleum of Lenin. Among the government and party leaders who saluted us as we passed were Stalin, Molotov, Orjonikidze, Kalinin and Budenny.

Back in my hotel room, I bathed my cold, tired feet and drank hot tea with black bread and cheese. I changed from wool to silk stockings and put on my most up-to-date costume, a two-piece knitted green wool dress which my friend, "O'C" (Miss May O'Callaghan, also a technical worker living at the Lux) had brought me from London. In place of the short sheepskin shuba I had worn in the parade, I donned the smart plaid wool coat with fur collar which Hugo Gellert's wife had given me. A felt toque in the latest fashion bought at GOOM, Moscow's biggest department store, replaced my fur-lined hat with ear flaps. Instead of heavy shoes I wore oxfords. Thus, properly attired, I hurried down the Tverskaya to report to my employer. Apparently he had not missed me. In the company of Scott Nearing, William Gropper, Dorothy Thompson, Sinclair Lewis and other noted American guests, he had watched the parade from the balcony of the Chicago *Daily News* office in the hotel.

"I saw you skipping along with those hordes," Dreiser told me, eyeing my costume with apparent approval. "I couldn't tell you from the natives. Wood had to point you out."

Louis Fischer dropped in to check a rumor that Theodore
Dreiser was being held virtually a prisoner by the government.
Relieved that the rumor was slightly exaggerated, he offered
to sneak the prisoner out for a visit with Walter Duranty of
The New York Times.

Duranty, regarded as the dean of American correspondents
in Moscow, lived and worked in comparatively spacious quarters across the river. The welcome glow of a grate fire in his
office was a sight seldom enjoyed anywhere in Russia, where
brick wall stoves prevailed. Hotels and public buildings had
steam heat piped from a central heating plant.

A number of American correspondents were already there,
cocktail glasses in hand, enjoying the hospitality of the urbane
Englishman. Among them were William Reswick of the Associated Press, Eugene Lyons of United Press and Wood of the
Chicago *Daily News*. Theodore Dreiser lost no time in questioning the dean of newsmen. Was this place rented to him by the
city?

"Each dwelling unit has its house committee responsible to
the Central Housing Department," Walter Duranty explained.
"In 1921 I was given a three-year lease on condition that I keep
it in repair. I had to make extensive repairs. This was the
house of a merchant in the old days. At the end of the three-
year lease the apartment reverted to the Housing Department
and I made a contract with them to pay $125 per month,
through the house committee."

"Who are on this house committee?"

"The tenants elect the members, meetings are held three
times a year to hear the report and check the accounts. This
system makes grafting difficult."

"How's that?" Dreiser inquired skeptically.

"Well, there's also the Workers and Peasants Inspection
which can drop in any minute and look at the books. It is a
check on every department of the government. It can clean
out a whole office force if there is evidence of graft or inefficiency."

Duranty conceded that the graft system in America made
for cheaper production, citing the price of canned meat at 10

cents in the United States compared to 39 cents in Russia.
Louis Fischer promptly pointed out that this was due to ratio-
nalization of industry rather than to the graft system.

Dreiser, who was inclined to agree with Fischer, then asked
about bureaucracy. Duranty replied cautiously.

"Bureaucracy is a heritage of past centuries, you know, and is
at least now recognized as an evil – not the natural way of life."

Walter Duranty was regarded as more reliable and impartial
than most of his colleagues who, not knowing the language and
confined to Moscow, relied on secretaries to translate the daily
papers. They then rushed to cable any scandals they could pick
up and were not above twisting reports to please the editors
back home. Duranty, on the other hand, wrote in the preface to
his *Duranty Reports Russia* (Viking Press, 1934): "I am particularly fortunate to have been given from the outset by *The
New York Times* complete freedom in my handling of news."
(He wrote the section on the 1917 Revolution in the 14th edition of the Encyclopedia Britannica.)

"Efforts are being made to reduce the red tape," Duranty
continued. "In 1922 it took 45 minutes to draw money from the
bank – now three minutes. There were 48 paper records in each
railroad report; now this figure has been reduced considerably.
There is so much unemployment that cutting down office forces
is difficult, and of course this encourages bureaucratic methods."

"Why is there so much unemployment?" demanded the loyal
chronicler of American industrialization.

"As a matter of fact," Duranty explained, "more people are
being employed, but more peasants are coming into the cities."

"Why are more peasants coming into the cities?"

"They can't use the available land because there is no money
to develop the land and build roads."

"What about Russia's foreign debts?"

"Russia says she is ready to pay any debts she really owes,
but not the ones she doesn't recognize. By the way," Duranty
added, "although the International Harvester Company lost
heavily through the revolution on account of being national-
ized, it is granting more credits than any other company."

The discussion finally got around to the fact that under NEP (New Economic Policy) people could have servants.

"So Soviet Russia has a servant problem," scoffed Dreiser. "I thought this was a classless society."

The other Americans laughed derisively, but Duranty calmly explained that domestic workers have the same rights as any other workers. They must belong to a trade union, and an agreement is drawn up between employer and servant and strictly enforced. "It is a phase of the New Economic Policy which was intended to be only a temporary letdown after the stringency of postrevolutionary military communism. But," Duranty added, smiling, "you'll have to ask one of their Marxian theoreticians about that."

Someone suggested that Mr. Dreiser see Bukharin. "He's the party theoretician—the 'sweetheart of the party.' An English translation of his book *Dialectical Materialism* has been published in the United States." (International Publishers, 1925.)

Someone else said he thought Bukharin was mixed up in the power struggle between Trotsky and Stalin. This idea only increased Dreiser's interest in getting an interview with the party leader.

"Make a note of this," he told me. "Ask VOKS to get me an interview with him."

The conversation grew livelier, with disputed points usually referred to Duranty. Then Dreiser asked him a challenging question.

"I watched that parade today. Why did all those people march? Why, millions of them poured past the Grand Hotel, hour after hour. Tell me, Duranty, were they really as enthusiastic as they seemed?"

Walter Duranty's sensitive face took on a quizzical expression. He shrugged. "The enthusiasm is not exactly spontaneous," he said cautiously. "I believe they are required by their trade unions to march."

I had been listening in silence and taking notes up to this point, but now I had to speak.

"I marched," I said. "I thought it was a privilege. Attendance at trade union meetings is compulsory, but taking part in demonstrations is voluntary. I don't believe a single one of them would have missed the parade today."

Walter Duranty looked at me with sudden interest. "I think you're right," he said slowly. Turning to his inquisitor, he went on earnestly: "I believe this thing will succeed in time, Dreiser — barring another foreign attack, with American help."

The truth-seeking American delegate was engrossed in thought as we walked back to the hotel in the bracing night air. He finally remarked that he had respect for Duranty's opinions. "He's given me something to think about," he said.

When we paused on the Iron Bridge over the Moscow River, Dreiser turned to look back at the domes and towers of churches standing out against the starlit sky.

"Let's start out early tomorrow morning without a guide. I want to go back across the river and ramble around among all those churches I can see from my windows. Those variegated domes fascinate me. There must be a thousand!"

"That's a good guess," I told him. "There are 800 Greek Orthodox churches in Moscow, but of course not all of them are across the river. There must be at least a dozen inside the Kremlin alone."

2. People and Places in and around Moscow

Next morning, we hired a seedy *izvozchik*. Seated in the one-horse sleigh we set out in a spirit of high adventure across the bridge to the oldest section of the city. On the other side of the street from the Grand Hotel was the Voskresenski Gate into the Red Square, known as the "holiest spot in Russia." In the center was the little chapel of the Iberian Virgin. As we approached the gate, I translated the inscription on the side wall: "Religion is the Opium of the People."

"They seem to be taking their opium," Dreiser commented, observing the picturesque beggars lined up alongside the steps to receive alms from the worshippers hurrying past them into the chapel. Inside, the lighted candles and the golden, bejewelled ikons gleamed. The black-bearded priest was mum-

bling the service while an assistant moved through the crowd
murmuring, "Lord have mercy."

"They won't be here much longer," I told Dreiser. "The Pre-
sidium is even now debating on plans to demolish the chapel."

Now, in spite of his cynicism, it was the colorful domes rising
in medieval splendor which drew him across the bridge. But
first we had to stop at St. Basil's at the opposite end of the
Red Square. It had been built in the reign of Ivan the Terrible
and was now a museum. Its fantastic "pineapple" domes had
been repainted in the original vivid colors for the tenth anniversary celebrations.

When we crossed the Iron Bridge, Dreiser was charmed by
the quiet streets of imposing old homes built in the 18th and
19th centuries by rich merchants. Some had survived the burning of Moscow in 1812 during the rout of Napoleon's army.
Alighting to look at a church with blue, gold-studded domes, he
noticed a small house nearby bearing a plaque which noted
that it was the birthplace of the famous playwright Ostrovsky.
Dreiser remarked that he was acquainted with a play by him
that depicted the dull, empty lives of rich merchants.

He marveled at the enduring beauty of the churches. "Harmonious in every detail!" he exclaimed, gazing at the Pokrovka
Church, of gray stone with black metal domes.

But he also wanted to see how the people lived. After all, it
was people he wrote about, not churches. At the gate of a graceful white church with gilded domes, he looked inside the
watchman's hut. A woman with a shawl over her head readily
answered his questions. She, her husband, her mother, and two
sisters with their children lived in one large room, which had
an entry and a shed. The only furnishings were a brick wall
stove, table, chairs and an altar. Our driver, jealously noting
our concern over these wretched living conditions, assured us
that his were "still worse."

Thus we continued our ride past church after church of an
intriguing variety of architecture and of domes—gold, silver,
copper, bronze, iron, or painted white, black, blue, green
and pink.

Following the canal along the river bank, we came upon a monastery. Beyond its walls and towers, which were falling into decay, we found a lovely ruined church with a graveyard — and, in the court, a box factory! The factory was closed for the day, but when I explained to the guard that this was an *"Amerikanski delegat,"* he showed us a factory school for illiterates, a workers' club and a library in the former living quarters of the monks. The *Amerikanski delegat* seemed a little depressed by the whole setup. He's had his "fill of churches for today."

We returned to his hotel by way of another bridge. Nearby was a landing from which, in the summer, steamers ran to Nizhni-Novgorod on the Volga.

"If only you had come in summer," I sighed, "we could have traveled by boat, but now the river will soon be frozen over."

In fact, his coming at the beginning of winter, determined to tour the country (even to go to western Siberia) was the main cause of all the troubles ahead. I believe he enjoyed this day of wandering about freely without an offical guide more than almost any other of his 77 days in the Soviet Union.

He was tired but still in a genial mood when we arrived at the Grand Hotel. He told me that he had invited Dorothy Thompson to have dinner with him. Would I order the meal to be served in his sitting room? I did so, and then prepared to depart.

"No, stick around," he said brusquely.

Miss Thompson arrived. She was, I decided, Junoesque in her smartly tailored wool suit. She had not been wasting her time wandering around town looking at churches. She had been spending her few days in Moscow more profitably with her colleagues, the well-informed correspondents.

When the impeccably attired waiter appeared with the loaded tray, I again prepared to depart, after giving him further instructions. The host stopped me with a gruff, "Sit down."

I sat on the sofa. On the wall above hung an enormous painting (possibly a Repin copy) of Napoleon standing in deep dejection at a campfire in the snow-shrouded forest outside Moscow.

"What are you doing over there with poor old Napoleon?" he demanded. "Come and eat your dinner."

I sat down with them but did not join in the conversation. The guest entertained her host with tales that Walter Duranty and her friend Junius Wood had picked up on their Russian travels. One story so delighted Dreiser that again and again on the tour he made jocular references to it.

According to Miss Thompson, it seems that a poor peasant once complained bitterly to the priest about his wretched living conditions. *Batushka* advised him to bring in the pig, and the pig was brought from the lean-to outside the hut. The peasant complained that conditions were worse than before. So the priest told him to bring in the sheep. Still worse. "Then bring in the cow." But this was unendurable! So the priest said, "Take out the pig." That was better. "Now take out the sheep." Much better. And finally, "Take out the cow." The peasant and his family were more than satisfied: "*Ach, batushka,* it is so clean and roomy now!"

The two tourists chatted about the sights in Moscow—the street peddlers with braziers dangling in the breeze, the beggars, the primus sputtering at apartment windows, the "nightspots" they had visited—evidently in the four or five days before I came on the scene.

After that wonderful day browsing around without a guide, Theodore Dreiser was summoned to VOKS (Society for Cultural Relations with Abroad), which was in charge of his visit and responsible for his safety. He was in a belligerent mood when we went by sleigh to the headquarters of VOKS, an ornate stone palace. He already had argued with them about plans for his tour.

The director, Madame Kameneva, Leon Trotsky's sister, at once expressed disapproval of his hiring a secretary without consulting them. Understandably, she objected to a private secretary who was not responsible to VOKS and, in her opinion, was not even qualified for the job.

Squinting at me out of nearsighted eyes, she declared in Russian: "*Ona nye sovsyem sovietskaya zhenschena.*"

"What's she saying in that blasted language?" he demanded.

Before I could respond, Trevis, a VOKS guide who was favored by Kameneva, eagerly translated for him: "She is not at all a Soviet woman."

"What do you mean by 'Soviet woman'?"

"That is," Trevis replied insinuatingly, "not entirely reliable."

Madame Kameneva, who could speak English when she wished, hastened to explain, "I meant she is a non-party technical worker...."

"Splendid!" interrupted Dreiser. "A perfect recommendation."

"But," she protested, "you will need a guide and interpreter, and *Tovarish* Trevis is fully qualified to serve as both...."

The American delegate began to shout. "You promised me a private secretary and a private tour. If I can't have what I want, by God, I'll leave and you can all go to hell!"

"Yes, yes," the treasurer, who was a reasonable man, interposed soothingly, "we'll all go there presently, but first let's settle this business."

Madame Kameneva took her fingers out of her ears and listened quietly to the treasurer's suggestions. The irate guest simmered down, too. It was finally agreed that he could keep his secretary at his own expense, and VOKS would furnish an official guide and interpreter when needed. Since he was the only foreign delegate to demand a private tour, it was explained, plans must be delayed until the end of the official holidays on November 15.

This meant that he was still free of official supervision, and that, with the exception of appointments VOKS would make for him to interview officials, he could go his own way in Moscow.

Sergey Dinamov, who meanwhile had stood ready to help when needed, invited the American author to visit his home.

He took us by street car to an old working-class section where he lived with his wife and two children in three rooms of a shabby frame house. It was occupied by two other families. The plumbing was primitive and the outhouse was in the courtyard.

At the tea table, Sergey answered Dreiser's questions about his own life. He told a moving story to the sympathetic chronicler of human woes. He had lived with his mother in only one of these rooms. From the age of 12 he had worked with his

mother in the nearby textile factory ten hours a day, earning
14 roubles a month. After 13 years in the same factory, his
mother earned 25 roubles.

"If Mama had lived she would be receiving 70 roubles a
month, all services free and an annual vacation in a rest
home."

"Did your mother die before the revolution?"

"No," Sergey answered, pride in his tone, "my mother was
killed fighting beside her fellow-workers on the barricades
during the revolution."

Dreiser was silent, a compassionate silence. At this point,
neighbors whom Sergey had invited to meet the American author came in. He questioned each of them in turn.

The welder worked in an auto factory. He received 35 roubles
a week, on which he said he was able to support his wife and
two children. They lived in one room.

"Ask him if he means he can feed, clothe and provide other
needs for his family on — let me see, a rouble costs me 52 cents —
so he gets about $18 a week." Dreiser looked skeptical.

The second worker, a nice-looking young fellow with two
children, was a semi-skilled worker, a stoker in the textile factory, who made only 18 roubles a week. But rent was set according to income, so he paid only 2.50 roubles a month.

In their leisure time these two men went to their factory
clubs and saw Living Newspaper and "Blue Blouse" entertainments, attended union meetings and political circles and the
kino. They participated in sports at their clubs — boating and
swimming in summer, skating and skiing in winter.

As for the children, the stoker said he had no particular
plans for them beyond simple moral instruction and anti-religious propaganda to counteract the teachings of their grandmother.

"What kind of anti-religious propaganda?"

"*Nu* . . . singing revolutionary and Young Pioneer songs instead of church hymns and influencing them not to go to mass
with *babushka*. But," he added with a grin, "they don't want to
go anyhow. Most people don't when they no longer have to."

Both workers said their children had elementary school education. If they wished to go higher or train for a trade or profession, they now had the chance.

"Do you have ambitions for your children to occupy a high position in life, such as that of a government official?"

It was all the same to him, the textile worker replied, shrugging his thin shoulders. They would get what they deserved.

"I don't care what they earn, as long as they're satisfied. As for my daughter, no, I don't have ambitions for her to grow up and make a respectable wife and mother. What she does with her life is her business. If she wanted to live with one man, all right. If she wanted to divorce him and take another – that's her choice. The important thing," the young father concluded, "is that she should be an independent person, able to support herself."

Dreiser motioned to me to "be sure and get all this down." But Dinamov, as host, seemed slightly embarrassed by the artlessness of the unskilled worker's remarks.

The bank clerk was a different type. He was of slighter build, smoother face, with more refinement of speech and manner. He was 27, made 130 roubles a month, was married and expected to be a father soon. He had been a shepherd boy for ten years, then had come to the city and, as an unskilled worker, had studied and learned office work. No, his job as clerk did not give him a superior social position. He still felt nearer to the *rabochee* (workers) than to the *sluzhishchi* (employees).

All three agreed that the present way of life gave them more comfort and security than they had known before the revolution.

"Now you tell us about Amereeka!" the unskilled worker proposed boldly.

The guest of honor warmed to his subject. He described the high American standard of living, the high stage of industrial development, and ended with a tribute to American capitalists.

"The world owes them a debt," he concluded.

"A debt for what?" Dinamov demanded, speaking in English. He seemed annoyed at the American guest's defense of capitalism for the benefit of his neighbors.

"For developing the industrial power which the world now shares."

The young Marxian literary critic's fair skin reddened. His blue eyes seemed ready to burst through their thick lenses. He started to retort. Fortunately, the tailor next door, who was in business for himself (permissible if he did not hire anyone), dropped in to invite us to a christening at the parish church. Since we had to walk some distance, we arrived too late for the service. But the sexton allowed us to come into the gold-domed edifice before he put out the lights. The ikons gleamed in the candlelight. The air was heavy with incense.

Dreiser gazed around at the magnificent interior. "Quite grand for a working-class neighborhood," he observed.

Still nettled by the American's glorification of private enterprise, Dinamov heatedly pointed out that for centuries the Russian masses had poured their substances into these glittering trinkets while living in wretched poverty.

Dreiser soothed the young man's ruffled feelings by wholeheartedly agreeing with him about the Russian state church, and they parted good friends.

In sharp contrast to Sergey Dinamov's home and neighborhood was the grand former palace of Kereshnikov, the sugar king. It faced the Kremlin on the opposite bank of the river. Here, at the Foreign Office reception for foreign delegates — attended by leaders of official Soviet circles — Theodore Dreiser met the genial foreign minister, Maxim Litvinov, and Ivy, his eccentric English wife. Madame Kollontai came and sat beside the American novelist on a small divan. The charming Soviet ambassador to Norway had set a precedent as the world's first woman envoy. Dreiser began at once to question her about her opinion of the progress made under the Soviets. She replied with wit and enthusiasm.

"To me," she told him in good English, "the most striking thing about the new society is the change of mental outlook of our people. The new generation, especially, thinks and acts socially and cooperatively, conscious of its responsibilities."

"What are the reactions of the teen-agers, let's say the 14-year-old?"

The slender, dark-haired ambassador smiled radiantly.

"Oh, the party is his guiding light — not a religion, but in place of religion. Duty to the Soviets is paramount in his loyalties. The party is his spiritual guide. Don't worry about our youth, Mr. Dreiser. They have something to believe in, at last! Another striking thing," Madame Kollontai went on eagerly, "is the position of women in the new society, their determination not to be parasites. They are conscious that there is a social stigma on the housewife."

Alexandra Kollontai was sent to Norway as ambassador and trade representative in 1922, and in 1927, to Mexico in the same capacity. She had just returned from Mexico and was at present back in the Commissariat of Social Welfare, where she had served as its first director in 1917.

"Oh, the number of women who come to my department begging for work — to have a part in the building of the new society!"

The novelist, who to my knowledge never had included an "emancipated" woman among his heroines, seemed tremendously impressed, perhaps more by her feminine charms than her feminist ideals.

Later in the evening all the guests gathered in the grand dining hall around a long table loaded with expensive foods — huge bowls of black caviar, smoked sturgeon, cold meats, pastries, coffee and wine.

Spotting Diego Riviera, Dreiser sat beside him and renewed their warm friendship. The old cronies laughed, gesticulated and had a wonderful time, although one knew no Spanish and the other very little English. On Dreiser's other side was Gorkin, editor of *Izvestia,* and the two discussed freedom of the press in their respective countries. The Soviet editor claimed there was more freedom of the press in his country than in the United States, because Soviet newspapers openly criticized and found fault for constructive, not destructive, purposes.

Across the table sat Anna Louise Strong, a large blond woman with a surprisingly soft, pretty face for a determined newspaper woman who had pushed her way into the farthest corners of the vast USSR and had written profusely about all of them. She rose to speak, and the words flowed as easily from her lips as from her pen. She related a long dramatic story about the penetration of Soviet power into an Arctic village.

Finally, Foreign Minister Litvinov rose, genially greeted the guests and welcomed them to the tenth anniversary celebrations.

"This beautiful mansion which serves us so graciously on this gala occasion, as you see survived the bloody battles of the October days. So also did that ancient landmark on Red Square — St. Basil's Cathedral. Which reminds me of a story about our illustrious Commissar of Education and the Arts."

The guests applauded and craned their necks to look at the scholarly commissar, Anatoly Lunacharsky, who combined old world culture with new social theories.

"In the heat of the revolution," Litvinov continued, "while the battle raged outside in Red Square, Comrade Lunacharsky paced the floor in a room of the Kremlin. He was weeping for the safety of St. Basil's. Comrade Lenin tried in vain to reassure him. At last, Ilyich said, 'Never mind, Anatole, we'll build you a new one.'"

3. Dreiser Explores the Theater, Interviews Stanislavsky

The Theater Arts were under the Commissariat of Education, and Commissar Lunacharsky's wife was a leading actress.

During his long stay in the Soviet capital, Theodore Dreiser gained considerable insight into the theater and some knowledge of the effect the revolution was having on the art of the theater. He saw a number of plays and interviewed leading directors.

One of his memorable experiences was a visit with Stanislavsky, revered director and co-founder (with playwright V. N. Danchenko) of the Moscow Art Theater.

At early dusk of the November day, we entered a graceful and unpretentious gray stone building on a side street named Kamergerski Peryulok. Stanislavsky was in his office and stood up to greet us, a magnificent man with thick white hair,

strong features and brilliant dark eyes. His secretary, a small, dark woman, spoke some English.

The American author asked what was to him, the most important question at once: "How has the revolution affected your creative work?"

"Of course, it has not been easy to adjust ourselves to the drastic social changes. But," he added earnestly, "the white line of art is eternal and passing conditions cannot change it. There have been deviations, especially in surface forms, but already the role of art is again taking the right path. We must take the good from the revolution and use it. During the upheaval we strayed far off in search of the new; that of value which we found becomes a part of immortal art."

The director recited a parable to illustrate this thought: A group of children strayed off the main road into the woods to gather mushrooms and flowers, and returned to the road to find that out of their treasures only one small flower remained for the immortal urn.

"What of the old have you discarded and what have you adopted of the new?"

"The chief role of the Art Theater has been to maintain the tradition of the transcendency of the actor's art. Decorations and settings are only important as a background for the actor's art; his being the inner, as opposed to the surface, art. The revolution has brought much that is new in these surface forms, but nothing to the art of the actor."

Stanislavsky maintained that the Art Theater was the only one which had continued to work in the sphere of inner creative art.

"The rest have been occupied with decorations, settings and other surface forms, and, most significant, in the new content of the plays. The aesthetic character of the old play has given place to the political in the new. We must have different voices for the old hymns and the new, and all this is now adjusting itself. But," the old director continued firmly, "I cannot feel that the plays of Shakespeare can be done in the present style. True, I do not say that the youth today do not have the right to see Shakespeare through their eyes, and produce as they

see the play. But to tamper with Shakespeare, do the plays
over...." He lifted his shapely hands in protest. "This is a
complete lack of understanding of creative art. Art conscious-
ness is a living thing. A person cannot cut off his hand and put
in its place his foot!"

The rich voice which had risen in uncontrollable emotion
became even again. It was once more the steady, tolerant, understanding voice of the creative artist adapting his art grace-
fully to the new order.

"But we profit by all this experimentation. The worst condition for art is to stand still; it is better to move even when
wrong. The union of the new with the old stands out in greatest
relief in this theater," he told the American writer proudly.
"When we returned from America we found that the young
people looked upon us as aged. But last year, and particularly
this year, they have begun to understand how much they do
not know and how much they can learn from the old order.
They have come to me from all the theaters, begging me to tell
them my secrets!" He was smiling in childlike delight. "For
this reason, we have decided that it would be most practical
for me to give a series of popular lectures on the art of the actor.
Indeed, I notice a tendency everywhere to revert to the inner
forms of art. People seem to be getting tired of the surface
forms."

Stanislavsky added hastily, as though wishing to avoid doing an injustice to the young Soviet art: "They are not neces-
sarily bad—some of them are very good—cubism, futurism,
impressionism—and a lot of nonsense and stupidity," he added,
in spite of his good intentions. Then he became reconciled once
more:

"So we must throw away the bad and keep what is good....
To the surface art of the actor has been added movement, gymnastics, dancing—all very valuable. Surface forms can be lik-
ened to the art of painting. The actor cannot go beyond his culture. He stands still. He cannot convey more than the painting.
When we learn to use paintings in our technique, they will be
of great value. But so far, in some theaters the decorations are
too advanced, premature, and the actor tries to act according

to the new settings, but is unable to do it and only spoils the effect. Either the actor plays in the old style and the decorations are the newest, or vice versa. Therefore, there is no harmony.

"Our theater," the famous director emphasized once more, "uses only such decorations as support the art of the actor. For the futurist actor we use futurist decorations."

Dreiser had been listening intently as both the secretary and I tried to convey in English the profound ideas of the great Stanislavsky on the art of the theater. His final question brought the subject down to concrete examples. It was a delicate one for the director to answer truthfully to an outsider in this period of social upheaval:

"Has communism produced any really great plays?"

"No," he replied without hesitation. Then he quickly added, "But *The Days of the Turbines* and *The Armored Train*, which we have produced, are good as chronicles of the revolution. They have introduced many changes in content. We are now preparing to produce a new play by Leonov which seems promising."

When we rose to go with his secretary to visit the Art Theater Museum, the venerable director's parting words were in commendation of the new order:

"Theater art is already playing a big role politically. In every factory there is a theatrical group which acts out the 'living wall newspaper'; in every workers' club there is an actor's circle such as the 'Blue Blouses.' They are the lively factory players who carry their costumes and props in suitcases and can just as quickly put on a play in a village as in the Grand Opera House." He smiled.

"All Russia is acting!" he declared with a parting wave of his expressive hand, which was like a salute to the New Order.

Later in the evening, the gracious secretary took us into the auditorium of the Moscow Art Theater, restful in its classical lines and soft gray tones. Its emblem, a white seagull, on the curtain, seemed to assure us of the enduring quality of the world-famous theater.

We sat in Stanislavsky's own seats, ten rows back, on the center aisle. The curtain had just fallen on the second act of

The Days of the Turbines. It had aroused a storm of protest from the younger generation. They demanded its suppression as a "White Guard" counterrevolutionary drama. After some alterations, the play had continued. One of the most important changes was in an early scene. During the Civil War, the sons of the old bourgeois family, the Turbines, had fought in the White Army against the revolutionists, and in this scene the family, celebrating the Christmas holidays, movingly sing the tsarist anthem. It was replaced by a ribald drinking song in the revised version.

The exquisite acting raised a not exceptional play to dramatic heights. The closing scene which we were seeing showed the Turbine family together again after the Civil War. The younger brother had turned Bolshevik, but the older brother was still bitter. As they decorated the Christmas tree, from afar came the stirring music of a marching band playing the Internationale, the new national anthem. The young Bolshevik defiantly sang the words:

> *Arise, ye prisoners of starvation,*
> *Arise, ye wretched of the earth,*
> *For Justice thunders condemnation —*
> *A better world's in birth.*

The others listened with mingled emotions as the music swelled, then died away in the distance. The new order had passed them by. They were only *sputniki* (fellow travelers) or, in the vernacular of that time, *bweevshee* (has-beens).

I tried to explain the play, which I had seen earlier, to Dreiser as we walked back to the Tverskaya. He was troubled by the implications in the Art Theater director's guarded statements regarding postrevolutionary restrictions on freedom of expression in the creative arts. He wondered why the revolutionary element had demanded suppression of this realistic chronicle of the Civil War era. It seemed to him quite harmless as tsarist propaganda. Was there anything in the play which could be said to present the cause of this likeable family as worthy?

"Of course, they're a losing class, a part of the old ruling class that had to go," he mused. "But that last scene — although rather touchingly nostalgic – showed they could still live, love and be happy together, or can they?" he added. "Maybe that ending was doctored by the censor. . . . "

Dreiser had given Stanislavsky the manuscript of his own dramatization of *An American Tragedy.* The director had said he would be glad to consider it for production.

The outcome, which I here relate out of chronological order, was that some time later, after our return from a trip to Leningrad, we went back to get the report for which the author had been hopefully waiting. The secretary again received us cordially and seated us in Stanislavsky's comfortable office.

The director looked very serious when he entered. He sat down and chatted with us politely, seeming reluctant to speak of the matter about which he knew the American author had come. After a few inconsequential remarks, he said slowly that he had read carefully the synopsis of the play prepared by the committee and had liked it very much.

"I certainly would be happy to produce it." He paused. Then he added that his specialists on censorship had decided the dramatization Dreiser had made of his novel could not pass the censor.

"But why?" the author demanded.

"First, because of the religious sections, and second, the relationship between employer and worker. I assure you, it is exceedingly painful for me to be forced to reject it. I would have liked very much to produce it."

Dreiser rose abruptly and with a grudging word of thanks strode out. He did not mention the other play he had brought along to submit, *The Hand of the Potter.*

I trotted after him, wishing I could comfort him. I had witnessed a scene that must have happened to him many times in American editorial offices. But the phenomenal success of his *American Tragedy* had given him confidence. I think he expected that, especially in New Russia, his dramatization of the novel would be readily accepted, as it had been in New York.

In the vestibule, the little secretary caught up with him. She eagerly assured him that everyone who had read the play had said it was wonderful. Dreiser did not respond. She put her hand on his arm.

"Perhaps," she said gently, "in another five years we might be permitted to produce it."

This experience with censorship seemed to antagonize Dreiser toward the Moscow dramatic theater. I thought he might get a broader view if he saw a play about the revolution from the communist point of view. I obtained tickets for *Cement*, a dramatization of a current novel, at "Korsh" (the trade-union theater.) The story centered about responsible party workers and sought to show the contamination of party members after the introduction of NEP.

One of these party men and his ambitious wife develop bourgeois tendencies. They profit from dealings with a foreign concessionaire, live in style, have drinking parties, exploit their maid. They are exposed and as they prepare to escape to Paris, there comes the dread knock of the Gay-Pay-Oo on their door.

This naive propaganda play was saved by several entertaining scenes which gave an insight into the everyday life of Muscovites. It also showed that the Russian sense of humor, or sense of the ridiculous, is very similar to the American. One scene which I found excruciatingly funny, because it was so true to life as I saw it, is set in an apartment house where a number of responsible party workers live. The three servants of three families are preparing meals for their respective employers in the community kitchen.

A large soup kettle on the stove interferes with the even larger roasting pan of a responsible party worker. The mistress of the roasting pan enters and haughtily demands that the soup kettle be removed. The maid of the kettle protests, at which point her mistress comes in and a quarrel between the two employers ensues. The mistress of the baking pan informs the mistress of the soup kettle that since her son and his wife are responsible party workers they are entitled to have their dinner on time. The mistress of the soup kettle tartly replies that she had noticed these responsible workers were terribly busy with important work far into the night, and the songs she heard them shouting didn't sound exactly communistic. A hand-to-hand combat for space on the community stove ensues. As the haughty mistress of the baking pan retreats, she is pushed into a tub of dirty water amid loud laughter and applause from the assembled maids.

Another scene in a crowded beer hall showed a number of Russian types — street cleaner, factory worker, professor — all dead drunk and pompously expounding their views on the revolution and NEP.

Dreiser laughed heartily over what he supposed was heavy burlesque. He agreed that the theater's greatest strength lay in its bold realism, its ability to place living characters on the stage. I assured him that the kitchen scene was as realistic as his own stories. I said he should visit the community kitchen on my floor in the Hotel Lux.

I told him about an incident when Roger Baldwin had spent a few weeks in Moscow in the summer and had visited me and my friend. Roger loved blueberry pie and bought a box of berries at a street stand. O'C and I furnished the other ingredients from our larder. He boldly went into our community kitchen to bake a pie. The servants of the foreign workers were watching their pots on the community stove. They gathered around the friendly American, chattering and laughing hilariously — and helping him, too. O'C and I went to my room to await the results.

Dreiser, who was no talker himself, but a good listener, enjoyed the story.

"Did the pie come out all right?" he asked.

"I don't know. Roger and the maids ate it all up."

In the American delegate's observation of the Moscow theater arts, he was introduced to the new "Lef" group (the cult of arts and letters). Meierhold, in his spectacular break with old forms, represented the theater in its experimental stage. His productions were the antithesis of Stanislavsky's. He created entirely new stage forms rather than new content. His staging of Gogol's *Revizor* (Inspector General), which Dreiser saw in the company of Sergey Dinamov, was in sharp contrast to the Art Theater's classic production. The mechanical construction of the stage, the rapidly shifting scenes, the innovation of

the turntable and acrobatic feats by the actors, combined
with a profligate use of the spotlight, were all motion-picture
techniques. Altogether, his production of *Revizor* was so utterly different from Stanislavsky's, in which Chekhov's nephew
played the role of the imposter, that it was difficult to think of
it as the same play. Liberties were taken even in the text of
Gogol's uproarious satire on the snobbishness and stupidity
of the old Russian society. But his stage sets outdid the Art
Theater's in richness. Out of a door in the polished wall rolls
a colorful miniature set on wheels, with the actors in their
places, looking like an old Dutch painting. The candles splutter
and smoke, the actors move and speak. . . .

Meierhold's bizarre production annoyed Dreiser. He disagreed with Meierhold's avowed aim to make the theater a living part of people's lives – not drama but theater, not dramatic
literature but theatrical production – craftsmanship in the service of the contemporary social structure.

VOKS made an appointment for him to interview Meierhold,
which he kept rather reluctantly. On the outside door of a
walled court was a sign: "Living Quarters of the Meierhold
Theater."

"Does this mean the actors, technicians, stagehands and
staff all live here with the director?" he demanded.

I explained that many cultural, business and industrial organizations had living quarters for their staffs and workers.
We went up a flight of stairs, down a narrow corridor and into
a large dormitory with rows of iron cots. Here we met a red-
haired young man who apologized for Mr. Meierhold's absence.
He had been called unexpectedly to a party conference relating
to a scandal in the theater.

Dreiser wondered if the scandal was about that crazy production of *Inspector General*. "I didn't want to meet him anyhow," he muttered, as we went out the gate of the big community house. I assured him he was not alone in his prejudice
against Meierhold. Furious debates raged in theatrical circles
against his extremism, especially in his handling of *Inspector
General*. Critics charged that the "Lef" leader had turned a
realistic social satire into a symbolical and mystical musical

comedy. However, Lunacharsky, representing official judgement, supported Meierhold.

The call on Meierhold was not altogether wasted time for the impatient delegate. Coming out, we walked down handsome Varovsky Avenue, "Ambassadors Row," past several embassies. We stopped at the Quaker House and had a chat with Miss Davis, who told us about the work of the Society of Friends in the villages, in matters of sanitation, the fight against cockroaches and bedbugs, and other important problems of rural communities. The Quakers had a proud record of relief work during the famine and typhus period.

Then came the real payoff, from my employer's point of view. The Museum of Modern Art, which we unexpectedly came upon, contained a small but valuable collection in the French Gallery – paintings by Van Gogh, Matisse, Gauguin, Picasso and Renoir.

"To think I might have missed this!" Dreiser told me almost reproachfully.

It was again his insatiable curiosity about "how the other fellow lives" – the main source of his creative writing – which impelled him to visit William D. Haywood.

The militant strike leader and head of the Industrial Workers of the World, had served many jail sentences. Given a long sentence, he had jumped bail and escaped to New Russia in 1920. He was in Moscow in March 1921 when Herbert S. Calvert, an IWW delegate to the first Congress of the Trade Union International arrived. Bill Haywood was enthusiastic about a plan being worked out by Calvert and S. J. Rutgers, an eminent Dutch engineer and friend of Lenin, who had expressed the wish to bring skilled workers and technicians from America. Lenin approved the plan and an expedition to explore the Kuznetsk coal basin in Western Siberia was authorized.

Bill Haywood in 1921 became the first manager of the American Autonomous Industrial Colony Kuzbas. By the end of 1922, the big coal-mining enterprise had developed to such importance that Rutgers took over as director. Bill returned to Moscow as a pensioner of the Soviet Government.

Most Americans who came to Moscow visited Bill Haywood. It was a pilgrimage of the faithful. He held open house in his room on the second floor of the Lux Hotel. Bill had diabetes, a heritage of his prison years, and so, on doctor's orders, could not share the drops of cheer they brought.

This November evening, some Wobblies, American Communists and union leaders, including several Negroes, sat around talking with nostalgia about the old days of struggles and victories. Bill had married a little Russian bookkeeper, amiable and intelligent. She had found romance in him, although he spoke only a pidgin Russian, and she knew little English. She still worked in the office, did the marketing, cooked on a primus, and kept the crowded room neat.

The two bulky, aging men sat on the bed and had little to say to one another. They had not met since the days of Bill's prime, when Dreiser was a reporter in Chicago. Always acutely sensitive to his surroundings and to the moods of others, he seemed depressed when we left.

In May, 1928, a few months after Dreiser returned to the United States, Bill Haywood died in Moscow. His ashes were placed in the Kremlin wall.

In spite of his impatience with Meierhold, Dreiser continued his examination of the theater arts. He had an appointment with Tairov, director of the Kamerni (Chamber) Theater, which specialized in foreign plays. Tairov had produced Eugene O'Neill's *Hairy Ape, Emperor Jones* and *Desire Under the Elms* — the last a remarkably realistic picture of a New England farm. Of course, a certain amount of unreality was to be expected, but the impressionistic sets avoided details, simply showing straight gray walls, the right wing thrown open to a lone tree standing against a golden sky. On stage were only a table, a stool, a bench. At left a staircase led to the two upper rooms, one always visible, the other closed except in night scenes at the baby's cradle.

Dreiser asked Tairov why he produced so many foreign plays. He replied simply that good modern Russian plays were scarce. "Soviet drama is in its infancy."

Bieberman, a New York theatrical manager, in Moscow at this time, told Dreiser he must see a play at the Jewish Kamerni Theater. The play that week happened to be *137 Children's Homes*, a takeoff on Gogol's *Inspector General*, based on contemporary bureaucrats and imposters. Dreiser told Bieberman it was a very clever comedy, but he'd had enough of the old imposter plot. Mr. Bieberman protested that this play did not do justice to the Jewish Theater and insisted that he go with him to see *200,000*.

The free evening gave me an opportunity to type the notes I was keeping for my employer. He had instructed me to use "I" to mean himself in writing the diary. But he left the writing entirely to me, except for an occasional reminder to be sure to make a note of this or that.

Next morning he dutifully reported his impressions of *200,000*. He said that since it was a rhythmic pantomime, understanding Yiddish was not essential to his enjoyment of the play. He told me Bieberman was planning to take this brilliant company to New York.

Lunacharsky's Commissariat of Education granted the largest government subsidy to the Bolshoi Opera House, where the imperial opera and ballet carried on in all their former splendor. But now sitting in the imperial box of the magnificent red-and-gold theater were working men and women, delegates from the factories. The government box was on the left side, near the stage. At the ballet *Esmeralda*, our seats were in the *bel étage*. At *Swan Lake*, which enraptured Dreiser, we had orchestra seats.

From where we sat we had a view of the darkened government box, in which I recognized the swarthy, heavy-featured face and cropped black hair of Stalin. The ballerina Semionova, as she ran off stage, curtsied when she passed the box.

On another evening, Dreiser took Anna Louise Strong to the Bolshoi to see the opera *Prince Igor*. But he preferred ballet.

4. The Soviet Cinema; Eisenstein Answers Questions

Thus far the American delegate had paid little attention to the Soviet cinema. Now he had an appointment with Sergey Eisenstein, the film director already famous abroad as the author and director of *Battleship Potemkin,* a story of the insurrection by the ship's crew at Odessa during the 1905 Revolution. Eisenstein was only 29, stocky, fair-skinned and blue-eyed, with a boyish face and a mass of curly hair.

His spacious room was one of six-rooms in a flat occupied by five other families of cinema workers. Noting the American's astonished glance about the place, Eisenstein admitted that he had decorated it himself. It was in startling designs and colors, with a bull's eye on the ceiling. On his desk was a placard advertising a new cream separator. When the guest asked him where he had found his "American" double bed, Eisenstein grinned. He had bought it from an American farming community where he took pictures.

In reply to his first question, the young cinema director explained that his basic theory in the scripts was "no plot, no dramatic story (but making daily life a drama); no actors, just people off the streets or in localities where the pictures are taken." His *General Line,* then in preparation, showed how a poor village was developed through collective efforts.

"In other words, you are a propagandist for the Soviet system. What would you do with your ideas in South Africa?"

"I would adapt them to local condition—deal with the colonial question, probably. And," he added, "in America, with your Negro question."

"So you are an uplifter," Dreiser concluded.

"As you please," Eisenstein retorted, smiling good-humoredly.

Answering questions regarding Soviet film production, he said only three or four great pictures had been produced in the past three years: one was his own *Potemkin*; another was Podovkin's *Mother,* from Gorky's novel. He considered that the method used in the German film *The Cabinet of Dr. Cali-gari* was a wrong approach to making motion picture. "Expressionism," he said, "is not adaptable to kino art." He was interested in individual stories only if they were on broad lines, illustrating general human principles. He was now working on the idea of filming Marx's *Capital*.

Dreiser shook his head in disagreement with this propaganda approach. Young Eisenstein laughed and began talking about the cost of production. For example, he had received 600 roubles for his scenario *The General Line*, which would cost about 75,000 roubles to produce. The heroine of *General Line* received a salary of 150 roubles a month.

"Of course," he added, "an old artist of the Art Theater like Leonidov receives 100 roubles a day."

Eisenstein looked around his modest quarters and admitted it was a very bad little studio—"but a new, modern one is under construction."

About the general organization of the Soviet motion picture industry, he said that it was owned by the government and came under Lunacharsky's department as a separate branch with a manager and a staff.

"There is strict control as in your country, only here it is political, whereas in the United States it is moral."

Before we left, Dreiser made amends for his apparently unsympathetic attitude toward the new social ideals. He made one of his unexpectedly optimistic forecasts:

"I predict that the Russian temperament is such that in 30 years Russia will lead the world. In America, to conquer our wilderness was the great impetus. Here, it is to make your social revolution work."

The film director was pleased by the change in his guest's tone and graciously offered to arrange a special showing of *October* and *The General Line* on the following day.

October proved to be a series of swift-moving scenes of the Bolshevik Revolution in Petrograd. Most stirring was the storming of the Winter Palace. In sharp contrast, *General Line* showed village scenes from real life—a model state dairy, a religious procession, a poor peasant asking a kulak for the

loan of a horse to harvest his crops. . . . The kulak and his wife
are rolling in fat and the primitive luxuries of feudal barons. A
symbol appears at appropriate times throughout the series of
scenes – the wax figure of a fat pig, whirling coquettishly and
bearing a ludicrous resemblance to the kulak's wife.

5. *The Visitor Discusses Agriculture with Experts*

Although Dreiser's interests and his writings were distinctly
urban, the realistic picture of village life he had seen in the
theater reminded him that Russia was essentially a nation of
peasants. Now, with the country in a critical stage of the reconstruction program, he recognized that the peasant problem
was of transcendent importance.

He had a long talk with the American farmer Harold
Ware, manager of a 10,000-acre farm in the North Caucasus,
which I had visited a year earlier. Ware was married to the
lovely, talented Quaker, Jessica Smith. She had come to
Russia with the Friends Service Committee during the Civil
War and famine. With her training and knowledge of Russian,
Jessica was a valuable assistant in the management of the
large-scale farming enterprise, as were others in the American
group, which included Quakers and American Baptist mission-
aries.

Harold Ware told Dreiser that he was introducing the latest
American farming methods and machinery. So successful were
his methods that Soviet representatives of regional agricultural stations came to see the results and consult with the Americans. Peasants came from villages in the district, bringing
their broken tools to be mended – magically, it seemed to them.

After his stimulating talk with Ware, the American delegate welcomed the opportunity to interview Commissar
Svidersky of the Land Department. Svidersky was a shrewd,
middle-aged man, whose father had been a rich landowner.

"So what did *you* do in the revolution?" was the American's
bantering first shot.

"Nu. . . " The commissar smiled broadly, responding appreciatively, as Russians always did, to the author's dry humor.

"I traveled from village to village commandeering flour for distribution to the needy. The famine did not end until 1923, but since then the improvement in the villages has been unbelievable."

Dreiser fired questions as fast as Svidersky could answer them. The peasant population? One hundred million. Land distribution? That depends upon the district and varies according to the number in a family. Does the government take a certain percentage of the peasant's production? It buys from him the products it needs but he is free to set the amount.

"Isn't this giving the city worker less freedom than the peasant?"

"No, because we pay the worker definite wages and expect a certain amount of labor from him. The labor of the peasant is on a different basis. He does not have the land free. There is an agricultural tax. The inspector comes to the peasant and decides the amount of his taxes, according to the number in his family. We consider that the larger the family, the richer the peasant. If he has eight acres of land and only two members in his family are able to work, he is poor."

"Why don't you take the land away if he can't work it?"

The commissar shook his finger at his inquisitor. "Remember," he declared, "our revolution gave the land to the peasant. Every member of a family has a right to a piece of land. We cannot take the land away even if he is not able to work it. We help the poor peasant with credits, etc. If we took the land away, he would get poorer and poorer, but if he has it he can still rent the part he does not cultivate."

Dreiser considered this for a moment. Then he asked, "Wouldn't it be better to apply Henry George's single-tax theory, for the state to own the land and lease as much as the peasant can use for a certain return? If he took more than he could handle, he would have to give it back, and if he was an incompetent farmer, he would have to go into some other work."

Svidersky shook his head. "No, such a system could not exist here. The peasant would own land according to his ability. George also believed in nationalization of the land, as we do, but according to his system there would not be equality among the peasants. We say the land belongs to all the peasants. Some families are very strong and work well. We try to help the weaker or less competent peasant so that he will be able to work alongside the others. The cooperatives give him credits to buy equipment; the district agronom gives him advice. If we can't increase the production of the poorer peasants with this help, then," he concluded, spreading his hands in a gesture of resignation, "then your theory is right. Right now we are testing the socialist, as opposed to the capitalist, system." He was referring to the controversy raging in the Central Committee of the party on the issue of introducing collectivization into the villages. "It is a crucial time for us. It is precisely on this question of the government's concentrating more on improving the condition of the poorer peasantry that there is all this conflict in our party today. If we help the peasant to develop, we can build up our industry. If not—then the bourgeois power will rise again."

Dreiser did not press him on this point.

"But," Svidersky added hopefully, "the peasant's standard of living has improved already, his consumption has increased 40 per cent—except in the Volga Region because of the famine. But the peasant is not satisfied with his standard of living, although it is much better than before the war."

The American individualist pursued his favorite thesis: the big mind, the naturally endowed, competent individual, gets ahead; the little mind, the incompetent, falls behind.

"What do you do about the incompetent peasant or the misfit?"

"He must take the initiative to get out. However, just now, the peasant youth in general are anxious to leave the village and go to the factories. The Young Communist organization is taking care of them."

"On the other hand, if the factory worker thinks he could do better on the land, does the government try to send him there?"

"Today we can't guide the individual. In the early post-revolutionary days, the policy was to let everyone go to the

Land Department with his personal problems – or see Kalinin. But we found we simply did not have the machinery to handle the masses individually. Now the organization of Young Communists, as I said, handles such problems. The Department of Education conducts schools for the young peasants and trains them to be social workers. A factory worker can, if he wishes, be transferred to an agricultural school."

"How does the Russian peasant compare with the peasant of Western Europe?"

"There is no comparison, what we call a peasant and what Western Europe calls a peasant are two entirely different types. Our peasant is small, Meester Drayzer; his enterprise is small. But," he added with spirit, "we are lifting him up. The peasant who comes to me now from my district had in my time no boots, no samovar, no manufactured goods, no schools, no hospital, no cooperative. Now he has all of these things."

"Are you reaching all the peasants with your new methods and equipment?"

"Yes, everyone, even the smallest nationalities, whose culture is very low, are being reached through the party, trade-union organs, cooperatives, radio. I got a surprise this morning," said the commissar, a ruminative smile spreading over his keen peasant face. "I received a delegation of 15 nomadic people from the Kazakhstan Republic in Central Asia. These nomads travel with their herds from pasture to pasture. But now they are beginning to want to settle on their own lands! They came to ask me, not for horses, but straightaway for tractors! Not one tractor, but many. They had to talk to me through an interpreter – they did not speak Russian."

Impressed but still not satisfied, his inquisitor asked one more question: "How long do you think it will be before the peasant will have a decent standard of living?"

"Now he wants the American tempo. We have a five-year plan, but personally I think the process of development will take ten years."

"What about the tempo of the Russian peasant being so much slower than the American farmer's?"

"There is no fundamental difference. It is only an old fable. There are many legends about the Russian peasant, but it is plain that he had enough energy to kick out the tsar and put in the Soviet power. He has acquired 30,000 tractors in three years. We were afraid that he could not run the tractors but our fears had no foundation. He has learned to run them."

He stood up and extended his hand. Dreiser rose and shook his hand respectfully.

6. *Brief Visit to a Candy Factory*

The American delegate visited only one factory in Moscow, a very pleasant one – the big candy factory Krasny Oktyabr (Red October) on the other side of the river.

It was his first introduction to the "fab-kom" (factory-workers' committee). In the committee rooms, he talked with the secretary, who explained that the fab-kom is elected by the local trade union members to look after their interests. Three of the 15 members devoted full time to their duties and were paid by the factory management. Fab-kom made a collective agreement with the management which was ratified at a local union meeting. A conflict commission, on which workers and management had equal representation, settled disputes. Should a worker fall below the set norm of production, the factory committee would support the management.

Each local trade union ("mest-kom) elected a representative to the Moscow Soviet. This representative sat daily in each factory committee office during the noon hour to talk with the workers. They ate dinner in the factory dining room. Each factory had a trade union club. In the same rooms with the fab-kom was the factory nucleus of the Communist party, which exerted the directing influence on the whole plant apparatus. Krasny Oktyabr had 2600 workers and employees.

This was Dreiser's first (but not his last) introduction to the ever-present factory day nursery. This well-equipped and attractive nursery was used by 88 per cent of the women workers. Infants and young children could be left here ten hours of the day. Nursing mothers were allowed two hours free time to feed their babies here. There were cribs for infants and trained nurses in attendance, a play room, beds for afternoon naps, a dining room and a glass-enclosed porch.

Although child care was not one of the American novelist's major interests, he conceded that this was a very well-equipped nursery. He added in a threatening aside to me, "But when I've seen one, I've seen them all." (That's what *he* thought.)

He was more interested in seeing the candy factory in operation, although he did not eat sweets, preferring, I suppose, to get his sugar from liquor. However, for me, underweight and craving sweets, the aroma that filled the air was ambrosial. The many varieties of candies—chocolates, caramels, hard candies—tempted me almost beyond endurance. Noting with amusement how I breathed in the aroma, pressing my hand to my solar plexus and rolling my eyes, my employer called the attention of our guide to my plight. He laughed, brought a paper bag and urged me to help myself from the trays. What a sweet memory!

Dreiser was interested in the modern factory machinery. The workrooms were clean and well equipped. The workers wore fresh white aprons, but the wrapping of assorted candies was still done by hand.

The workers gathered around us and asked questions about candy factories in America. The guest admitted he had never seen one, and was no authority on the subject of sweets (as was his secretary) but he thought this plant might compare favorably with the best in the United States.

He asked them one challenging question: "What about graft?"

A chorus of voices answered that graft was practically impossible in this factory or any other because of the strict control by the factory management and workers committees, as well as workers and peasants inspection.

Out in the frosty, exhilarating air, we hailed an *izvozchik*. Dreiser loved to bargain with the drivers and had been quick to learn the exchange rates.

"Ask him how much to that porcelain museum."

"Three roubles? Why, that's a dollar-and-a-half. He's nuts—offer him half."

"*Nyet, nyet, barin. Dva-peedeesat.*"

"Two-fifty, he says? Okay, make it two."

That settled, the great American financial expert leaned back contentedly in the narrow seat of the sleigh. I squeezed in beside him and tucked the fur robe about us, and we skimmed over the slippery cobblestones.

The porcelain collection was in a fine old mansion, formerly the home of a textile manufacturer. Inside, the spacious rooms were richly furnished and harmonious in style and color. An exhibit that was most pleasing to Dreiser was a collection of porcelain figures in bright-colored native costumes.

The old driver was waiting outside, walking up and down and slapping himself to keep warm, so we decided to ride to a large sculpture museum on the Volhonka. There we dismissed the *izvozchik* with an additional rouble.

Dreiser lingered over the exhibits. He mused before the classic figures, some in heroic size, and murmured, "Nothing so perfect as the sculpture of ancient Greece has since been conceived. This is pure beauty unmarred by gross material conceptions."

In the section devoted to foreign paintings, he declared solemnly, "These Dutch masters have never been equalled."

The Tretyakov Gallery gave him a good impression of pre-revolutionary art. He spent some time in the two rooms devoted to Repin's historical paintings, especially the huge canvas depicting Ivan the Terrible after he had murdered his son.

"Those haunting eyes," he muttered, as he turned away.

7. TD Settles Literary Matters with Gosizdat

Meanwhile, the American author was able to attend to personal business relating to the publication of his literary works in the Soviet Union. Sergey Dinamov, always eager to help, arranged a conference with Ossip Beskin, head of the

Department of Foreign Literature, of which Dinamov's Anglo-American section was a division. Dreiser came to Gosizdat (State Publishing House) in the belligerent spirit he had habitually assumed in dealing with American publishers. He was annoyed that some of his books had been reprinted in Russian by Soviet publishers without his consent.

My role as interpreter at this interview was a delicate one, since I was also employed parttime by Gosizdat. Dreiser was aware of this relationship, but showed no concern. He trusted me.

Ossip Beskin was a suave, blond young man of bourgeois background, who had been educated in prerevolutionary schools. He spoke no English, for French had been the foreign language of cultured Russians.

The negotiations began haltingly. The American author at once brought up the matter of the cheap paper editions of some of his novels and short stories which had been printed by Soviet publishing concerns — *Sister Carrie, American Tragedy, Jennie Gerhardt, Lynch Court, Free and Other Stories.* He was also aware that Gosizdat had published two books in abridged editions: *Color of a Great City* (titled *New York)* and three sketches from *Twelve Men.* Several more of his works were in preparation.

Gosizdat now asked for exclusive rights to all his works, past and future. Beskin offered 750 roubles for the two books they had published already.

The author glowered. "I refuse to accept your offer. You can take them as a gift."

Ossip Beskin's fair skin reddened to the top of his prematurely bald pate.

"We don't want them as a gift. We want to clear up back debts and start relations on a fair business basis. Your texts were abridged to lower production costs in order to make small paperbound books more accessible to the workers — 65 kopeck for *New York,* 15 kopecks for *Twelve Men.* (A kopeck was half a cent.) So, Meester Drayzer, be so kind as to say what you will take to settle the old account."

"One thousand dollars."

"Good. Now let's discuss your contract."

Dreiser was very firm about terms. He agreed to give the State Publishing House exclusive rights in the USSR and to send copies of his books to Moscow one month after publication in the United States and England and also to send them all his published works up to the present. Rejecting a lower offer, he insisted upon advances of $600 to $1000 on each book, semiannual royalty statements and payments in dollars at ten per cent of total sales to be made through the Chase National Bank in New York.

For the immediate future, the author mentioned that he wanted $1000 advance on *Chains,* now in preparation, and *A Gallery of Women*, which would be ready for publication in New York in 1928. It was so agreed.

When we rose to go, Ossip shook my hand and whispered, "Good girl, you helped us."

The staff gathered around to express their good wishes to the American author, who was already widely known in the Soviet Union. He never had received a penny for the books that were published by small concerns—especially in Leningrad—but the State Publishing House kept this agreement. In fact, Dreiser told me about 1933 or 1934 when I visited him in New York that payments always came through promptly, and his dealings with Moscow had been more satisfactory than with his American publishers.

This statement appears to contradict what Helen Dreiser wrote in *My Life with Dreiser* (p. 293), "while he had not received any payment from the U. S. S. R. since he first drew up a contract with the state publishing house in Moscow in 1927, he did not care to demand an accounting because he had such a desire to see Russia succeed in its experiment—" When he learned that payments were being made to several authors in the United States, "he dictated a long personal letter to Premier Stalin—" Two months later, she added, without mentioning the year (probably 1944), he received through his bank $34,600 from Moscow. In addition, after Dreiser's death, a Soviet government representative "personally delivered" to her "seven thousand dollars in cash."

Obviously, she was not informed about the payments made in the nineteen-thirties, and did not know that he had refrained from asking for an accounting only before and during the agonizing years of the Nazi occupation.

During the period up to the end of 1966, his works had appeared in the USSR in 15 languages, in 170 printings totaling over 12 million copies. Eleven editions were printed in English. The last 12-volume edition of Dreiser's works was issued in 200,000 copies (figures from *Soviet Life,* May, 1967).

Now that his professional relations with the Soviet Government were on a business basis, Dreiser went to see Novokshonov, president of the All-Russian Federation of Writers. Several writers' organizations had headquarters in "Dom Gertzena," the former home of the Russian writer Gertzen.

When we entered the reception room, a tall, lean man with a gaunt face was signing papers at the Federation of Writers desk.

I whispered to Dreiser, "Isn't that Henri Barbusse?"

Dreiser started toward him, but the author of *Under Fire* hurried out without seeing him. Novokshonov recognized Dreiser at once. They sat down together.

"So this is a writers' union. A great idea. We could use one in America. Does it function like the other trade unions?"

"Yes, its function is to protect the interests of members in concluding agreements with publishers and in fixing norms of pay. It also provides legal defense."

"What if the publisher reneges on his contract?"

"Our lawyers give advice and conduct cases in the people's court free of charge. The union has a representative in the people's court, as well as in the Moscow Soviet."

Dreiser remarked that he'd have to take up this matter with the AFL when he got back.

There were 1100 writers and journalists in Moscow, according to the union's president, and about 10,000 throughout the Soviet Union. "And growing," he added. Members paid two-and-a-half per cent of their earnings in dues, receiving the usual workers' benefits. They had their own rest home at Sochi on the Black Sea.

Dreiser decided on the spot to join the Writers Union. It pleased him to have his name follow Barbusse on the roll. After taking leave of the federation's president, he looked about the headquarters of *his* union. There was a library, a lecture hall and an attractive dining room, which now, at mid-morning, was empty. The small, round tables looked cozy for intimate chats over a glass of tea. A brass samovar stood on the counter. A sign said that meals for members cost 40 kopecks — about 25 cents.

"I bet this is a lively place when it's full of writers," TD commented a bit wistfully, perhaps remembering his lonely years as a struggling writer. "We'll come back here for a meal sometime."

As we walked toward the center, we suddenly had a full view of "one of the noblest shrines of Christendom," the stately white stone Cathedral of Christ the Savior, which stood on a broad plaza near the Moscow River embankment. Its great central dome and four encircling cupolas, all five topped with the Greek cross and covered with gold leaf, gleamed in the morning sunshine.

Dreiser stood still and gazed in awed silence at the exquisite building, which was like a piece of classic sculpture. Presently, he said this was not his first view of the cathedral. One night, shortly after his arrival in Moscow, he had gone inside with Scott Nearing, Dorothy Thompson, William Gropper, Junius Wood and William Reswick. Why did it look newer and more modern than the other churches?

I explained that Tsar Nicholas I had ordered construction of the church in 1837 to commemorate the defeat of Napoleon's armies. But it was not finished until 46 years later.

I inadvertently remarked that a debate was now going on in high government circles over a proposal to tear it down.

He was aghast. "You mean they are talking about tearing down this magnificent monument to their victory over Napoleon? Are they nuts?"

I said Stalin and his supporters argued that it was not fitting for a church to occupy the loftiest site in the capital, clearly visible from every point of approach to the city. Stalin wanted to build in its place a Palace of the Soviets which would be the highest building in the world—higher than the tallest New York skyscraper.

"I'd like to talk to Stalin," Dreiser muttered, "but," he added glumly, "I guess I won't get a chance to interview him." He walked away in moody silence.

8. Meeting with Mayakovsky; Banquet for Foreign Writers

We had dinner with the "poet of the revolution," Vladimir Mayakovsky. He lived in a shabby but comfortable apartment. Breek, a literary critic, was there with his wife Lilya, who acted as hostess. She was exotically slim and charming. Also present were Tretyakov, author of the new play *Roar, China!*, and his talented wife. All were leaders of the "Lef" group, in which Meierhold was a controversial figure. A friendly bull terrier, the first household pet I had seen in crowded Moscow, gave me a homey diversion.

The table was loaded with *zakuski,* a variety of smoked and pickled fish and cheeses, stuffed eggs, cucumbers in sour cream, cold meats—and vodka and wines. Our host had a large income from his popular writings and lectures. Not being a party member, he was not restricted in his earnings. A large bowl of caviar brought a side remark from the American guest, which I did not translate although it would have amused the poet:

"Good Lord, that would cost at least 25 dollars in New York!"

Then the main courses appeared—oxtail soup with *piroshki* (rolls stuffed with meat), goose with apples, and other delicacies which further astonished the guest. But what astonished the hosts was the guest of honor pouring his glass of vodka over the whipped cream on his prune preserves.

"A great epicurean discovery!" the handsome young poet of the revolution proclaimed. "We shall call this concoction *Krem Drayzera* and thereby immortalize his name!"

I find that my translations do not do justice to the sparkling wit of the "Lef" literary leaders. And Dreiser, too, entered into the spirit of the conversation and was very gay. After the food and liquor, the jokes became embarrassing for me to translate and Dreiser remarked on the disadvantages of having a female secretary.

"Perhaps a eunuch would be more satisfactory," said Mayakovsky, "but I'm afraid you won't find one in Moscow."

The gay party accompanied us to the tram. Dreiser shouted from the steps a word he had learned "*do-sveedanya!*" (till we meet again).

We met again sooner than we expected. Gosizdat was giving a banquet for foreign writers at Dom Gertzena that evening. Upon entering the dining hall, the first person we noticed was our erstwhile host, Mayakovsky. The young giant, looking more like an American football hero than a revolutionary poet, loomed up at the head of the long table. He saluted the American author with a comradely gesture.

Among the American writers toasted were Anna Louise Strong, Professor H. W. L. Dana, Albert Rhys Williams and Mary Reed. After I had translated Theodore Dreiser's brief and simple speech, Mayakovsky shouted:

"Meester Drayzer is the first American ever to admit he has not reached definite conclusions. After a few days in Moscow, they write whole books about our country." (Loud laughter and applause.)

Dreiser was intrigued by the exotic appearance of the man sitting across from him. I whispered, "That's Khalatov, president of Gosizdat!"

The president of the State Publishing House was dark-skinned, with sparkling black eyes and full black beard. A round embroidered Caucasian cap sat jauntily on his shoulder-length black hair. His full red lips were smiling, his expression was half-childlike, half-cunning.

Theodore Dreiser fired questions across the table at him. Finally, the publisher came around and sat beside him. But persistent questioning revealed only that he was "Armenian, 33 years old, a born revolutionist." Dreiser, the reporter, still tried to get at the man but in reply to every question the president of the largest publishing company in the world only added another post, another long title. Finally giving up, Dreiser consented to have his photo taken with his wily publisher.

"You see," he told me as he rose to go, "I have to get on the good side of this fellow."

Khalotov made the major speech of the evening. He boasted that in the decade since the revolution, Gosizdat had printed "not thousands, not millions, but half a billion books!" For the benefit of the foreign writers present, he gave statistics on foreign literature translated and published up to 1928: Of American authors, more than 50 fiction writers were in print, averaging in first editions 5,000 to 6,000 copies. Among the most popular was Sinclair Lewis's *Main Street,* which sold 30,000 copies. The total copies sold of the complete works of Upton Sinclair had reached 485,000; the complete works of Jack London, 1,300,000; Sherwood Anderson's *Triumph of the Egg,* 14,000.

Finally, with a sly smile in our direction, Khalatov announced "Gosizdat has just signed a contract with Teodor Drayzer for exclusive right in the USSR to all his past and future works." Loud applause. Still clapping, Mayakovsky rose and shouted, *"Molodetz* (bravo) Drayzer!"

It was 2 a.m. when we rode by sleigh to our hotels in a driving snowstorm.

9. Pilgrimage to Tolstoy's Home

After this festive evening in the company of his fellow-writers, Dreiser was in the mood to take a sentimental journey to Yasnaya Polyana, 100 miles south of Moscow. It was the 17th anniversary of Leo Tolstoy's death (November 21, 1910). At 1 a.m. of a bitter-cold night, we boarded a crowded train. No seats in *myaki,* the soft coaches, nor even in *zhestoki,* the hard coaches in which one could rent bedding. The only space left was in fourth class, dubbed "Maxim Gorky." When we entered, we understood why. It was packed with the "lower depths" of the population. Standing room only for us. In the candlelight we saw rows of booted feet hanging from the upper tier of shelves. One fellow had taken off his boots and his bare feet dangled in the glowering face of the American delegate. Pungent odors filled the airtight coach.

Actually, his discomfort on his first journey outside Moscow lasted only two hours. At the first stop, we jumped off (no passage between cars) and ran to the first soft coach, where the *provodneek* (car porter) kindly allowed us to occupy his tiny compartment. We sat dozing until our arrival at Yasnaya Polyana at 7 a.m.

Here was a real Russian winter scene, an old village deep in snow and surrounded by a snow-laden forest of pine and birch. We were very tired and hungry. Seeking breakfast, we went to the watchman's hut and were kindly received by a young peasant woman wearing a red kerchief. Built into a whitewashed log wall was the brick stove for cooking and warmth. The young father of the two children lay in his boots on the shelf over the stove which served as a warm bed in peasant houses. Against the side of the stove were a birch-twig broom, a poker, and long-handled iron prongs for sliding earthen pots and tin pans in and out of the deep oven.

While the American author watched curiously, the woman prepared the brass samovar. She brought a bucket of water and filled it, then dropped pieces of charcoal down the inside pipe and lighted them. Next, she inserted a piece of stovepipe in the top and put the other end in the stove flue.

While the water was heating, she scrubbed the table on which she had kneaded the loaves of bread just out of the oven. By this time, the water was boiling. She removed the stovepipe and put four eggs to steam in a sieve on top of the samovar.

Meanwhile, she had put a spoonful of tea leaves in a small earthen pot, poured boiling water from the spigot of the samovar over the leaves and, removing the eggs, placed the pot on top to steep. Now she deftly threw a white embroidered linen cloth over the table, moved the steaming samovar to the table, set two bowls, two glasses and spoons, brought stools and seated us, with the customary invitation: "Please sit and drink tea."

She cut thick slices of the warm black bread on a wooden board and invited me to pour the tea. Pouring some of the strong essence from the little pot into our glasses, I filled them with boiling water from the spigot. Our hostess used pincers to break off chunks from a hard lump of sugar for our tea and set a bowl of apple preserves before us.

Dreiser ate with gusto, enjoying the breakfast of fresh bread and butter, perfectly soft-boiled eggs and hot tea.

"I never ate a breakfast that tasted better!" he declared.

After Dreiser had paid her, she gave us directions for finding a sled to hire. The primitive sledge quite amazed the American guest. A straw-filled basket was tied to birch runners and drawn by a horse with a high-arched yoke. We sat on the straw and bumped over the dirt road to Tolstoy's home, now a museum. Down an avenue of trees stood a two-story white frame house looking very much like my grandfather's farmhouse in Oklahoma.

The old caretaker, surprised to have such early visitors, showed us the unheated rooms, left exactly as when the family had lived in them. There was a grand piano, shelves of books and family portraits in the large living room. Tolstoy's bedroom had a narrow cot, a washstand and chair. An old dressing gown hung as he had left it on that winter night 17 years earlier when he set out with his youngest daughter on his last journey, searching for peace. He had become ill and in the watchman's quarters of a small station, much like the one we had just left, Tolstoy had found eternal peace.

Unaware that relatives were living in another section of the house, we decided we should make ourselves known at the village Soviet. We asked the driver of the sledge who was waiting outside to take us. As soon as we came into the log building of the village Soviet, there was great excitement. Why hadn't we sent word we were coming? A messenger was dispatched to the Tolstoy house to bring news that the great American author had come to attend the anniversary observances. Tolstoy's daughter asked that we brought back at once.

We were chilled in the ten-below-zero temperature and very tired when we entered the warm, comfortable living quarters. I went straight to a cushioned seat against the tiled stove.

Sinking into it, almost purring with pleasure, I began to thaw out like a frozen stray cat. Presently, the elderly niece of Tolstoy brought a tray with bread and cheese and hot tea.

After we had rested, we rode in a sleigh to Tolstoy's grave, following the procession of peasants and their children who were walking along in deep snow almost to the tops of their felt boots. It was a simple, fenced-in mound of earth in a grove of birch trees. Children from the village school, which had been founded by Tolstoy and was now directed by his niece, laid pine branches and autumn flowers on the grave. A chorus of sweet young voices sang the old dirge, *Vechnaya Pamyat* (Eternal Remembrance). Tolstoy's daughter Olga spoke, and one of the peasants recited poems. Then the procession, all chanting the moving dirge, filed back to the village.

When we returned to the farmhouse, our thoughtful hostess took us upstairs to rest before dinner. There were two other guests, including Tolstoy's old friend Milyukov. Learning that he was well informed about agricultural problems, Dreiser questioned him, dwelling on his favorite theory — the incompetence of the poor peasant. Milyukov promptly countered with the argument that the great advantages the revolution was bringing to the poor peasant would in time raise the level of his competence.

At the close of their discussion, Milyukov asked the American delegate to deliver a letter to President Coolidge from the peasants of Yasnaya Polyana. The letter begged him to prevent American interference in the development of the Soviet experiment. At the time Dreiser showed little disposition to carry out the mission, and, as far as I know, the letter was never delivered.

In the evening, villagers came to the memorial program in the big living room. Records were played of Tolstoy's voice speaking in Russian, English, French and German. His words rang out clearly in the hushed room. The peasant children sang another lovely song. His niece played Tolstoy's favorite pieces — Tchaikovsky's "Pathetique" and Chopin's "Funeral March." A visiting woman scientist read from Stanislavsky's memoirs his tribute to Leo Tolstoy as a playwright, and then told of her own personal memories of Leo Tolstoy, the man.

The ragged Tolstoyan peasant who had recited poems at the grave still wore his grimy old shuba, a knapsack on his back and huge felt boots. He had learned to read only seven years ago and he now recited his own poems.

Dreiser wrote of him: "on his face was a childlike and quite seraphic smile. Some mute, inglorious temperament. . . . "

One of Tolstoy's stories about his little nieces was read, and everyone laughed, especially the niece who was present. She spoke English and talked to Dreiser about her life. She had lost her wealth in the revolution, was in prison for two months, was released as harmless and came out with only one dress. But she was quite philosophical about the New Order, believed it would succeed, and was content to be permitted by Tolstoy's daughter to live in one room of the house for the rest of her days.

The American author had a long and, in his own words, "wonderful" talk with Olga. She told him about her work in the village school and of the new Tolstoy school under construction.

At 10 that night, we bade farewell to our kind hosts. In order to avoid the Maxim Gorky coaches, we hired a sleigh to Tula, a 20-verst ride in the bitter cold. Enveloped in sheepskins, we were snug from the icy wind and dozed most of the way. At Tula, famous for the manufacture of samovars, we were able to get places in an International coach and arrived in comfort in Moscow at 6:00 the following morning.

10. Interviews with Radek and Bukharin

After this pastoral interlude, we learned that VOKS had arranged several interviews with officials to keep the impatient delegate occupied while waiting for the main tour. They no doubt were planning it with care and trepidation. Before the scheduled interviews began, Dreiser had an unscheduled visit from a high-ranking member of the Central Committee of the party.

At 9 o'clock one evening, as I was leaving my employer's suite after a busy day, Karl Radek dropped in, unannounced.

Dreiser had telephoned him several times at his apartment in the Kremlin without reaching him. Radek now hurriedly explained that no individual foreigners were admitted to the Kremlin nor could they be connected with residents by telephone.

"So I came to you," he concluded with a bow and a smile. He was of stocky build, with a fringe of reddish hair about his face that receded from a broad forehead. Horn-rimmed spectacles added to his owlish look.

Radek was an "Old Bolshevik." In 1915, with Lenin, Zinoviev, Trotsky and other Russian revolutionary leaders, he had attended an international socialist conference in Zimmerwald as representative of the Polish Socialist party. Until recently he had been editor of *Izvestia,* the government newspaper. Now he was virtually a prisoner in the Kremlin. After Lenin's death, he had been a prominent figure in the bitter struggle between the two power groups on the Central Committee, led respectively by Stalin and Trotsky. The struggle had reached its climax when it became clear that the New Economic Policy adopted in 1923 as a temporary measure in the transition period from war communism to peaceful socialist construction, was strengthening the position of private traders and prosperous peasants.

A crisis had developed in agriculture, especially in grain farming. The Stalinist group maintained that small peasant holdings must be organized into collective farms, allowing a peasant family to own only house, garden, cow, chickens and one horse. A collective farm would be owned jointly by the peasants in a village and machinery, labor and earnings pooled.

The *kolkhoz* (collective farm), organized and operated by a group of peasants, was owned and run by them for their own profit. On the other hand, the *sovkhoz* (state farm) belonged to and was operated by the government, and the peasants worked for wages.

The Trotsky group favored large-scale farms, of which there were already a few. These applied mechanized agricultural methods and utilized the competence of the more prosperous (middle) peasants and the kulaks. The Stalinists labeled the two plans "socialist vs. capitalist" farming.

Considering Dreiser's views on the problem of the competent versus the incompetent peasant, expressed in his interview with Svidersky, it seemed likely that the American visitor would favor the state farm. Sensing that a major crisis was developing, he wanted to get some basic facts about the issues in order to find out "what these Russians are up to." But to his disappointment, Radek avoided any reference to the conflict within the party or to his own precarious situation.

Radek had been very close to Lenin in the days before the October Revolution. He was in the group of Russian political exiles who traveled in a sealed train from Germany to Petrograd in April 1917, with detailed plans for a series of revolutions already mapped out. According to Krupskaya's *Memoirs* Radek was one of the exiles who traveled under an assumed name — "Pripevsky" — given him humorously by Lenin, "pripev" meaning refrain of a song. Radek sang well, besides being very talkative and full of jokes — which sometimes annoyed Lenin.

Now here was "Pripevsky" talking freely to Theodore Dreiser about world politics, literature, art and music, gesturing with his delicate hands. There was reverence and tenderness in his voice when he told of his personal association with "Vladimir Ilyich." He spoke of Lenin's classical interests and tastes, and his utterly unscientific mind.

"He wouldn't use a fountain pen because he didn't know how to fill it," Radek said, laughing. "Yet he saw clearly the need to industrialize Russia."

Radek spoke of Lenin's dislike of the jarring noises of cities, while realizing the need for building industrial centers. Dreiser remarked that evidently he was a lover of music.

"Not classical music but peasant folk songs and ballads — village melodies. What he disliked was the old Russian operas, dwelling on the luxurious life of the nobility."

Dreiser said he agreed with Lenin on that score. He was grateful for the visit, enjoying the conversation on subjects nearest his heart.

"I hope we can get together again," he said, when Radek was leaving.

But he never had another opportunity to talk with Radek. Not long after, by vote of the 15th Party Congress — controlled by Stalin—Radek, together with Trotsky and Zinoviev and other Bolshevik leaders of the opposition, was expelled from the Communist party.

Because of its historic relevance, it seems appropriate to describe, though out of chronological order, another of Dreiser's most important interviews, in Moscow.

After our trip to Leningrad (see next chapter), on the morning of December 5, VOKS informed us that Nikolai Bukharin might be able to see the American delegate after the session of the 15th Party Congress that day. While Bukharin was not one of the bloc of "Trotskyites and Zinovievites, such as Radek," which the Congress had voted to expel, at the moment he, too, was in a precarious position.

In the afternoon, Trevis came to accompany us as interpreter. As we showed our passes at the main gate, the American delegate was exulting that at last he was to get into the Kremlin. But he had little opportunity for sightseeing after he was inside the crenelated walls. We hurried to the Kremlin Palace, where party plenums and congresses were held. Passing through several great halls in the vast former palace of the last tsars, we entered a vestibule where we removed our wraps. I noticed my employer had forgotten his bow tie. This upset him, but Trevis assured him Bukharin had too many important matters to worry about to notice such a small detail. He impressed upon him the fact that Bukharin was president of the Comintern, the leading Marxian theoretician and the "darling of the party" because of his comely face and sweet disposition.

Thus properly impressed, we solemnly entered the large, comfortable reception room. Soon, a small man entered quietly. His fair, wavy hair was thinning and fell in wisps over his high forehead. His face was boyish, his blue eyes childlike. He greeted us in a charmingly affectionate manner. This genial Russian intellectual knew English but preferred to have a translator. Trevis was an able interpreter and left me free to take notes.

Unawed by the noted Marxian scholar, the arrogant American launched his planned attack.

"Does the Soviet Government follow Marx closely, and how have you diverged?"

If he was taken aback by this sudden onslaught, Bukharin did not show it. "We have not diverged at all – but I think we have modified Marx to meet our problems."

"If you have not diverged, why then does the individual own land, horses, houses, automobiles?"

"Marxism is not a set doctrine which lays out a plan for the future society. Marx never denied the transition period."

"Then you can adapt Marx freely?"

"It is not a definite, detailed plan, but he recognized the transition period – in the *Communist Manifesto* there are 11 or 12 points dealing with the period during which the socialization of industry would take place."

"We are moving toward that in America."

"Yes, but under the dictatorship of the capitalists."

"Here you also have a dictatorship."

Bukharin smiled indulgently. "Yes, but of another class – the workers (not the private owners)".

"Is there any difference?"

"Yes, of course. But we must consider that any form of society must develop. Capitalism had several stages in its history – primitive, industrial. Socialism is not a fixed order. Like capitalism, it will develop."

"Like a tree?"

"Quite so. And the present stage is the dictatorship of the proletariat. I read various economic theories. For example, Thomas Nixon Carver said that the economic revolution is taking place in America, not in Russia, that it takes the form of labor banks, employee stock ownership, etc., which are entirely transforming the capitalist system."

"This is true," Dreiser assented quickly, in the tone of a debater who has scored a point.

"No, it is an illusion. You have several layers of society – skilled workers, poor farmers, rich farmers, Negroes, and the standard of living of some of these classes is very low. You have only three million organized workers, out of 25 million. And these labor banks and profit sharing are only for the labor aristocracy; these privileges only for a few. This exceptional situation is due to world economic conditions such as affected England earlier and resulted in the evolutionary development of the English laborer. Now England no longer has such exceptional conditions for the workers, while in America the machine process is the basis for the benefits, which accrue chiefly to the capitalists and the labor aristocracy. But the present system in America is only a moment in the constellation."

"Do you maintain that the situation here is final?"

"No such thing. It can change."

"But in what direction? You don't think it could change into an intellectual despotism?"

"No. . . "

"But aren't there millions who don't agree?"

"No — not so many. . . "

"If 51 per cent of the population were communist and 49 per cent were not, what would the government do?"

"This is an absolutely abstract point. We must look at problems concretely, because we have no abstract situation. The real situation is not one which can be stated as for or against communism, because the leading force is communist. As in your society, the great number are with us; the rich peasant is against us, a third section is neutral, or passive."

"That is the mechanism of life. But please answer my theoretical question — 49 against 51."

"But this question is not possible in such a simplified form. . . "

"I mean only the mental attitude."

"You cannot divide populations by mental attitudes, but on actual social conditions."

"But you do have a dictatorship. . . "

"Yes, of the city proletariat. Our relationship to the peasants is different."

"But your peasants do not always agree, and if they don't, you lead them anyhow?"

"Your mistake is that you think only in a static, not in a dynamic, way," Bukharin replied patiently. "In great questions, the peasants are with us, and from this important base of agreement we lead them to other questions. For example, I received today a photo of myself when I was in prison 20 years ago. I can recall that at that time if you spoke against the tsar a peasant would knock you down because traditionally the peasantry were for the tsar. But by a careful propaganda approach we were able to show the peasants that only fools would support the tsar. We came to the peasants and said: 'What are you suffering for?' and they replied, 'We need land.' Then we showed them that the tsar had most of the land, and so little by little we led the peasants nearer to us."

"Isn't this what you do with the child, take him and teach him certain principles? The child knows nothing, so what you teach is to him true. Doesn't the success of your system depend upon your teaching the child?"

"In a way, yes. But on the radio you can receive on more than one station. In the same way the apperceptions of one class are one thing, and another class, another. When we try to transform the child we have the problem of various tendencies."

"But if you take the child and say this is true, it is, and doesn't the success of communism depend upon changing the psychological attitudes of the child? Doesn't the Catholic Church do this?"

Bukharin pointed out here the obvious fact that any society rears its children in its existing economic and political system. The freer the society, the more freedom the growing child has to think for himself. Oligarchies have not survived, he pointed out. "Old Greece and Babylon were destroyed," he concluded.

"But not Greek civilization," Dreiser protested.

"True, and we inherited that."

"Aristotle is as great today as he was then," Dreiser declared.

"No, not as great. Do you know that in the Chinese we can find almost the whole process of Greek civilization?... Modern capitalism confronts us with this problem: If we have two or three more world wars, we will disappear. There is only one force which will save us – the dictatorship of the proletariat."

Somewhat frustrated, Dreiser doggedly returned to his original question: "Why does the individual own land, houses, automobiles?"

"Under the New Economic Policy it is true that bourgeois tendencies appear. But they can be controlled by the iron dictatorship of the workers. The Social-Democrats oppose this control. Such bourgeois tendencies will always lead inevitably to the collapse of socialism."

Impressed by the logic of the Marxian dialectician, the American individualist said earnestly, "I'm not against the Soviet system. I came to see if it would work. The question troubling me is: Should the big mind rule the little one?"

"Ah, this is the question of intellectual aristocracy. In reply, I shall explain the real communist society of the future and then return to your question."

"But," the inquisitor persisted, "what about the big mind and the little mind right now?"

"Well, if we need the advice of a statistician, we go to a good statistician. It is not possible that all people have the same nose, eyes, or the same quantity of brains."

"You are right," the individualist interrupted, "there are a few gigantic minds and many little ones."

"But if we take the present capitalist society, there is a standard of intellect, a monopoly of education . . . "

"No, that's not true!"

"But it is a fact that in capitalist society the proletariat is oppressed culturally. Yet if you compare the quantity of brains of the oppressed class with the brains of the capitalists, you will find that there is no difference. It is a matter of opportunity."

"From where do you get these statistics?" Dreiser demanded.

"From scientific sources."

"Can you mention a great mind from your proletariat?"

"In our country today the intelligent and the unintelligent are not divided into classes. Part of our great minds are from the pre-revolutionary intelligentsia and part from the proletariat, to whom the dictatorship of the proletariat now gives greater opportunities. All forces in bourgeois society are against the proletariat. They do not have the advantages of education. . . . But today the Soviet Government gives more advantages to the working class, so we are always getting new forces from their ranks. That is not possible in capitalist society. Here, we have big minds which do not work against the working class. Take me, for example, I am the expression of the dictatorship of the proletariat against the bourgeoisie."

"Does Marx rule your mind?"

"I am a Marxist, if that is what you mean. But this relationship is not analogous to your question, which, as I understand it, is whether the more clever should rule the less clever. But a more important question is class relationships and not whether the proletariat or the bourgeoisie are more intelligent."

"But if in Soviet Russia the clever mind rules the less clever, you have an intellectual aristocracy."

"But the relationship is entirely different. There was, for example, an intellectual aristocracy in Judea made up of the privileged classes. In Egypt the rich were the intellectuals."

"In Soviet Russia there are two classes," Dreiser insisted, "the intelligent and the less intelligent."

"But they are not classes. . . "

"Yes, they are!" He gestured toward the windows. "Down below there is a street cleaner of very low intelligence. Do you mean to say that his position in society is the same as yours?"

(In an aside to me, Dreiser muttered: "I'll die but I'll get this out of him!")

"Yes," Bukharin replied calmly, "in our social system he has the same opportunities as I have and the same rights."

"Then what are you doing here? You agree you would rather be here?"

"Certainly. We can't class all men as blondes and brunettes, rich and poor, fools and intelligent. I am not the same as the man in the street, I agree. But today we make it a government policy that all manual workers must be educated the same as the intelligentsia. Already, we see results. Ten years ago, we had in the Central Committee of the party five or six intellectuals to two or three workers. Now we have 60 members of the Central Committee who are workers. There is no intellectual difference between them and us."

"Did these have special training? You can't tell me that these 60 men are typical."

"Yes, now there are masses of them. I have worked among them a great deal and our masses are very intelligent."

The incorrigible individualist did not give up. He recited again his code of life: "I think big minds will always sit in high places and have comfortable rooms and lead the little

minds in the street. If your country gets rich and everybody
has money, who will sit here and who will work in the mines?"

"The old intelligentsia will die, and the new generation
will all be workers."

"Yes, but who will do the dirty work? All can't sit here."

Bukharin paced the floor, his comely, boyish face showing
the strain of suppressed impatience. Then he brought out an
English edition of his book *Historical Materialism*. Turning
the pages, he handed it to his guest. "Read page three-o-nine
of my book."

Dreiser read the page: ". . . the incompetence of the masses
will disappear, for this incompetence is by no means a necessary attribute of every system." He closed the book and handed
it back to its author. "Incompetence will always be," he repeated.

The Marxian scholar put his hand to his head. "Oh, my God,
I can't stand this!" he groaned, speaking in Russian. Then
quickly recovering his poise, he continued in a quiet tone:

"We will always have differences in intellectual qualifications, but in a situation, for example, where a big scientist
says to me, 'You must produce more in your department,' there
is no oppression, no suggestion of my incompetence in this."
He added, "We think that through large-scale development
of economic resources we shall succeed in machine production
without capitalist competition. There will be the same competition between two workers as between two writers or two
managers of state factories."

The visitor curled his lip in a cynical smile. "So you think
there will be no unhappiness, no disappointments, no tragedies?"

The Marxian shook his head. "There will always be unhappy
love, individual tragedies, perhaps even idiots and defectives
for whom we will build hospitals. But individual ambitions will
disappear because they will have no basis. There will be another type of personal ambition — to best serve society, not for material gain but for personal satisfaction and a place of honor
in society." He went on gravely: "We Communists today are
a product of the old society. We must often fight against old

traditions in ourselves. When a child learns to read he must make an effort. But later he reads unconsciously and without effort. And this relationship between man and man — without competition for material possessions — will finally be as easy as learning to read."

"So you're going to have a perfect world, against human nature," the author of *The American Tragedy* flung back at him. "And you think God will accept it? That's the bunk! Contrasts will remain forever, that's what makes life interesting. That's the way the universe is run, is spite of your Marxian theories."

"My God, take him away!" Bukharin muttered in Russian to Trevis. "I can't stand any more."

But on the surface, gracious and charming to the end, he escorted us to the door.

When we left the Kremlin, outside the gateway to the Red Square we ran plump into a street cleaner engaged in sweeping the cobblestones with a birch-twig broom. When his labors carried him in front of the Chapel of the Iberian Virgin, he removed his ragged fur hat, dropped his broom and crossed himself.

"I suppose next year he'll have Bukharin's place," Dreiser muttered.

11. TD Meets Mikoyan

It is pleasant to record here Dreiser's interview with the Commissar of Trade, Anastas I. Mikoyan, who was destined to become President of the USSR in 1964.

Mikoyan's spacious offices were in the big building occupied by Narkomtorg (People's Commissariat for Commerce) within the crumbling brick walls of Kitai Gorod, built by Boris Godunov in the 16th century. One wall skirted Red Square.

The dark, slender, young Armenian, with his clipped black mustache and khaki uniform decorated with medals, was an imposing figure. He politely motioned the guest to be seated in the deep leather chair facing him across his great carved desk. On one side sat a mild little man; on the other, a pretty blond girl. Both secretaries knew English and took turns translating — for which I was thankful, since the subject matter consisted largely of dry facts and figures.

Dreiser wasted no time in asking for the information he wanted. His questions were keen and well chosen, which is not surprising when we recall the Cowperwood novels, chronicles of the businessman, stockbroker and banker in the epoch of the growth of American capitalism and the building of industry. At the time of his pilgrimage to the first socialist country, the author's challenging approach reflected a sympathetic identification with his hero Cowperwood.

After asking about the functions of Mikoyan's department, Dreiser then inquired:

"Don't you ever use the policy of stimulating buying by selling luxuries?"

"No, we can't even supply the necessities as yet. Even so, people buy the luxuries when they can get them. We ourselves produce many more luxuries than were produced by Russian industries before the war. However," he added, "Russia will never be a luxury-consuming country. Luxury," he said in a matter-of-fact tone, "can only lead to the destruction of communism."

Dreiser asked about trade within the country.

"The government buys grain and other food products from the peasants," the commissar replied in measured tones, to permit almost simultaneous translation alternately from his two alert young aides, "and industrial materials at their source from the area trusts. There are two or three great organizations from which we buy special products like cotton, grain and coal. Prices are fixed at a maximum or minimum and strictly adhered to. Price fluctuations such as you have in America are impossible. A certain level must be maintained — not too high, which would be hard on the worker; not too low, for it would ruin the peasant. For example, in your country, prices fluctuate greatly in the past year; in Russia, they have remained stationary for two years."

Surprisingly, the loyal American accepted this statement without argument. Mikoyan evidently had impressed him as a coldly practical, implacable Communist public servant. For the first time, and perhaps the last, in his interviews with Soviet officials, he did not display his American sense of superiority, his assumption of the right to say what he pleased and do what he pleased when a guest in a foreign land.

He asked only one more question. "Does the government demand a profit above wages and upkeep?"

"Yes," Mikoyan replied simply. "The government has a minimum profit. In the grain trade there was an income last year of 700 million roubles and a profit of only eight million.

Mikoyan added, "The government takes only amortization from industrial profits and 40 per cent from the profits of state organizations, which it uses for operating the Union of Soviet Socialist Republics."

The Commissar rose and bowed us out with military formality.

Theodore Dreiser was in a subdued mood as we walked out of the ancient walled trading center and left the Red Square by the Iberian Gate. Continuing on the strip of park which skirted the Kremlin wall, we entered the boulevard and circled around into Strasnoi Square. Pushkin's statue stood at the intersection facing the Tverskaya.

It was only four o'clock in the afternoon, yet already it was twilight of the November day. A full moon shone on the red-cheeked children who were out with their sleds, bundled up like teddy bears in the frosty air. Pushkin looked benignly down on the happy scene.

It amused Dreiser that the old monastery across the square was now an antireligious museum. He walked quickly through the arch in the tower gate. Inside, he stopped short and gazed long at what I called "my favorite church." Its domes were an exquisite shade of blue, studded with gold stars.

"You are right," he said softly, "it *is* the loveliest. It may be the magic of the moonlight, but its medieval grace soothes my nerves."

I was thankful that the Museum of the Godless Society was closed.

12. *Conversations on Trade and Cooperatives*

On the following day, the fact-finding delegate was back to the gruelling interviews by which he hoped to learn the official Soviet position.

Klimokon, vice-president of the All-Russian Cooperatives (the existence of which before the revolution was a helpful preparation for the present social structure), was a young man, rather commonplace in appearance. He spoke excellent English and answered questions with keen understanding. At the outset, he explained that NEP was now on its way out.

"What is the percentage of private trade at present?" Dreiser inquired.

"About 22 per cent. The cooperatives now handle half the trade, mainly in small shops operated by consumer groups. Private shops get their goods from the state, because our government has a monopoly on foreign buying. The cooperatives also buy through the state. The government's share of the trade diminishes as the cooperatives increase their power to handle it."

"What is the controlling principle in your trying to sell to the public? Do you try to stimulate trade? Do you want the co-ops to make a profit?"

"No, we work on a small margin. We do not trade for profit but to supply the people with the necessities of life."

"Would you prefer to restrain their demand for luxuries?"

"Not if people can afford them, but imported luxuries are heavily taxed."

"I have heard that the private shops are using more initiative and are more popular with the people," Dreiser remarked.

"Actually, their business is decreasing," calmly replied Klimokon.

"Does private buying by the NEP men produce private capitalists?" Dreiser inquired shrewdly.

"I regret to say it does," the official answered gravely. "But they are on the decrease. The agricultural co-ops organize wheat pools, for example. The private dealer pays more, but he can make a profit sometimes by selling in local places. However, such speculation is on a small scale because all transportation facilities are in the hands of the government."

"So you think there is no danger from the private trader?"

"Of course, there is danger—they might have seized trade with one blow. During the Civil War, when the cooperatives were weak, private traders were a great danger. But financial pressure from the Soviets deprived them of their capital, and foreign private capital could come in only with difficulty." He added, "Capital in the cooperative societies was accumulated during the first period after the revolution. The government told the cooperatives they must compete with private trade and beat it with lower prices."

"Do you think your production costs are excessive?" This was the American writer's chief criticism of Soviet economy.

"Yes, especially for clothing and shoes. Too much of the work is handicraft in shoes, and much of the raw material must be imported."

The American delegate suddenly popped one of his loaded questions: "When Soviet Russia is rich will your people still wear cheap clothing, eat cheap food? Mikoyan told me just the other day that Russia will never be a luxury-consuming country."

Dreiser added, "He said luxury can only spell the death of Communism—inspire show, waste, vainglory... I wonder."

Klimokon did not comment on the commissar's statement. He said simply, "Poor people don't live that way from choice, Mr. Dreiser. Only now we are poor. We are supplying only 75 to 80 per cent of the people's needs. In the cooperative shops there is always a mass of people buying cotton because they know if they come late none will be left. Of course, if a man has money he can go to a private store, pay more and get material. But," he amended optimistically, "the government hopes to supply this remaining 25 per cent in five years. As for the present standard of living in our country, the demand for white bread has increased 250 per cent since the war. Butter also. This figure is for workers—the bourgeoisie doesn't count."

"Don't you think too much red tape is the cause of the delay?"

"Yes, there is too much red tape, too much bureaucracy, but far less than before the revolution. But obviously," Klimokon added with asperity, "it can't be blamed to any degree for our not accomplishing miracles in supplying the whole population with a decent standard of living in ten years!". . .

Reproved on that score, the defender of private enterprise fell back on some of his pet theories. "What about private initiative? Won't absence of advertising and other stimulants to buy take away the spirit and color of life?" Klimokon answered patiently until the American had nothing more to say. He rose to terminate an interview which had given little support to his theories.

However, on the following day, he came up freshly primed for a bout with the People's Commissar of Post and Telegraph. Commissar Lubovitch was rather stout and had a good-natured almost jolly face, round and smooth-shaven. The son of a carpenter, he had finished elementary school and, after trying several professions including teaching he became a telegraph operator. His present career began in 1917, when he seized the Petrograd telegraph office by force.

Since Lubovitch spoke fluent English, the exchange of ideas was easy. His interviewer led off with a broad question which Stalin himself might have avoided answering. But this man, it seemed, was used to facing (or circumventing) big questions with self-assurance.

Dreiser: "What is your plan for Russia for the next 25 years?"

Lubovitch: "We have a five-year plan, but since technology, fortunately, does not stand still, it is difficult to keep to even such a brief period of planning. We find it necessary to change the technical details every year. Our plan for the Postal Department has actually lagged behind our accomplishments. We have been able to cover 60 per cent of the regions of the USSR, whereas before the revolution only three per cent were covered by the postal service."

"Was all this under your direction?" Dreiser asked, with a quizzical glance.

"Yes, I was the originator of the system," the commissar admitted modestly. "I studied systems in Europe and installed the best here. At first the postman made his rounds only two or three times a week, traveling about 25 kilometers (15 miles) a day on foot. Today, 60 per cent of our postmen travel on horses. There are still few automobiles in the provinces, with the exception of the Crimea.

"Since the revolution," Lubovitch went on proudly, "the postal service has been transformed. The postman is a walking Soviet encyclopedia, incorporating every kind of service in himself. He takes orders for goods, periodical literature, books, money orders, telegrams, registered letters. If he can't answer a question, he goes to the local Soviet and brings the answer next time.". . .

Dreiser kept prodding. "How long before the remaining 40 per cent of Russian territory will have full postal service?"

"At present this territory has a third line of communication not belonging directly to the Postal Department, a kind of individual messenger service you might call it. But in the next five years we expect that all of the 40 per cent will also be connected by radio, telephone and telegraph."

The commissar went on the explain that the Postal-Telegraph Department of the government operated not only wireless stations but also radio, most of which was international.

"Does the government use all these means of communication for education and propaganda?"

The commissar replied emphatically, "No. We furnish the technical apparatus, and social organizations use it as they see fit. We have nothing to do with the ideology, only the technique."

Finally, Dreiser suggested with his crooked smile:

"Perhaps you would like to ask me some questions."

The response was explosive. "Why didn't the Congress on Telegraph now being held in Washington invite us to participate? I believe we could help them."

The American delegate's reply was unexpectedly frank: "Because those in control fear Soviet influence on the workers."

Thus encouraged, the commissar continued with equal frankness: "If the American people really wanted culture, they have the most complete apparatus in the world for it, but they use their rich resources for luxurious living."

This time the American delegate responded as a loyal American is expected to do: "The average American loves his government and if anyone speaks against it, he yells 'Bolshevik' and wants to have him arrested. Why? Because he gets good wages, has an auto, wonderful roads, every farmer has a telephone and radio, every farm girl has silk stockings."

"Yes, democracy does exist in America," Lubovitch commented drily, "but it is under the control of your financial rulers." He reflected a moment. "You see, I have a brother in the United States who worked in a Ford plant."

"Is that so!"

"Yes, he was ashamed of his brothers in Russia and after a long controversy he and I stopped corresponding. But not long ago, my other brother, who lives in Odessa, had a letter from our brother in the United States saying he had been out of work for a year and needed 200 dollars for an operation. Our brother in Odessa could not, of course, send him American dollars, but he answered that he also had needed an operation. It was performed without charge in a state hospital, with a leave of absence on pay."

The American delegate had nothing more to say. He rather sheepishly shook the commissar's hand and thanked him. Out in the street, I ventured a comment.

"Things must have changed a lot since I left home."

"Now what's on your contentious little mind?" he inquired irritably.

"Are you sure all the farmers have telephones, cars and radios, and all the farm girls have silk stockings?

"What do you know about conditions? You haven't been *home* for more than five years!"

One evening in late November, Sergey Dinamov came to present the final draft of Dreiser's contract with Gosizdat for his signature. The author was annoyed that it did not specifically mention, in the clause guaranteeing publication of new editions of all his works, the abridged editions put out by Land and Factory and other independent small firms.

"I refuse to sign the contract until a clause to that effect is added," he declared.

Sergey protested that "all his works" of course included those already put out in abridged editions. But when Dreiser remained firm in his demand, Sergey agreed to return the contract for revision.

The pleasure Sergey had anticipated from this visit was spoiled. Not only had he looked forward to concluding the contract but also to bringing the good news that VOKS had completed arrangements for the awaited trip to Leningrad. He coldly announced as he prepared to leave that "reservations have been made on the late train tomorrow night."

"Why didn't you tell me before?" Dreiser shouted.

"You gave me no chance," Sergey replied stiffly. "Trevis will accompany you. He has the reservations and will call for you at 11 tomorrow night."

He opened the door and started to leave. Dreiser was hurt. He counted on the young man's warm friendship and readiness to help.

"I can see that friendship between individuals means nothing to a Communist," he muttered.

Astonished at this unjust charge, Sergey began to protest. But his efforts to find English words to defend his political ideology only caused annoyance to the rampant individualist. Without waiting further for his Russian friend to express his views, Dreiser launched on his favorite "cult of the individual" theme, as Sergey had once labeled it.

"But can man be made to work as enthusiastically for others as for himself?" he argued. "Under communism would Rockefeller or Gary be paid the same as a swineherd? You want to bring every human being down to the same level."

"We want to raise every human being to higher level!" the young Marxian retorted. "You are advocate for intellectual aristocracy versus mass rule. All you hear and see in Soviet Union teach you nothing. I am ashamed for you, Drayzer."

"Drayzer" came back at him with another blast. According to my diary, "the poor fellow was completely exhausted by the ordeal, but he (Sergey) staggered up time after time with a fresh onslaught."

Finally, when both men had relieved their minds of some of their accumulated differences of opinion, I reminded them that the hour was late and tomorrow we had to prepare for our trip. Soon, the old individualist and the young socialist were laughing over their heated argument. Regardless of some disagreements on social theories, they vowed they would always be friends.

So the following night, theoretical differences put aside, Sergey Dinamov saw us off for Leningrad. We were accompanied by bumptious, flashily dressed Trevis, the VOKS interpreter. I distrusted him, suspecting that he was sent to keep an eye on me as a "not entirely Soviet woman."

He gave me reasons for my suspicions. On the marble stairs, as we were leaving the Grand Hotel, Trevis took my arm and said in a confidential tone: "We'll be traveling together for several weeks, I hope. Between us we ought to be able to manage the old man — right?"

We traveled International on the de luxe night train, in separate single compartments. From beginning to end, the Leningrad trip was to be the most comfortable and enjoyable of the long tour.

CHAPTER II

Leningrad

1. "He Had Never Seen Such a Beautiful City"

At ten o'clock on the following morning, November 26, we arrived in Leningrad. The head of VOKS, a scholarly looking young man, whose father was the director of the city public library, met us. We were taken by automobile to the magnificent Hotel Europa.

En route, the honored guest looked about him delighting in the cultivated beauty of the former tsarist capital, the broad avenues flanked by fine buildings and the modern Western European atmosphere — in contrast to the decaying medieval splendor of Moscow. Uniformed porters opened the car doors. Inside the hotel the air of grandeur and the obsequious and well-ordered service were understandably soothing to the frayed senses of the American. He had been depressed and irritated by the shabby lobbies, poor service and leaking plumbing in the faded sumptuousness of the Grand Moscow Hotel.

Each of us was given a private room and bath, and later I accompanied my employer and our guide to the restaurant on the roof. It was a charming place, with potted palms, brightly decorated walls, shaded lamps. A brisk reporter arrived to interview the American guest while he ate a breakfast of cold meats, rolls, butter and cocoa.

Later, sitting in an open car, Dreiser gazed about him and declared he had never seen a more beautiful city. The cold, gray fog which habitually hangs over Leningrad partially curtained the grand palaces and the gilded domes of splendid churches. Marble columns and monuments were coated with frost, giving a satiny texture to the stone. Finally, there before us rose the Winter Palace, recently restored to its original white and green.

In the granite mass of the Cathedral of St. Isaac, the scaffolding still remained for the unfinished mosaic work inside the lofty dome. It had been interrupted by the October Revolution ten years before. The priest who conducted us said money could not be spared to complete it. On the altar in a glass case was an object which prompted Dreiser to ask, "What's that—a bird's nest?" Trevis quickly explained that it was a crown of thorns brought from Jerusalem. From the gallery inside the great dome we had a fine view of the city and the surrounding country as far as the Fortress of Kronstadt and the Gulf of Finland.

Crossing the Neva River to the central district, we came to the classical Smolny Institute. Erected in 1808 as an "Institute for Noble Maidens," the exclusive finishing school was seized and used as revolutionary headquarters. Lenin occupied Room 95 on the third floor. The building had become the administrative center of the city and region. Although Leningrad lies farther north than any other large industrial city in the world, the climate is tempered by its close proximity to the Baltic Sea. It was in 1927 the largest industrial center of the Soviet Union, with a population of three million.

We crossed bridges over the canals, turned into a graceful court and stopped at the beautiful mansion by the river which housed VOKS. There we had tea elegantly served by our charming hostess. Refreshed, we left for the notorious Fortress of Peter and Paul, now a section of the Revolutionary Museum. It runs along the water's edge, and its foundations were the first to be laid by Peter I when, in 1793, he began to build the city which bore his name for 200 years. But first we stopped at the cathedral which is the burial place of the tsars. Trezinin, the designer of the cathedral—which has a gilded spire 200 feet high—also built the fort.

Crossing the courtyard through the deep snow, we entered the ruined fortress, a Russian bastille during the 19th and 20th centuries. Its damp, dark cells had held political prisoners who participated in contemporary revolutionary movements. Vera

Figner and many other revolutionary martyrs were once confined in this dreadful place. Cell followed cell in chill monotony — each a stone room with a high, barred window and containing only an iron cot, an iron table and a washbowl.

In each heavy iron door there was a narrow slit of glass through which the guards could look into the cell, and a small door through which food was passed. The prisoners were completely isolated; no sound came to them through the thick walls but they learned to communicate by tapping on the walls. One cell was used for solitary confinement, another for punishment. A solid panel was dropped over the window to leave the room in complete darkness.

Dreiser was shaken by the vivid picture the fortress brought to his mind. He wrote poetically of it later in *Dreiser Looks at Russia* (p. 108): "... with a feel enduring to this hour of many, many lives that withered here; old miseries whimpering about each and every room! I heard them."

He turned away in brooding silence. But as we rode down the long, straight avenues, his spirits rose and he began to take an interest in the groups of magnificent buildings which had been designed by the greatest architects of the 18th and early 19th centuries. From almost every viewpoint we could see the slender, gilded spire of the Admiralty. The beautiful building, where military units and a naval museum were housed, was in Empire style, with two long wings reaching to the banks of the Neva. On one of the avenues radiating from the Admiralty stood the stately Kazan Cathedral with its graceful colonnade. On the way back, a Mohammedan mosque fascinated Dreiser. Its cone-shaped dome was inlaid with tiles of blue and white porcelain, like the mosques of Samarkand — which he had expected would be on his itinerary.

In the evening, Trevis, who was conducting the American delegate with a grand flourish, sparing no expense, took us to the opera, *Eugene Onegin*. To my disappointment, for I loved the romantic story of Eugene Onegin in Pushkin's dramatic poem, Dreiser found it so boring that he wanted to leave after the first act. He remarked that the plots of old operas were very insipid and that he did not approve of the operatic form.

At the hotel, the cabaret on the roof where we joined our hosts was in full swing. A jazz band, labeled by Dreiser as "imitation," was making a terrific racket and the guests were bravely trying to dance the fox-trot and Charleston. Here were NEPmen, the new bourgeoisie, in full bloom. The American guest, who said he didn't care for even the real thing in New York's night life, strode out. As I trotted at his heels, he remarked over his shoulder, "No wonder the party leaders think it's time to crack down on the NEPmen!" He added, before the omnipresent Trevis had caught up with us, "But I can't see why they have to cut one another's throats over the problem." He had been worried, and with good reason, about the possible fate of Radek ever since the ousted party leader's memorable visit.

On the following day, he saw a relic of imperialist Russia in all its decadence. We traveled by automobile to Tsarskoye Sielo (Tsar's Village) ten miles from Leningrad. It had been renamed "Children's Village." Many of the palaces and mansions had been converted into sanitariums, rest homes and nurseries. There were splendid palaces here, former homes of the imperial government officials. We had time only to go through the Tsar's Summer Palace, which had been preserved just as Nicholas II had left it suddenly more than ten years ago. On the tsar's desk, the top page of the loose-leaf calendar read: "Monday, July 30, 1917."

Our conducted tour of the Alexander Palace occupied two hours. The stately building had been erected by Empress Catherine, and the beauty of its architecture remained unchanged. But the original interior except for the marble hall—which had been done over by the last tsar, was richly decorated in very bad taste. After trudging through a hundred chilly rooms, Dreiser concluded it was the worst palace he had ever seen.

"An affectation of grandeur resulting in a show of bad taste and ugliness. I see now why it was necessary to get rid of these people."

There was a whole apartment for the last heir, a lovely child, who was a cripple. Several rooms were filled with his playthings. In the bathroom of the heir to the Russian throne were only a bowl and pitcher and a toilet, — and on the tables all his braces and straps.

"Poor child!" the recorder of human woes muttered. "Poor crippled conclusion of worn-out royal stock!"

It was good to get out in the clear air again. A sleigh waited, drawn by a *troika* of three spirited gray horses, and we were taken for a brisk drive around the stately grounds of Alexander Park. The flying hooves kicked snow into our faces. Indignant residents, not accustomed to being forced off the public paths into snowdrifts, shook their proletarian fists at us. One old woman even suggested with an expressive gesture that we should be hanged from a tree. All this delighted the American delegate. In *Dreiser Looks at Russia* (p. 114), he describes the scene:

"Glorious!" I thought. "In these proletarian days to be thus berated, or hung here, say. I seem as bad as the Czar — hence as good. Glorious! And I sank back, suffused with a royal calm. . . . But what mental lightweights and lunatics that Czarist crew must have been! Literally to throw away — and all for the pleasure of a little tyranny — the vast, magnificent Empire that was theirs!"

2. Leningrad's Industry, Education and Housing

His disgust with what he had seen of tsarism was dispelled that evening by his boyish glee at the State Circus, although this was a heritage from Old Russia. As in Moscow, it was a permanent, high-domed building with tiers of seats in a circle around the pit. The program changed weekly, and the performers were traveling troops, many of them from abroad. The circus was operated by a subsection of the Theater Arts under Lunacharsky's Department of Education.

Our seats were in a box near the pit. Tickets cost three-and-a half roubles. There were ten numbers on the excellent program, including marvelous feats by acrobats, jugglers, performing horses and riders, and two very funny clowns. The climax was heralded as an "American attraction" — a young man shot from a cannon high into the air and landing on a mat. The spectators covered their ears for a protracted period before the explosion came.

It did not seem to me so different from my childhood memories of the traveling circus in Oklahoma, the big tent, the dust, the smell of horses, the clowns—

"But," protested my fellow American, "where are the elephants, the savage lions, the seals—the peanuts? I must speak to Lunacharsky about this!"

Perhaps the Commissar of Education did get the message. Next morning, Trevis, a rather clever young man we had to admit, quoted Dreiser's complaint to the Vice-Chairman of the Leningrad District Soviet. This introduced the interview with Ivan Ivanovich Kandrataev in a jovial spirit. Kandrataev's post was like that of lieutenant governor of an American state, a very responsible post, since Leningrad was now the largest industrial center in the Soviet Union.

Ivan Ivanovich was a plain-looking young man, who had been a metal worker before the revolution. He took in his stride the long series of Dreiserian questions, which were (as usual) a bit blunt, sometimes a bit arrogant.

The novelist was most interested in the human aspects of the various phases of the new society. "You yourself are a worker. What difference do you notice in the energy of the worker today as compared with the worker under tsarist rule?"

Kandrataev's plain face lighted up. His speech became animated. "In the whole mass you feel a great enthusiasm. The worker feels that he is the boss, that his wish is the command of the government. The whole administration is changed. The worker, even if he is not politically intelligent, feels this. Under the tsar, the workers' welfare was not the business of the state; the worker had no interest in production."

"How soon do you think you can liquidate unemployment?"

"That is difficult to say, due to the abnormal conditions at this time, both nationally and internationally. At the same time, however, we are short of skilled workers and must train them to fill these needs."

"What is the Soviet Government going to do with the loafer?" the American persisted. "Would he eventually become a beggar or a bandit?"

"There is very seldom such a problem. Among the criminal element we do educational work and they are taught to work in special institutions."

"What about housing for the workers? In Moscow I saw that their living conditions were very bad. Even in new quarters they are living five to seven in one room without a private bath. Doesn't the government want to raise the living standards of the workers?" Dreiser concluded. "Isn't it better for families to have separate quarters?"

Ivan Ivanovich displayed surprising patience.

"When the workers made a revolution they didn't do it for bathtubs, but for political power. We are poor; there are many tasks before us. Only through the efforts of the broad masses of the people themselves can we satisfy the cultural demands of the workers. But we feel this must be done. As you say, the conditions in Leningrad are better than in Moscow; yet you must realize that even here, in what was the most cultured center of tsarist Russia, the wealthiest and most aristocratic people not only did not have bathtubs; they also had outhouses in the yard."

After a pause, he concluded, with feeling, "We would gladly build three-room apartments with bathrooms, but that would cost 12,000 roubles. With the same money we can supply housing for many more people. Moreover," he added with emphasis, "the Russian is used to the *banya* (steam bath) and still prefers it to the private bathroom with tub. You see, if we had to deal with an already educated and Westernized people, the problem would not be so great. Now the demand for education is tremendous among the workers. Before, it was only the church for the woman and vodka for the man."

Kandrataev now called in the head of the Commission for Construction of Workers' Dwellings and asked him to show the American visitor what was being done by his department. The blond, rosy-cheeked young man seemed very eager to show us the new workers' dwellings. The local Soviet furnished a car to take us around.

First, we visited a large apartment house of 415 rooms, which had been constructed by a cooperative building group, at a cost of one million roubles. The exterior was very attractive — plaster painted in soft tones of gray, lavendar and pink. The courts were not yet finished. The apartments already occupied had one, two or three rooms, but no private baths.

The American guest questioned our guide closely on the subject of baths, although, after Kandrataev's clear and indisputable statement, he did refrain from derogatory remarks. He was told that there was a bathroom in each section serving 40 persons, each entitled to two hours a week. It was proposed eventually to keep these bathrooms for the children only, and to build a steam bathhouse in the courtyards.

Each corridor or section had a community kitchen. Dreiser was keenly interested in looking into one, after what he had seen and heard about the custom in Moscow. This one presented the same picture of communal life. The large cookstove was full of pots and pans, boiling soup kettles, and frying meat. Half a dozen women stood around the stove, stirring, watching their kettles and frying pans, and chatting. A sign read: Hours from Five to Eight Reserved for Working Women."

We visited a few apartments. The walls were freshly painted; everthing was new and clean. But the furnishings for the most part were cheap and unharmonious. Dreiser expressed shock at the number of persons occupying each apartment.

"Good God, where do they all sleep?" Dreiser had wondered in a one-room apartment where five people lived. In another apartment with two rooms, however, the solution pleased him. In the second room there was a crib, two children's cots and a couch for *babushka*. In the living room, the wife pointed with pride to a good, new, double bed.

"Of course, we are satisfied," she declared. "Before, we slept on the floor in a damp basement room; now we have a nice, warm, clean place, two rooms — and look at our beautiful new bed!"

On each floor there was an alcove for social life, a "Lenin Corner." There were dormitories for factory workers in the same building. We found one of the boys at home in a large, clean room which held a row of comfortable iron cots. He was a sturdy, dark-skinned boy of 16, with bright brown eyes and a turned-up nose. He told us he had come from White Russia. His brother was working in a Leningrad factory and had sent for him to come to the factory school. He was studying to be a machinist (four hours of work, four hours of study each day), received 22 roubles a month and paid two roubles a month for his place in the dormitory. He hoped to be earning good wages in a few years.

The boy had been writing a letter to his family when we came in. His handwriting was beautiful. After hesitating shyly, he permitted Trevis to translate it aloud:

"Dear ones," he began, and told how satisfied he was in school and how nice were his living quarters. "I live with two other boys in a large, clean room with central heating. I have a comfortable bed and find it is very good after sleeping on the floor at home. . . . "

Dreiser put his arm about the boy in parting. Perhaps he recalled the sordid living conditions at home in his boyhood and his struggles to earn a little money at this age.

We visited a group of large cement houses, all in pleasing colors, connected by arches, with inside courts. Dreiser commented that even inside new buildings he detected the familiar pungent odor compounded, he speculated, "of boiled cabbage, sheepskins and vile-smelling mahorka tobacco."

Before he took leave of the eager young housing official, Dreiser wrote a statement of his impressions (see Appendix).

After the tiring day, it was relaxing to attend a private showing of two new films at the Sovkino Studios. Dreiser liked *Storm*, a tragic love story of the Civil War in south Russia. The plot was interesting, he said; the photography was good and the technique excellent.

The second picture, *The Women of Riazan*, he pronounced a "gem." He said he had never seen more beautiful photography. The story was compelling, the characters and scenes

in the village realistic. Its grim realism was in the manner of
his own stories. The leading figure was a big, stern peasant
with a long beard who ruled his household with an iron hand.
When his eldest son was killed in World War I, he took his
son's widow for himself. He violated the bride of his younger
son after he had gone off to war, and she bore him a child.
When her husband returned she threw herself into the river.
After telling her brother the truth about his father, the old
man's daughter took the baby to the new Soviet children's
home in the village. Although the social propaganda was obvious, the American critic did not condemn it as such.

3. Visits to a Rubber Factory and to Sovkino

The following day, spent at the largest rubber factory in
Russia, turned out to be as exciting as a movie. The Red Director, Alexander Adamovich Zhanen, one of the most dynamic
Soviet officials Dreiser met in the Soviet Union, had risen to
this post after working at the bench in this plant for 21 years.
(A Red Director is a Communist party member who has come
from the workers and has been trained by the government.)

Zhanen was a heavy-set man with curling mustaches and
heavy brows arching keen gray eyes. His broad face wore a
shrewdly good-humored expression. He wore a baggy old gray
suit and walked with a limp. I can picture him now, limping
ahead as he conducted us on a tour of the plant. But before the
tour there was a long interview in his office, which the American delegate prolonged with his persistent questioning.

The factory employed 16,000 workers on the whole process
of rubber production. The rubber article manufactured in largest quantities was overshoes. Rubber tires were still produced
here in small amounts, to supply Russian needs. This was one
of three such plants of the All-Russian Rubber Trust; the
others were in Moscow and Odessa.

"Yes, we have had some specialists from America, and we
make regular trips there for investigation and study. But,"
Zhanen added with pride, "our 108 engineers are all Russian.

Since 90 per cent of the materials are imported, mostly by water, this location is ideal."

Dreiser suggested that Odessa might be a better place, since it has an open port all year.

"But Odessa is too far from the center, and our port is open long enough during the year."

"Is what Rykov says true, that production costs are two-and-one-half times higher in Russia than in America?"

Zhanen shrugged. "Not that much."

"Why is production so expensive here?"

"Because we have so many expenses not incurred abroad. Of every rouble of production profits we spend 32 per cent for the welfare of our workers – health and unemployment insurance, vacations in rest homes, pregnancy, cultural advantages."

"What is your salary?" Dreiser asked bluntly.

"Two hundred twenty-five roubles a month and a four-room apartment. There are certain workers who receive more. (At that time, 225 roubles was the maximum salary a party official could receive.) Zhanen added that the best technicians received 600 roubles per month and quarters, and the lowest paid worker, 60 roubles.

"We have the piece work system, so actually there are only about 18 workers getting as little as two roubles a day. We have an eight-hour day, and if the work is dangerous or injurious to health, six hours, or even four, as in the case of underground miners."

Dreiser now pressed his pet theory that free enterprise developed better leaders and qualified workers. "You were a worker under the tsar. Is the worker better qualified and more intelligent than before?"

Zhanen retorted, "In ten years the qualifications of workers as a whole could not change much, but we have technical schools to train a new army of qualified workers who will take the places of the old. Remember that before the revolution 60 per cent of the workers in this plant were illiterate, now only *one* per cent."

"How do women compare in productive power with men?"

"Forty-nine per cent of our workers are women. We have

here a type of production which needs the work of women, requiring not so much physical strength as delicate craftsmanship."

Did he consider women workers as valuable as men?

"Certainly. There is no difference in pay as in capitalist countries, where women are used for jobs because their wages are lower."

Suddenly the Red Director shot a question at his inquisitor: "What about social conditions in America?"

The American delegate replied smoothly, "The basis of our government is the welfare of the masses, and American workers are the best-off in the world."

"Yes, yes," Zhanen agreed, with a quizzical look that belied his ready assent. "But consider what Russia has accomplished in ten years under an administration of simple workers. The capitalist system we inherited was underdeveloped. We had an imperialist war, followed by revolution, civil war — in which several foreign countries invaded us to help the counterrevolutionists — then came famine and pestilence. . . . How much do you think we might have accomplished under the Soviet power if we had inherited the industrial development of America?"

The American delegate responded in the best tradition of an emissary loyal to his government's political system. He was eager to prove its superiority to his hosts (as well as to himself). At this point, I turn from my diary notes to the version Dreiser himself gave of his reply to the Red Director's challenging question, in *Dreiser Looks at Russia* (p. 153), in which he added words he *wished* he had spoken:

"Choosing to disagree with his arraignment of capitalism, I went on to inquire where America would be without its capitalists, money geniuses, inventors, and what not else, and I traced the rise and services of various financial giants — Colonel Cornelius Vanderbilt and the railroads; Jay Cooke and the financing of the Civil War; John D. Rockefeller and oil; Pullman and the sleeping car; Carnegie and the steel industry, and his libraries; Armour and the meat industry; Ford and his cars; Hearst, Crocker, Stanford, and others, and the Union Pacific.

"I explained what they had done for a land that then needed to be developed quickly by genius functioning individually and for gain. I insisted that always the big brain had powers and capacities for service which the little brain had not, and which it must respect, though I held no brief for exploitation, and least of all for tyranny. The lion and the lamb, I said, should lie down within at least a reasonable distance of each other."

I detected, after checking with my diary account, similar very human embellishments of his report (in *Dreiser Looks at Russia*) on Zhanen's reply:

"But he would not agree with me. No, no. All capitalists were bloodsuckers riding on the backs of the workers. . . .And please God here in Russia it was so if a man wanted position, he must serve for the same wages as the little man. I agreed that this might be made true if the proletariat continued to maintain an armed dictatorship and could not be outwitted by a strong man with a big brain. . .at times the individualistic animal preyed and thrived on the herd. Zhanen replied if this was true, the individual should be exterminated! I responded, 'be it so, only catch your children early. . . and train them to kill the individualist.' He replied, 'We will catch the individualist and train him to believe in Communism."

Dreiser did not include in his book a passage I put in the diary which quotes him as having said, in a burst of eloquence:

"I answered at length about the unselfish work of scientists and the achievements of American financiers in building up industry, 50 per cent income tax, gifts of rich men to the country, improvement of social conditions to a high point. . . . And perhaps the next step will be the Soviet system, and I believe if this system were put to the masses in America, they would accept it."

To which Zhanen, according to the diary, replied cynically: "Are not these steps being taken to entrench capitalism and deceive the masses?" The American's reply was an explosive "No!"

Smiling, Zhanen rose and offered to conduct us through the plant. We walked for two hours, seeing all the processes of preparing the raw rubber and all the different products—tubing, water bags, dolls, overshoes, and yes, "overcoats"—enough to supply all Russia, using the Ford system. All at once, here we were in a separate room. A score of girls were at counters rolling thin rubber over black plaster forms. This reminded Dreiser of a story. I dropped behind and the men went on, the director laughing heartily as Trevis translated with gusto.

When we returned to the office, Zhanen ordered tea and plates of white bread and bologna. Refreshed, Dreiser started off again on the matter of the director's salary.

"Is it true that you receive only 225 roubles?"

"Nu. . . " Zhanen ruminated, twisting one end of his mustache. Then he thought of something. "Besides," he admitted, "I can use one of the factory's automobiles any time day or night for business or private purposes."

The American evidently didn't think this privilege amounted to much. "Why does a Red Director receive 225 and not 1000 roubles?"

"Marx has said that living with people develops the mind. If I as a Red Director would get ten times more than the average worker, it would withdraw me from their sphere. Our policies must develop along with the intellectual development of the masses. . . . "

"If you had the choice, would you rather be at the bench or here in the director's chair?"

Zhanen spread his hands in a disparaging gesture. "Personally, I think under our present conditions it is easier to be a worker than to direct a factory."

"That's not answering my question."

"I am a member of the party," the Red Director said simply, "by birth a worker but by present conditions a director. I must decide where I am more useful and work there. I consider that I can be more useful as a director than a worker."

This did not satisfy the American individualist, who was trying to get at the man himself. "But as a human being, what is your wish? Put aside all this duty to the party and so forth. Here is Zhanen, the man."

"Very well, I put aside all considerations of the party, and so forth. Here is Zhanen, the man. But first let Meester Drayzer answer one question: Can you as a writer believe it is possible to look on a man only as a human being, an individual, independent of his environment?"

"No," Dreiser replied unsuspectingly.

"Very well. Why are you a writer?"

"I was born a writer."

"Then I was born a director."

They both laughed heartily. This should have broken up the debate, but Theodore Dreiser did not give up so easily. He had made a bet with Trevis that Zhanen would not answer his question on whether his personal choice would be the bench or the director's chair. Now, in an aside to Trevis, he said, "Give me my five kopecks." But he was determined to have the last word. As a parting shot he reminded the Red Director of the debt New Russia owed America for its industrial technique and machinery.

Zhanen shrugged, his gray eyes narrowed shrewdly.

"There is a proverb: Nothing existed in the beginning. God made the first man and hung him on the wall to dry. From where did America learn the capitalist system? Yours is an international people. Your capitalists, financiers, scientists, builders, came from every country in the world. You admit that your capitalists had nothing in the beginning, so that is why America is a democracy. They were poor immigrants who risked all in coming to the New World. There, the rich natural resources gave them the opportunity to develop industry."

The Red Director, a most unprepossessing figure in his baggy old suit, stood up to give his final thrust: "Take Samuel Slater, for example. You may remember that when he came to America from England, he copied from memory the secret design of the English textile machinery and built it in New England — only a few years after your revolution."

Dreiser's silence was eloquent. He shook his host's hand respectfully. When he went out, he wrote in the guest book:

"I have talked with and learned from an able man."

On the following day, Timofayev, the manager of the Sovkino Theaters in Leningrad, showed us the club of the 400 workers employed by Leningrad Sovkino, which operated 800 motion picture theaters in the *gubernia*. It was an extensive club, with all the characteristic activities and sections: wall newspapers, Lenin corner, radio, meeting hall, library, shooting circle, medical training corps, cooperative, a department covering work in the villages and aid for homeless children. Then there was an insurance department, a Communist party local, a medical dispensary, a cultural department and educational circles. Workers also voted at their place of employment.

Timofayev said he had just come from a factory meeting of 800 Young Communists at the Red Triangle rubber plant. They had gathered to discuss the kind of pictures needed. There was a big debate, in which the Sovkino representatives took part. The Red Triangle rubber workers expressed their demands as to pictures. They wanted more films about young people, young factory workers like themselves, as well as about village life.

"I'll bet Zhanen had a hand in that," Dreiser remarked to me. He also commented that this club was additional evidence that a worker's life centered around his job.

From the club we went to the factory of Sovkino. It was in a building which had been a great amusement palace in the old days. The skating rink was now the main studio, where 40 scenes could be taken at the same time. Sets were standing for street scenes and interiors. Small scenes were being shot on the side – close-ups, for example, of a Red Army officer with a revolver. The property rooms were like a vast junk shop – all kinds of furniture, pictures, dishes, bric-a-brac. In a separate, well-lit building their sculptor made furnishings, statues, paintings, and other props and decorations on order for the sets. Using plaster on wood, he was making a good imitation of a stone structure.

By the time we returned to the comfortable office, the director had arrived. Greenfeld was a small, keen-eyed, middle-aged man who spoke English fluently. Tea was served, and he was quite startled when Dreiser asked, "Where's the vodka?" When

Greenfeld replied that to his regret they didn't keep liquor around the studio, Dreiser expressed surprise that a kino factory could run without it. "I know *I* can't," he declared. "You say you work 16 hours a day without vodka?"

Laughing, the director sent a clerk out with an emergency order. Soon, a boy dashed in with a bottle, and the guest poured a generous portion in his tea.

"M-mm, I've discovered a wonderful drink!"

I suggested that since Mayakovsky had named a whipped cream dessert *"Krem Drayzera,"* Director Greenfeld might name a beverage in his honor *"Chai Drayzera"* (Dreiser's Tea).

"It will be done," Greenfeld agreed solemnly, making a note on his desk pad.

I also made a mental note to carry a bottle of vodka in my coat pocket to add to his tea on the winter tour when his spirits were low and his flesh weak.

4. Palaces, Museums, Libraries, Pushkin's House

In the crisp, dry air of Moscow, the invalid doomed by a Berlin doctor to die on the Russian trip, had thrived, but the perpetual Leningrad fog was bad for his chest. Nevertheless, he had been so comfortable and happy here that he had as yet suffered no attacks of coughing nor of bad temper.

An inspiring interlude was a visit to the Hermitage, the famous art museum adjoining the Winter Palace.

The vast Winter Palace, a monument to the architectural genius of Rastrelli, had been renamed Palace of Art. Part of the Palace was occupied by the Revolutionary Museum; the remainder was now the State Hermitage Museum. Its priceless collections were displayed in a series of galleries two miles in length if laid end to end, according to our guide, Alexander Vasilevitch Suslov. The paintings by Western European artists held Dreiser's attention—French and Dutch landscape painters. 40 Rembrandts, Dürer, Leonardo de Vinci, Michaelangelo, Rubens, Raphael, Titian, Corot.

We had to drag him away to look at the other exhibits. One room was devoted to old ornaments and jewelry excavated in the Crimea, and dating back to the fifth and sixth centuries, B. C. There was a display of crown jewels, diamonds, pearls, rubies and emeralds, which, Dreiser muttered to me, might just as well be sold to buy tractors—without robbing the world of art treasures. However, he conceded, the sale should not include the collection of the cameos of Katherine the Great, some made by the empress herself, whose devotion to art was responsible for the marvelous collection of foreign paintings.

As for the crown jewels, "Mere jewels treasured by dubs," he wrote in *Dreiser Looks at Russia* (p. 107). "Yet remaining here—untouched and apparently sacred—a memento of grasping taxes and impositions which afflicted the peasants and workers of a former day."

At last we passed over into the palace itself. From the windows of the salon of Catherine the Great, Dreiser enjoyed a fine view of the river and the needle-like golden spire of the Admiralty shining in the light of the hitherto unseen sun. He looked down on lovely parks and gardens, where there were many famous statues, including "Grandfather Krylov," the Russian fabulist. A succession of beautiful palaces ran along the quay, among them the Marble Palace, which had become the House of the Scientists.

From a window on the other side, we looked down on the Square, scene of the most important battles of the October Revolution. Like the Red Square in Moscow, it was now the place of mass demonstrations.

The VOKS hosts persuaded their guest to visit the Leningrad Public Library. We recalled that the chief librarian was the VOKS director's father. It was, the head of VOKS said, the second largest library in the world (first was the Library of Congress) and contained five million volumes. After the revolution, the acquisition of private collections had doubled the number of books.

The stately building that stood on the corner of the Third of July Street was one of the most noted works of the architect Rossi, last of the classic school (1835); it stood among a group by the same master. There was also a monument to Catherine the Great in the garden.

The interior of the library wore an air of dignity and grandeur. A large collection of rare books in glass cases included Voltaire's entire library, purchased by Catherine after his death. There were many original manuscripts of Russian writers, among them Leo Tolstoy and Dostoyevsky. Shelves of leatherbound books reached to the ceiling.

Attended by solicitous library assistants, Dreiser expressed to them his great interest in the books. What subjects were of special interest to him? they asked eagerly. What department would he like to see? It was difficult for a man who was interested in every branch of human knowledge to choose one on the spur of the moment, but he did — the philosophy department. Forthwith, the head of the department was summoned, a white-haired lady who nervously suggested that since the collection was very large, she would be pleased to direct him to the branch of the subject he had in mind.

"A-a-a, witchcraft," he stammered in desperation.

Immediately, he was led into a large inner room. The head of the witchcraft section and his assistants were bringing in stacks of aged volumes in French, Latin, Greek and Russian, and a few in English, which he began perusing. "Sorcery, magic, spells, exorcism, abracadabra — I love that word," he whispered to me. His interest in the general subject was genuine, for there was some mysticism in his complex nature. But to spend an afternoon mulling over this pile of musty volumes!

"Get me out of here!" he urged Trevis. "Tell them these books are fascinating, but I can't spare the time just now — tell them anything, but get me out!"

Our guide, a solicitous and energetic young man, insisted upon showing the guest the Academy of Sciences. He resisted, but the appointment had been made and he had to submit. Our stay was brief at the impressive academy. Dreiser asked a few polite questions of his host, a gentleman with fierce mustaches.

"Fortunately," he muttered to me as he went out, "no more important personage than the assistant director wasted his time on me."

The next appointment was at the House of Pushkin. Again our charge protested and finally explained that the reason for his impatience with libraries, academies and museums was the obvious fact that "it's the first sunny day we've had since we came. The city looks so radiant with the bright sunlight on the snow and the golden domes and spires, it's a crime to go inside!"

The chauffeur obligingly put down the top and we went to Pushkin's House, on condition we would not linger. The museum had been moved recently into a very attractive gray stone building. The director himself graciously conducted us. The American author showed more interest when he learned that the exhibits included material on all the Russian writers of Pushkin's era.

The main exhibit showed the periods of Pushkin's life from childhood to his tragic death. Dreiser had not known that Alexander Pushkin's grandfather was a Negro, a page in the tsar's court. He saw a remarkable resemblance to Pushkin in the grandfather's portrait.

When we came out, the winter sun was setting.

"My first Leningrad sunset!" he exclaimed.

Yet when we crossed a bridge, he insisted upon turning from the sunset's glory to look at a Buddhist temple, an èxact reproduction of temples in India, Siam and Mongolia. In fact, it was a friendly little Mongolian who showed us the interior, which was even more impressive than the exterior. Dreiser stopped short with an exclamation of wonder and awe. Facing him was a huge idol of brass. The walls were covered with panels of Oriental silk, and paintings of Oriental figures hung on either side of the carved door.

"Well!" he exclaimed. "I hardly expected to be suddenly transported to a mystic Indian temple."

He stood awhile, musing.

5. Archbishop Platon Discourses on the Church

A two-hour interview with Archbishop Platon, head of the Russian Reformed Church, was a fitting sequel to the cultural program of the day before. Dreiser was keen on probing the state of religion in new Russia. The interview was arranged by VOKS and recorded by their stenographer.

Platon wore a simple black robe. His brown hair fell to his shoulders, his brown beard covered his chest. He had a serenely beautiful face lighted by large, brilliant, gray eyes. His face wore the Christlike expression often acquired by priests.

The following abridged conversation is based on my own, not the official, notes:

The American delegate's questions were, as usual, well-chosen and bold.

"How many people did the old Russian Church represent?"

"Eighty-two per cent of the population."

"Was this the state religion of Russia?"

"Yes, it was obligatory on all citizens. I now represent only part of the Russian church. Thirty-two per cent of the religious population are my adherents, 68 per cent the old church."

"What percentage of the population today adhere to the Russian church, old and new?"

"About half of the former adherents, or 40 per cent."

"You mean that 60 per cent are unbelievers. Why did your third of the religious population separate from the other two-thirds?"

"After the October Revolution, the situation of the church was one of non-conformity to the New Order. The church leaders expected to use the old church to build Christian life in accordance with the old faith. This leadership in the old Greek Orthodox Church came into conflict with the new form of government. As a result, there was a full break with the old church, and this brought political terror on the part of the Soviet Government against the leadership. Tikhon, patriarch of the old church, showed that he wanted to save the old order, when the general lines of the old church were defined in the decisions of the congress held after 1917. In 1922, some church leaders addressed a petition to Tikhon stating that if he continued the old policy and did not try to cooperate with the new social order, it would have a very bad influence on the Russian church.

"I must say that this petition was inspired by the wish to organize a church which could satisfy more adequately the living needs of the masses. The so-called reformed church today is the result of a movement which began in 1905... The better representatives of this movement wanted to change the superstitious minds of the people and place less emphasis on formalities. The new leadership had a new social outlook as well as a new religious view. The religious mass was reactionary and conservative in their political point of view. Some of their leaders had been an arm of the tsarist government and were opposed to political change. For this reason, the church was in a serious political situation after the 1917 Revolution. . . .

Our group split with the old church, headed by Patriarch Tikhon, because he did not try to cooperate with the new social order. Indeed, the old church recognized the Soviet Government only in July of this year (1927) and now will be legalized.

"Then you are sovietizing the church?"

"No, we are only returning to the old customs when the dignitaries were the elected representatives of the congregation. But the church itself never destroyed this system. It was the tsarist state which put her own high officials in the church in positions of power. Now that the church is again free from state domination, it can restore this system. One of the tasks is to make the old orthodox services understood by the masses by changing the language from Slavonic to Russian. While maintaining the old dogma, an attempt should be made to abolish the deep and meaningless superstitions."

"Will the state allow the church to develop as you wish, or will it interfere?" Dreiser asked point-blank.

The archbishop replied in slow, measured tones, conscious of the verbatim record being made of his words and the danger of misinterpretation:

"Our church realized that it must repair old mistakes. In answer to the anathema of Tikhon, we made a statement recognizing the legality of the social revolution and supporting the Soviet Government. Therefore, the government gave full legal rights to this reformed church. After six years we can say that there has been no interference of any kind on the part of the Soviet Government. Also, on our side there is no interference with the government. . .

"As to dogma," he said in reply to a question, "we stand on strict Eastern forms and close contacts with the Eastern Greek Church. There has been no change in dogma. It is a purely orthodox church, part of the Orthodox Eastern Churches, whose official representative to the new Holy Synod is considered the real representative of the real Russian Orthodox Church."

"The new church believes that social welfare must be created by the people themselves, by social revolution, which can some day bring about a society like the reign of God on earth. This belief in the social revolution is an important fact in the ideology of the new church. That is why some followers are leaving us, because they say that revolt is not right, that it is never right for classes to be in conflict with one another. But we say that revolt by the oppressed against their oppressors is a natural condition; and we are against the oppressors, not the oppressed. In this we follow the old Bible prophets. . . ."

"Don't you believe that when a man is educated in Soviet schools your dogma will conflict with his education?"

The archbishop answered calmly: "If, when a man has finished a broad cultural and technical education, he cannot agree with our dogmas, then it means that the church will die. If we believed that such a thing could happen, we could not go on with our work, for the need of faith in something will always remain." He paused, then continued thoughtfully, "In relation to the eternal conflict between the Hegelian and the religious

theory, between the theory of the divine mind and the materialistic mind, I firmly believe, should the thesis of materialism predominate, that an antithesis will arise in the spirit
of man."

"Will there, then, be a new interpretation of life from two
viewpoints – the spiritual and the material?"

Platon did not answer this question directly, but closed the
interview with a restrained and sober appraisal of "the church
movement as it exists ten years after the revolution." He warned that "this is only my personal opinion and must not be in-
terpreted as that of the church in matters of such deep philosophy. . . ."

Archbishop Platon concluded: "Now the minority is with us
because we don't want big crowds. What we want is well-train-
ed and cultured people who will understand spiritually our
faith. Our material conditions are bad; the old church or-
ganizes a material boycott against our church and even seeks
to deprive our followers materially when possible. So we are
very poor. But our organization is very strong and has con-
nections with foreign churches and nuclei among Greek Orthodox churches abroad. So," said Platon, rising and stretching
out his hand in solemn farewell, "with full faith and peace we
face the future."

6. The Theater for Young Spectators

That evening we had the most entertaining of our Leningrad
experiences, in my opinion. We visited the Theater for Young
Spectators.

The director, Alexander Briantsev, was a little man with a
round, rosy face and bright blue eyes. His scanty blond beard
looked absurd on his childlike face.

Boys and girls were crowding eagerly into the auditorium
to see a play by Schiller, *The Bandits*, which the thin young
stage manager, Eugene Hackel, had revised somewhat for the
youngsters. He had written a prologue to each act depicting the
life of the playwright in relation to his play. Hackel quickly

gave Dreiser an outline of the plot before the curtain rose. He was very proud of the results of his revision.

Broad seats in a semicircle gave every young spectator a close view of the stage. The young actors themselves quickly changed scenes by shifting long silver pillars, swinging from ropes, and changing or moving props. This intimate, behind-the-scenes view delighted the children. Throughout the fast-moving scenes they expressed their enjoyment by noisy applause, laughter, sighs and tears.

After the first act, Dreiser said he had become accustomed to the shouting and rapid-fire action and had come to the conclusion that this style of acting suited the play—and certainly suited the audience.

He met the pedagogical head, who studied the needs of the children and their reactions to plays. The children filled out forms stating their opinions. These, he said, as well as his observations of the spectators during performances, were the basis for future programs.

When the play was over, we returned to the director's office. On the way, we went behind the scenes and met the actors, who were still in their grease paint and costumes. They gathered about the American author. One girl stepped up and said in fairly good English: "Please, Meester Drayzer, we want to play in America!"

"Fine," he replied. "I'll be glad to see you all. You are good actors."

The smiling director of the theater was waiting in his little office with steaming tea and *pirozhnie* (luscious French pastries). The indefatigable inquisitor began firing questions as soon as he had finished his first glass of tea (without vodka).

"What morals do you teach the children?" the American moralist asked.

"Not just communism," retorted the director, aware of the implication in the American's tone. "We teach the general principles of personal conduct, not to strive for personal good fortune but for the benefit of the community, and to live together with others. But our chief aim is to present pure art, not to teach morals, and we get our inspiration from our audience. Ours was the first children's theater to be established here and in Moscow. Now the local soviets come to us for advice."

"Is this kind of theater a part of the government's educational plan?"

"This is a provincial theater and so does not get direct support from the center, although our local Soviet supports us. This theater costs the government 250,000 roubles a year. We try to educate the spectator so that when he grows up he will be trained to attend adult theaters with discrimination and understanding. The founders were a small group, including actors, who had been dreaming of a children's theater for a long time.

"During the famine," Director Briantsev continued reminiscently, "we received only bread and herring. For two years the actors gave 30 per cent of their salaries to the theater fund. After this pioneer group, a steady line of actors applied for places in the company. We take only qualified graduates of dramatic schools, and these must show they are inspired with the ideal of the children's theater."

Dreiser was interested to learn that the children's theaters followed the system of Stanislavsky.

"How do you apply Stanislavsky's principles to a theater for children?" he inquired, somewhat puzzled.

"We do not imitate him but we accept his discovery of the fundamental principle of the theater – the art of the actor. For young spectators especially, the actor must use facial expressions to convey emotions to the audience. His speech must be perfect. Vocal training is very important, especially through choir practice. The third requirement is motion as a means of expression. The actor must be nimble and graceful. For this we have rhythmic gymnastics, physical culture, dancing, fencing, acrobatics. They have these lessons before each rehearsal."

"And of course they have a trade union," Dreiser said dryly.

"Of course," Briantsev responded, matching the guest's tone. "According to the trade union rules, the actor's working day is six hours, but our actors manage to get away with working eight hours and even more. Besides, there are special meetings every week to discuss all aspects of our work.

"In the matter of stage settings, we do not create special sets for each play, but adapt our one set. It is an original idea I worked out myself," he added modestly. "I decided upon the amphitheater and arena also, because I have always believed that for the youth a stage must have a dynamic character and allow complete freedom for the actor as well as an unobstructed view for every spectator. Of course, such a stage is poor for a play which requires many changes of scenery, so we added some principles of the medieval stage."

I could see that the relentless inquisitor was not listening attentively, probably thinking up a question that would provoke a controversy with this contented little man. It was not long in coming.

"I see you have *Uncle Tom's Cabin* in your repertoire," the guest remarked as he glanced through the list of productions scheduled. "How do you handle it?"

The director grinned sheepishly, making his round, rosy face appear even more childlike. "*Nu* ... as you can see, we must adapt plays to our audience. Of course, certain traditions of the book have been kept. . . . Only the direction is changed. In our production, the attention does not center on Tom, who is a passive character, but on the active hero, George. . . . "

Dreiser looked very grave. "I'm afraid when my government hears of this, there will be trouble."

The director began to suspect that the American was pulling his leg. He went on boldly, "Sinclair does not exist in the play. . . . "

"No Sinclair? Well. . . I'll do my best to prevent war."

"The sentimental parts are thrown out. I regret to say that Eva doesn't exist. . . . "

"No little Eva? No ascent into heaven? Good God, I'm afraid I can't prevent war! What else did you leave out?"

"Tom and George help Eliza to escape, but. . . there is no ice. . . . "

"No ice! I'm not even sure I want to prevent war!"

The director went on, enjoying this bit of impromptu play-acting. "Legree sells the dying Tom, and Ben, the little Negro boy, takes the revolver and shoots Legree...."

"Curtain," yelled Dreiser, and everyone burst out laughing.

We departed with handshakes, embraces and mutual felicitations.

On the following morning, we were back to workaday facts and factories again. But the factory Dreiser visited with Trevis had an exciting history—it was the famous Red Putilov works, which produced locomotives, rolling stock, tractors and heavy machinery. The heroic Putilov workers had played a decisive role in the October Revolution. Lenin ordered them to put armor-plate and guns on the engines and cars and send them to the front.

I stayed in my hotel room to type the notes I had been taking during our stay in Leningrad. It was a full day's work which kept me busy until dinnertime.

At 11:30 that night we left for Moscow in an International coach. It was a restful twelve-hour journey—on the eve of a stormy encounter.

Jubilee Emblem for the 10th Anniversary of the October Revolution.

CHAPTER III

Return to Moscow

Back in the Soviet capital we parted with Trevis, who said he had to report to VOKS. Dreiser reminded him that he expected plans to be completed for the main tour. Trevis promised that he would have everything arranged for his departure by the southern route the very next day, if possible.

The impatient delegate was somewhat mollified, but still distrustful of the smooth VOKS interpreter. He asked me to find something relaxing to do in order to fill the hours until we heard from Trevis.

Meanwhile, he decided not to go back to his pretentious suite in the Grand Hotel at 20 roubles a day (which his hosts were paying). He asked at the desk to be given a more modest room.

I telephoned my friend, Miss O'Callaghan, and asked her to think up something relaxing for my irascible charge to do for a few hours. Always resourceful, "O'C" suggested we take him on a sleigh ride to Petrovsky Park.

Soon we were skimming over the snow in a roomy sleigh. Bright sunshine, crisp air, beautiful wooded countryside and the clever remarks of my Irish friend all combined to put our guest in high good humor. He declared that the dry Moscow air made his chest feel better already, after the days of fog in Leningrad. We rode out broad Tverskaya through the Triumphal Arch, built as a memorial of the War of 1812. Beyond the gates, the Tverskaya became Leningrad Highway. We skimmed through festive crowds walking from the busses to the Hippodrome for the horse races.

Dismissing our *izvozchik* at Petrovsky Park, we took a brisk walk through the thick woods to the picturesque lodge of the

Dynamo Sport Club, where O'C and I had taken skiing lessons. Because there was so much level ground, we had to learn the *"Finnsky shag"* (Finnish step). Miss O'Callaghan complained to Dreiser that she always seemed to fall hard, "but Ruth lands like a feather and doesn't even have a bruise."

"Well," he commented drily, "I guess she lands on the only upholstered part of her anatomy."

He enjoyed exchanging witticisms with O'C and even after the long bus ride back to the center was in excellent spirits.

But the storm was brewing. Trevis telephoned the hotel to tell him he should take a droshky to VOKS headquarters at once. Assuming this meant they would discuss plans for the tour, he insisted that I go along.

I felt a coolness in the atmosphere as soon as we entered the palatial reception room. I began to suspect that Madame Kameneva's open hostility toward me meant that she had received an unfavorable report from her favorite guide. Ignoring me, she addressed her remarks to the American delegate. She said she had reason to believe his secretary was not giving him a good impression of conditions.

"I am told that Miss Kennell showed you the worst housing in Leningrad. On the main tour, I suggest. . . ."

Without waiting to hear more, Dreiser shouted that Trevis had lied and he refused to let him go along on the tour. They were trying to take his secretary away from him, and if he couldn't have the secretary of his choice, he would return to New York. He added that there was a plot to prevent his choosing his itinerary and seeing what he wanted to see. And also. . . "

At this point, Yaroshevsky, head of VOKS' Foreign Affairs Department, gently intervened. He assured the delegate that their hesitation in making plans for an extended tour was due solely to concern for his health. He denied that they were trying to take his secretary away from him.

Without any reference to the wily Trevis, VOKS assigned a woman to be our official guide for the remainder of the tour. I was pleased to have another woman with us and even more pleased to learn that she was Dr. Sophia Davidovskaya, house physician at the Lux Hotel, who, it was explained, would look after the delegate's health. She was a kindly, dependable woman and we were good friends. She had often visited in my room and had been helpful in the care of my little son, who had left with his father and grandmother a few months earlier for a stay in England.

Dreiser was in high good humor when we left VOKS. While waiting for the main tour to be arranged, we would take a side trip to Nizhni-Novgorod on the Volga the following evening.

Poor man! He was now completely at the mercy of two women. Because he had difficulty in pronouncing her name, he at once called her "Davi."

"Doctor what's-her-name," he jeered, before choosing the nickname. "Eminently suited for the job."

I reminded him that since she was a doctor and a trained nurse as well, perhaps she had the most needed qualifications for this winter tour—considering what that Berlin doctor had predicted. I assured him that she was a good, conscientious person. But the fact that Madame Kameneva had chosen her as an "altogether Soviet woman" prejudiced him against her from the beginning.

When he started calling her "Davi," I decided upon a more convenient appellation than "Mr. Dreiser" to use for him. I called him "TD" (Tee-Dee). In our frequent correspondence through the years up to the day of his death, I always started my letters: "Dear TD," and he signed his letters to me: "T.D."

We arrived in Nizhni-Novgorod at 9:30 of a crisp, sunny morning. This was the birthplace of Maxim Gorky, renamed "Gorky" after his death. The station was clean, cheerful and lively. We ate bread and butter with sausages and had glasses of hot tea at the station buffet. As planned, I had a small bottle of vodka in my coat pocket, from which I poured a little into Dreiser's tea. "Davi" looked shocked. She never got used to the eccentricities and moods of our charge. While we ate we watched the crowds passing through the station. TD said there was something homey about the place.

We took a streetcar which carried us a long distance to the House of the Soviets. It was on the other side of the Oka River, which flows into the Volga. Standing on the platform we looked at the passing scenery. TD decided it was a very attractive city, up-to-date, with broad, clean streets. As we crossed the bridge we had a wonderful view of the other side—picturesque old buildings, beautiful churches and the towers of the walled Kremlin against the white hills. One Kremlin wall formed a side of Soviet Square in the center of which was a lovely white church with a silver dome.

We found our hotel, New Russia, nearby and were assigned two musty rooms. The American delegate, at Davi's insistence, had the more imposing of the two. Its black upholstered couch and chairs gave it, according to the victim, "the look of a gambling hall."

Davi went to the House of Soviets where, she reported, they were excited to learn of the distinguished American's arrival. Soon a representative came to the hotel to show him the city.

We rode in a small automobile, one of three we saw during our stay. As we drove along the river bank, we saw that the middle current was still flowing through the ice, although the boats could no longer navigate. The more Dreiser saw of Nizhni-Novgorod, the better he liked it. He said there was a snappy air about it, along with the charm of old landmarks.

We stopped at a handsome new building of workers' flats. On the door leading into one unit a sign informed us that "Railway workers Master Mechanic Vorosov and Assistant Kraskov" lived here.

"They never get away from their work, do they?" Dreiser mused. "Seems to be the most important fact about these men."

"Isn't your work the most important fact about you?"

After thinking this over, he said, "I guess you're right at that." He added wonderingly, "You know, you're the most sensible person I ever met."

He was impressed by the attractively finished corridors and rooms of the flats (each with its own bathroom), the polished floors—everything spotless after a month's occupation.

We looked at a group of new log houses for workers, built in the factory district, and visited the nearby textile factory, Krasny (Red) October, employing 3700 workers. Among the workers filing out there were many women, some carrying small wooden tubs on their heads. They always went from work to the *banya*, our guide explained. They looked gray and tired; their labor in the dust from the raw material was unhealthful. All workers had a month's vacation; a special ration of butter and milk for tuberculars was provided. Inside, the guide called our attention to the new ventilating system which had been installed this year, at a cost of 400,000 roubles.

We ate breakfast next morning in the little buffet near our rooms. Davi ordered fried eggs and the waiter brought us at least 13 in a huge omelette. This super-abundance annoyed rather than pleased our charge. He argued that this was a profligate use of good food which the Russian people needed.

After breakfast, our local guide arrived, ready to take us to a village. With him came a lively young reporter seeking an interview. Fortunately, his subject, having eaten heartily of the bountiful omelette, was in a good humor and dictated a glowing statement on his impressions of the city. The bright young newsman, Pavel Pavlovich Schtatov, who reminded TD of an American cub reporter, as he himself had been many years ago, was so delighted that he decided to accompany us to the village.

Dreiser mentioned to him that an American correspondent in Moscow had told him a tale about pigs and other animals living with the peasants in their houses. Then, as we put on our heavy wraps to leave, Dreiser exclaimed: "And now for the pigs!"

The reporter thought the remark so funny that he wanted it written in phonetic English (in Russian letters) for his article, which he said would bear the title, "Now for the Pigs!" I lettered it for him.

We started off in high spirits. The cold was intense. When we were out on the wide open steppe, I suffered so keenly in the icy wind that I put my head under the fur robe. But whenever my employer made a remark about the passing scenery, I lifted my head to look.

"She's afraid she's not earning her salary," said TD.

Blizhni Borosovsky, nestling in the deep snow on the plains looked like a Christmas-card scene. Although only 15 miles from the city, the village seemed quite isolated. When we entered the small log house of the district Soviet, the warm, dry air felt deliciously soothing. A crowd of women, children and old men, hearing of our arrival, pushed into the room and stood listening with rapt attention as we talked. The heads of the district Soviet and of the local Soviet, both young fellows, were eager to answer questions.

In reply to Dreiser's question about the reconstruction program of the district, the director said the aim was to unite small farms or to subdivide larger farms to meet the needs of the community. However, the tendency was to keep farms intact.

"What about the incompetent peasant?" the American individualist asked, pursuing his usual line of thought.

The young director asnwered with a specific case. "For example, three sons inherit a farm, the Soviet tries to see that the most capable has the management, or if one is entirely incompetent, to deprive him of any control. But the land cannot be taken away from him. The chief work of the Soviet is to help the population with their problems and protect their interests.

"They bring all their troubles to the Soviet House," he continued. "If a cow dies, they get insurance. If the cow gets sick, the district veterinarian is called in. The Soviet is the carrier of culture and enlightenment to the peasants: it fixes and collects taxes, and this money goes to the district Soviet, which finances the schools. The direction of schools and clubs is in the hands of the higher Soviet (volost), which hires teachers and promotes cultural activities. Two members of the Soviet are paid; three are volunteers."

"If the peasants want tractors, what do they do?"

"Artels are organized to buy machinery in installments. This Soviet bought fire apparatus. It gets good seed, feed for stock, implements, and sells milk, but grain is handled by the co-operative. However, here we have only enough for local needs, and no white flour. Our water supply is also not good."

"What else is this particular village trying to do?"

"There are three problems: (1) to supply fuel, since the woods are sparse; (2) to have crop rotation every three years; (3) to organize the peasants for communal work in production and distribution — that is, the collective farm movement."

"What about private enterprises, stores, factories?"

"This is a matter of economic conditions," the district director replied cautiously. Echoes of the storm raging in Moscow over the question of continuing the New Economic Policy no doubt had reached this rural area.

"This Soviet has the power to decide whether they want a factory," he went on, "although they must go to the higher organs for support. If it is a small business, the local Soviet can give permission. We have telephones put in by the district Soviet, and we can speak to Moscow, Leningrad. We have a radio here in the Soviet House. The population is very much interested, and the cooperatives have radio study circles. Of course, the local Soviet manages all the affairs of the village," he concluded. "No, we do not have electricity, but there is a great desire for it."

We went out for a tour of the village. An ever-growing crowd trailed along behind us down the white street. The first log house we stopped at was the home of a poor peasant. It had one large room and a tiny kitchen. There was an entry, and a very low door led into the living quarters. The wide boards of the floor were scrubbed clean, the usual whitewashed brick stove filled one corner and an altar stood in the other. Six people lived here.

"I can't for the life of me make out where they all sleep," Dreiser fretted.

I pointed out the bed on top of the stove, the clean floor.

This family had four dessatines (about 14 acres) of land, had earnings of 264 roubles a year and paid 7.60 roubles in taxes. They owned a horse, with which the man worked for neighbors. They had no rent to pay; but wood was scarce and they had no home industry and no cow.

"But we do have a radio," the woman announced proudly.

A neighbor stood in the doorway smiling at us as though he thought the whole thing was a joke. His shaggy red beard and

matted red hair looked damp. He had just come from the
banya, this being Saturday. He invited us into his house – two
rooms for eight persons.

"What, no pigs?" TD exclaimed. He had made a show of
looking for pigs in the parlor at the other place. "Not even a
chicken! I'm beginning to think my trip was for nothing."

When I translated this, the reporter burst out laughing. TD
turned to me, "Do you suppose Dorothy was pulling my leg?"

"Oh, no," I assured him. "Miss Thompson got it from the
American newsmen. They know everything."

Next, we visited a middle peasant who had a better log house,
with fancy wood carving on the window frames and a little
porch. Attached to the sturdy cottage was a covered shed for
the horse, cow and chickens.

We went inside and saw three very nice rooms, a large kitch-
en, a comfortable living room with upholstered furniture –
and a bedroom! Five in the family, about 15 acres of land, income 400 roubles a year.

Dreiser asked the Soviet official who was guiding us if he
might visit the village priest. A boy carried the news to the
priest's house.

The villagers were still coming along behind us as we walked
to the home of the priest. Dreiser was afraid the whole procession would follow us inside, but the Soviet official told them to
stay out. Even so, we were six people altogether who crowded
into the comfortable three-room cottage. The large, cozy living
room showed signs of culture.

The priest, a slender, scholarly looking, short-bearded man
in a black robe, greeted us nervously. The interview began
haltingly. Dreiser asked him how many followers he had before the revolution, and how many at present. Dr. Davidovsky
translated the question.

The priest hesitated, looking at her with obvious suspicion.
"What nationality are you?" he asked.

"I am a Polish Jewess," she replied simply.

In a tone of annoyance, the *batushka* remarked that it seemed all the translators these days were "non-Russian." Then,
watching me as I wrote, he answered slowly and cautiously.

"It is a difficult question. The church must have not less than 50 members to exist. I suppose we have about 300 now. How many of the faithful have become unbelievers I cannot say. The tendency to drift away from religion is especially strong among the youth."

"Do you think the condition of the village is better or worse since the revolution?"

"I cannot give my opinion. You must ask the local representative of the government. But personally my condition is worse than before."

"How does the church exist materially?"

"We live on the income from funerals, weddings, holy day ceremonies, masses... I have no personal income and this house is the property of the church."

"Is there danger that religion will die?"

There was bitter irony in the priest's voice when he replied: "I refer you to Trotsky's interview with the American labor delegation, published in *Pravda* (Aug. 24, 1927), for my answer."

Determined as Dreiser usually was to get at the truth on controversial subjects, I was glad he relented in this case. He turned to Davidovskaya and said it was evident we were torturing the priest, who could not talk freely before so many people.

"End the interview as quickly as possible and thank him for me for his courtesy."

When we were outside in the bitter cold, I realized at once that I had forgotten my fur gloves and ran back to the house. The *batushka* looked at me imploringly when he brought them.

"Please explain to the gentleman that I would gladly have answered his questions had we been alone, but before a Jewess, and the government representative, and a newspaper correspondent..." He drew his finger across his throat.

We returned to the Soviet House and in the room of the caretaker we were served tea from the samovar, bologna, black bread, boiled eggs, pickles, candy and wine. The guests sat around the table, while our official hosts and the villagers stood behind us and watched us eat.

TD whispered to me. "Here I am the 'Inspector General' again." And in the gay manner of Gogol's young imposter, he called upon the villagers to sing.

At once, as though he had been waiting for an invitation, a jolly young fellow stepped forward with his accordion. The secretary of the village Soviet led the chorus, and TD remarked, "Like all Russians, they sing well." They led off with the familiar "Volga Boat Song" followed by lovely village folksongs.

It was growing dark when we came out into the cold again. But there was one more thing to see—the schoolhouse. We trailed across a ravine, sometimes sinking into deep snow, to a new frame building. . . . As we noisily tramped into the classroom, the startled teacher came out of her living quarters carrying a lamp. There was symbolism in the picture she made. In the lamplight we could now see the clean, orderly room. The teacher eagerly showed us her pupils' work on the walls, the wall newspaper they had prepared. There were items of news, poems, compositions and drawings, including a political cartoon of a fat capitalist, a kulak and a priest, photographs of Lenin, Stalin and Lunacharsky, and banners with Communist slogans.

"But, oh, those little schools!" wrote Dreiser. "In little cabins in the villages, tucked away in the snow. . . "

In my preface to the Russian edition of *Dreiser Looks at Russia*, published by Gosizdat late in 1928, I quoted a passage (pp. 87-88, U. S. Edition) as an example of my statement that the book had "occasional flashes of rare understanding":

"And here in this ancient village of huts, in the midst of the vast fields of snow, was stirring a movement which was intended to teach these people to lift up their heads. . . and as you looked. . . and thought of the thousands of gilded churches with their ikons and gold and the comfortable priests of an earlier day teaching their people tame and unthinking submission to an indifferent and parasitic autocracy, you said, 'All hail to the Communist dreams! In God's name, may they not try for a better day?"

Now we were ready to depart. The whole village saw us off, including the serious young teacher, who threw a shawl over her head and joined the children. The youngsters cheered: "*Oo-rah, Amereekanski delegat!*"

The automobile set off across the pathless snow fields until it reached the main road. I kept my head under the robe all the way home.

We had dinner with beer in Dreiser's room, the "gambling hall" being appropriate for our ribald festivities. Pavel Pavlovich was still in high spirits. He caught me afterward and whirled me around in a fast Russian *valse* until my head was spinning, and I sank down at last out of breath.

The American novelist watched us with the contemplative expression which, I had come to suspect, meant he was storing a scene away in his capacious memory for use in a story.

Our cub reporter ("a youth to fortune and to fame unknown") recited some of his own poems, told peasant folktales, and was a first-class entertainer. Sonya Davidovskaya, tired and sleepy after the strenuous duties of the day, sat very straight in a black-upholstered chair, trying bravely to share in our gaiety. She was thankful when her difficult charge was in a happy mood.

Pavel Pavlovich was still gay when he and the city Soviet representative saw us off on the 9:30 train. I never saw the article he wrote for the local newspaper, headed, "Now for the Pigs." But I am sure it was a masterpiece.

CHAPTER IV

The Main Tour

1. The Rigors of Travel

Dr. Davidovskaya and I were summoned to VOKS to make final arrangements for the main tour. Dreiser went to the bank to get $1000 in greenbacks which his New York agent, Mr. Bye, had cabled for expenses on the trip — including my salary and expenses.

Sergey Dinamov remained with Dreiser at the hotel until our departure. Davi, who had bought our tickets, said our train would leave at 8:25, so 8:00 was the time we should be at the Alexandrovsky Station. We stopped at the Lux to pick up my bags and the good doctor, our official guide.

Arriving at the imposing station, we discovered that the 8:25 was not our train. Ours would leave at 11:25. Poor Davi blamed herself. I tried to save her from TD's wrath by saying I should have checked the train time. We were relieved to note that both men were in a genial mood — Dreiser because at last he was starting on the main tour, and Sergey because he could have a little more time with us. We decided to wait in the station restaurant.

During a late supper in the buffet, TD became ever more expansive over his vodka-spiked tea. He suggested that Dinamov come to the United States and he would arrange a lecture tour for him. This idea was very pleasing to the ambitious young literary critic.

"Write a short account of yourself for me to take along now, Sergey — you know the sort of thing, background, titles, various posts," he added, recalling his interview with the wily president of Gosizdat.

"Yes, yes, I shall do it at once," Sergey assented. He produced a pocket notebook and earnestly set to work.

Presently observing that he was still writing diligently, TD remarked to me behind his hand: "I'm afraid this beeg man won't finish his autobiography before train time." To Dinamov he said, "Don't rush for us. You can sent it package express to me in New York, and I'll get it when I arrive."

I laughed, assuming that Sergey would know he was joking, but when he gravely agreed and returned to his painstaking writing in English, TD began laughing, too. Before we could stop, we were in paroxysms of mirth. Sergey was pleased to see us so gay but a little puzzled about what had amused us. He continued to write with grave concentration. Dr. Davidovskaya sat in silence, also unable to comprehend what was so funny but grateful that her difficult charge did not blame her for the long wait.

Thus, the time passed quickly. At 11 p.m. we boarded the train. Dreiser bade a warm farewell to Sergey Dinamov as he pocketed the sheaf of notepaper. The troublesome delegate was leaving Moscow for the last time. He would never see the capital city nor his faithful young friend again.

There was no diner on the train and we had failed to provide food and supplies for the first lap of our journey, as all Russian travelers do — tea and kettle, glasses, silverware, bread, cheese, bologna. . . . I reproached myself for having forgotten to prepare, as I had in the past when traveling long distances on trains that had no diner. I had even carried a blanket roll.

A very friendly young Turk on his way back to Constantinople shared our four-place compartment, which the *provodneek* (conductor) already had made up with pads and bedding. Next morning, he insisted upon our having breakfast with him. Among the implements and food he brought out of a hamper was a can of peppers he was determined to open, although he broke his knife on it and almost broke TD's. When Dreiser tasted the stuffed green peppers he declared they were delicious. We enjoyed the breakfast of bread, cheese and peppers, our vodka and the host's wine. . . .

We were now in the Ukraine. We saw only villages half-buried in snow.

At 8:25 that evening we arrived in Kharkov. When we changed trains for Kiev, we bade a warm farewell to our friendly traveling companion. There was no time to buy food at the station nor to see anything around us. We hurriedly boarded the train and sat in our coupe, gloomily aware that with the obliging Turk left behind we had no prospect of food until morning. Luckily, however, there was soon an eight-minute stop. Sophia and I alighted and bought black bread, cheese and a bottle of Narzan, the popular mineral water which, next to vodka, had become TD's favorite beverage.

2. Kiev's Sights and People

We traveled in comparative comfort to Kiev. Arriving at noon, we ate dinner in the fine station – the usual borsch, beef and tea. An old automobile took us to the Continental Hotel. Even in the fog and drizzle, Dreiser said there was a charm about this Ukrainian city, one of the oldest in Europe, with broad streets and fine old buildings. Our hotel was not only handsome on the outside; it was quite magnificent inside. The broad stairway with red carpeting, a stained-glass window at the landing and a reception room decorated with elaborate wood carving made the place look like a cathedral, TD said.

One of the two rooms we were assigned was quite tastfully furnished. Davi pronounced it a "ladies' room." The other, she declared, was more suitable for a gentleman. It was a huge chamber, which, besides the usual marble-top stand with bowl and pitcher, had fat, red-upholstered furniture. Not being the gentlemanly type, our charge found it not only frightfully ugly but damp and cold. Still wearing his fur coat, he burst into the "ladies' room" and threatened to move in with us if we didn't find him better quarters. Horrifed at this prospect, Davi did find two rooms on the third floor. The one we took was not so nice but the gentleman's was very warm – with a bathroom!

While our official guide went to look up the local Soviet, TD and I took a walk. The heavy fog still persisted, the sidewalks were slippery and it was bitter cold. Yet there was a liveliness and an air of culture about the crowds that warmed our hearts. The more Dreiser saw of Kiev, the more it reminded him of Paris. The shop windows were attractive, the women were well dressed and good-looking, which, of course, pleased him.

Turning off the main thoroughfare into the Third International Square, we found a path that led up to the high bluffs along the Dnieper River, overlooking the densely wooded countryside. After we had climbed the steep slope, we came to a park deep in snow, where children were sledding. A side street led us to the well-preserved home of Taras Shevchenko, the famous Ukrainian poet. From here a flight of steps took us to the Old City.

Dreiser stood gazing about him almost reverently. In the street stood an ancient statue of Irina, dating back to the 11th century. From there we came into Golden Gate Square. A plaque said it was the scene of bloody battles in January 1918. Continuing down Golden Gate Street, we finally found what TD really wanted to see—the 11th century Sophia Cathedral, which had suffered little damage in the intervening thousand years. Inside, he was moved by the great beauty of the mosaics and frescoes, and the 12th-century marble sarcophagus of Prince Yaroslav.

"Who needs a guide?" he remarked smugly as we found our way back, after stopping to get a magnificent view of Kiev and the river. On the high bank there still stands a statue of Prince Vladimir, founder of the city in 988, bearing a cross.

Davi was waiting for us at the hotel with a schedule of sightseeing, but TD told her curtly that we already had seen most of the points of interest.

That evening, an English-speaking reporter came to interview the American delegate, who asked Davi to order dinner for them. Davi and I had tea in our room. Later, a brisk young man arrived from the Educational Department to take the delegate to the opera. Davi went along, but I stayed in our room to type my notes. I had not finished when they returned.

"He did not like the performance of *Faust*," Davi announced in an annoyed tone. "He wouldn't stay after the second act."

"It was abominably done," he muttered. "I don't like opera, anyhow."

Fortunately, the samovar in our room was still steaming, and he enjoyed a late supper of good bread, cheese and tea (spiked).

We were late getting started next morning. TD complained that our guide had blithely promised to come at nine o'clock and here it was already ten. He suggested that Davi wait for him and they could meet us at the city's greatest tourist attraction, the ancient Kiev-Pecherskaya Lavra, a citadel of religious fanaticism founded in the Middle Ages.

When we alighted from the tram, we saw the high walls and golden domes on the hill. "Museum Town" occupies a picturesque site on the high bluffs above the Dnieper. As we climbed up the road, we met many cripples on crutches – some legless, others without arms or lacking one arm or leg. We learned there was a home for war invalids in the monastery, as well as a factory manufacturing artificial limbs for the victims of war and civil war. During the revolution there had been heavy fighting around the Lavra.

The strong walls surrounding the monastery were erected by Mazepa, the hero of Alexander Pushkin's poem, I read from the Russian guidebook. I remembered Byron's "Mazepa's Ride" in high school English.

When we passed through the archway of the gold-domed tower, Dreiser stopped to exclaim over "one of the most magnificent cathedrals I have ever seen." The outside walls were covered with religious paintings in rich colors. The structure had the usual five domes – four points forming the corners, with a large dome in the center.

Inside, an old priest in a long black robe and black hat greeted us. Dreiser muttered that his gray-bearded face wore a far from priestly expression. He sold us tapers at 10 kopecks each and conducted us through the church. In the dim light, the gilded and jewelled ikons and the gold cloth on the altar gleamed faintly. We followed the priest through a trapdoor into a dark, dank chamber. By the light of our tapers, we saw a tomb and in it a figure under a gold-embroidered cover. The priest mumbled a prayer, kissed the cover and lifted it to show a withered hand — this was the mummified body of the Metropolitan, he said. It was the rarest sight he had to show us in the church, he told us. Now we must see the catacombs.

But Dreiser declined to visit the subterranean caves and catacombs in which lie the mummified bodies of the monks. For centuries pilgrims had prayed before the niches containing the relics of saints.

"I've seen the Metropolitan," TD argued. "You can't go higher than that — so why go lower?"

It was good to be outside again, TD said, taking a deep breath of the cold air. From the highest point on the wall we had a wonderful view of the broad river and the ancient city, which had been built around the Lavra, the highest institution of the Greek Church. "Hundreds of years ago, priests were inspired to erect the grandest mortal edifice to God," one of the crippled young men told us as we stood on the wall. "From here you get a direct train to heaven."

"Ask him when the next train leaves," said Dreiser.

Dreiser wanted to see the Antireligious Museum. It contained relics, emblems, symbols and treasures of the great religions of the world. So what was antireligious about that? I asked. TD explained that the purpose was to show the similarities, weaknesses and superstitions of all religions.

"And they've done a good job," he concluded.

Outside, we met several priests carrying their baskets of produce from the market. One thin old fellow with a wisp of hair falling from under his black hat passed us carrying a teakettle of boiling water for his tea. We asked him about the bullet holes in the walls. Yes, they were from the fighting during the revolution. But, he added, crossing himself, God had spared the ikons — "not one was touched."

While we were listening to the priest, the local guide and Davidovskaya caught up with us in an automobile. We went with them for a drive around the city, passing through the factory section along the river's edge. We visited a planting ma-

chine factory which produced 2000 machines a year for beet
sugar plantations, a new tractor plant with a capacity of 50,000
tractors a year and a tobacco factory. My fingers were so numb
that I was unable to take notes. My employer kindly assured
me that I need not worry—there was nothing of importance to
write about for him. Toward evening, our guide insisted we
must visit a wholesale bakery. It was deliciously warm inside.
My fingers thawed and I was able to take notes. The director
proudly showed us the plant. Two kinds of wheat bread were
baked here. The aroma was delectable and it was a homey
sight to see the golden brown loaves rolling out of the new German ovens.

We had dinner with our local guide and chauffeur in the
beautifully decorated restaurant at the hotel. Later in the
evening we had a samovar in our room and then, at TD's request, another ride up the hill for a last look at the glorious
view. After that, the eager guide insisted upon showing the
guest a new housing project for workers. Davi went along to
translate and I stayed in the hotel to type my notes.

At 10 p.m. we left for Kharkov.

3. Kharkov

The weather was gray and cold when we arrived back in the
new capital of the Ukrainian Republic at noon the following
day. TD had formed a prejudice against Kharkov, strengthened
after seeing the old cultural center of Kiev. At the Hotel Krasnaya only one room was available. It was long and narrow like
a corridor and there were no conveniences. Discouraged, we
walked as far as the telegraph office with Davi, who had to
leave us to visit the local Soviet. The colorful, lively appearance of the streets cheered our moody charge. In the open
square in front of our hotel stood a line of *izvozchiks*, their
sleighs gay with bright-colored carpeting and red and green
upholstery. There were little tinkling bells on the high-arched
yokes of the horses. Dreiser brightened at seeing this festive

display. He wanted to climb into a droshky then and there for an unscheduled ride about town.

However, the travel bureau (a branch of "Derutra"), where he wanted to get information about the remainder of the trip, was next door. At the desk he was advised to go to "Donoogel" (Donetz Basin Coal Trust) to inquire about a trip to the Donbas. We wandered around for some time in this enormous, imposing graystone building looking for the right department. Finally, through an open door we saw a large modern office.

"This is it!" exclaimed Dreiser. "This is the American Commission."

He had seen at once that there were Americans in the room. Their appearance was unmistakable. He eagerly strode up to the group with outstretched hand. They were five American engineers who had been in Russia only a few months. But they were able to be of great help and were full of friendly suggestions about the trip to the great coal basin. One of them, upon hearing of our difficulties in finding hotel rooms, offered to use his influence right away at the Hotel Krasnaya.

We had cocoa and rolls in a bakery lunchroom crowded with businessmen, officials of industrial trusts and private traders.

At the hotel, we found Davi and we three had a somewhat festive dinner, with orchestra music, in the hotel dining room. Our cheeful conversation centered on our hopes for a warmer climate on the shores of the Black Sea. In the Ukraine we seemed no neared our dream than in Moscow.

When we returned to our corridor, we learned that the efforts of the American engineer on our behalf had been fruitful. There was one large, comfortable room available upstairs. Since no second room was found for his ladies-in-waiting, the gentleman invited us to share this one with him. Thus was established a precedent for coping with room shortages in the future. Our motto was: one good room is better than two bad ones.

Hard-working little Davi had stirred up the local Soviet by presenting her VOKS letter and an article by Sergey Dinamov clipped from *Vechernaya Moskva* (Evening Moscow) about the distinguished guest. A cultured young man came from the Education Department to take charge of our program.

That evening he accompanied us to the Drama Theater, which was presenting a dramatization of the opera *Rigoletto* in the Ukrainian language. The Drama Theater was on the plan of the Bolshoi in Moscow, with three tiers of circular boxes above the main auditorium — which were almost empty when we came in. We were placed in a box in the lowest tier. Soon, several hundred soldiers from the local base crowded in and filled the boxes.

TD was surprised at the excellence of the production and the high quality of the acting. Our local guide explained (with Davi eagerly translating) that the Ukrainians were noted for their artistic talents, which had been suppressed under the tsars. The official language had been Russian, although the masses spoke only Ukrainian. Now that their own native language had been made the official tongue, under the new government policy regarding local languages throughout the Union of Soviet Socialist Republics, the guide said that the natural talents of the Ukrainian people were bursting into bloom.

When the guide suggested that we leave after the first two acts, Dreiser protested. He was really enjoying the play, preferring the dramatic to the operatic form. But the eager young man explained that the guest really must see the State Opera and he would not have another opportunity.

Dreiser agreed that it was indeed a beautiful opera house. Here, another foreign opera (not a dramatization) was presented in the Ukrainian language. He was just as enthusiastic about the production of *Carmen*. He said the voices were beautiful; that the Carmen was one of the best singers he had ever heard in the role; in fact, he went so far as to say she was *the* best.

He was in high spirits when we rode back to our hotel, in a gay sleigh with bells tinkling, to our comfortable room with private bath — and a steaming samovar.

It was thawing and foggy next morning when we set out with the local guide in a very good automobile. Kharkov was a booming industrial city; feverish new construction was going on — new buildings, new roads, new pipelines on waste land.

We passed through a district of new housing for workers — one-and two-story red-brick buildings which were very attractive in appearance. Kharkov, like every other city, had a housing problem, with a population increase from 200,000 to 450,000 in ten years. Its proximity to the Donetz Basin, rich in coal and iron, its network of railroads connecting the principle industrial centers and the Black and Caspian Seas gave Kharkov commercial and industrial importance.

The electromechanical plant we visited was the largest in the USSR. Dreiser asked about the high cost of production in Russia. The engineer admitted that production costs were much higher than in America, but pointed out that high compensation and social benefits to workers accounted for much of the increased cost. A lower tempo of labor, which conserves the workers instead of wearing them out, must be taken into account. He insisted that production, when estimated per capita, actually cost 30 per cent less than in the United States.

As we moved along through the vast, high-roofed building, with a crane overhead and a new German instrument-making machine humming, a growing crowd of workers followed us. They surrounded our group and wanted to know about America. Dreiser expanded. He told them about the superior wage and living conditions. They replied that here the worker was better protected, had free medical care, vacations in rest homes and sanitariums, nurseries for working mothers. . . .

Dreiser continued to question the technical director, a Lithuanian engineer, attempting, it seemed, to prove that American workers were much better off. The director continued his argument that while wages were lower, social benefits were greater; for example, workers in the foundry had a month's vacation annually, and the plant was closed two weeks of the year for the general vacation period.

"What, then, is your personal opinion of the Soviet system?" the American patriot inquired. "Will it have to be modified in time?"

The director, who was a nonparty, foreign employee, said he

was sure it would not be. It was a going concern, the workers supported the system and he saw no reason why it would need to be changed. He added that he had stayed on simply because he was satisfied with his material conditions. "I pay 40 roubles for my two-room apartment, but a worker would pay perhaps five roubles for the same thing because his wages are that much lower."

Dreiser gave up the interrogation, which was not convincing the Lithuanian that the American way of life was superior.

He reluctantly consented to inspect the day nursery for children of working mothers. He agreed that the conditions here were quite as ideal as in the Moscow model nursery.

"The idea's wonderful," he told me in a threatening tone, "But I don't want to look at any more nurseries."

He was in an irritable mood when we returned to the hotel room. The samovar was still standing as we had left it and we sat down to glasses of lukewarm tea. With Davi out preparing for more sightseeing, TD started to argue with me on his favorite theme of "the intelligent fellow always ruling the dub."

It was a welcome interruption when our little doctor and the local guide came to take us to an exhibition of Ukrainian art. It was held in a building under construction, where the offices of the great industrial trusts would be located. Our colorful sleighs sped merrily through the city streets and turned up a hill onto a brand-new boulevard. It ended on the edge of a meadow where foundations for several structures were being laid. Before us stood a great unfinished gray stone building 14 stories high.

The chronicler of American industrial development stared at this "skyscraper" in amazement.

"This building looks like it had been lifted out of Manhattan and set down on these snowy plains! It symbolizes the industrialization of old Russia!"

The exhibit was also unexpectedly thrilling. Some fine pieces of sculpture stood in the bare halls. Many paintings hung on the white walls, which glistened with frost in the unheated building.

"An art alive and strong," Dreiser commented.

He asked the price of a woodland scene done in bold, rich colors. The title was "Reading the Letter," by S. Simonov. The price was 350 roubles. He arranged for its purchase and shipment to New York. He also bought several bowls and vases.

A number of rooms were devoted to architectural plans and drawings of buildings now under construction and projects for the future. The present building was the first of a number of similar structures to be built around a court called "Dzerzhinsky Square," one of which would be the offices of the city government. Dreiser told our guide that the drawings for the project gave promise of a beautiful civic center.

"Here is a city dreaming wonderful dreams," he said. "It is easy to believe that, in ten years, there will be a Ukrainian Chicago here in Kharkov."

As I copy these words from my diary, I remember that this prophecy did come true. A new Chicago was, in fact, built in ten years on these empty meadows. Before the German invasion in June, 1941, Kharkov had become the third largest city and the third largest industrial center in the Soviet Union, with a population of 900,000.

4. Stalino

As we left Kharkov that evening, we had to walk a long distance on the station platform to our coach, and we boarded just before the train started. Dreiser was feeling tired and ill after the thrilling but exhausting day. There was no bedding for rent, so we spent an uncomfortable night. We were somewhat refreshed by two bottles of Narzan which the *provodneek* bought for us at a stop.

At ten the following morning, we arrived at Stalino, a new mining town in the center of Donetz Basin. The town itself (population 110,000) was 12 versts from the railway station. We hired a droshky which was on wheels because the roads were rivulets of melting snow.

As we rode along in the chill fog, our unpredictable charge, who had been coughing all night, showed signs of revival.

"This place looks like it's going to be interesting, after all," he remarked, gazing about eagerly. On all sides rose steep hills of slag, like pyramids. Down the sharp incline of a shaft a coal car was moving. "What a desolate place – yet how alive!" he exclaimed.

This first impression proved to be a lasting one. The American author also made a lasting impression on the mining center (renamed Donetsky). In a Reuters dispatch from Moscow (*San Francisco Chronicle,* April 11, 1968) there was a news item headed "DREISER STREET:" "A street in the Ukrainian coal-mining center, Donetsky, has been named for American author, Theodore Dreiser, who visited the city 41 years ago, the Soviet news agency, *Tass,* reported yesterday.". . .

In contrast to the hovels around the station, as we neared the city there were new dwellings. Soon we were in the city itself, splashing through the mud. Crowds of men, women and children were walking to the Sunday bazaar. The hotel was new and, as the porter at the door assured us, "charmingly clean." The small rooms were light and comfortably furnished – four roubles per room. But since we insisted upon an upper sheet for each bed, the cost was 50 kopecks extra for each one.

We ate breakfast in the cooperative restaurant next door, where an interesting assortment of people were dining – women with gray shawls over their heads, rough-looking men, and a few well-dressed persons. TD and I enjoyed our first American food, hot dogs and mashed potatoes with gravy. Sonya chose *gefilte* fish, which she pronounced good.

While she was telephoning to town officials and getting them all stirred up over the arrival of the distinguished American, that modest gentleman walked with me through the muddy streets. He was pleased with the lively atmosphere and the well-dressed townspeople, although the air was raw and damp and the town looked depressingly dreary and ugly to me. Spread out on homespun cloth in the slush and mud were the traders' wares: dry goods and notions, books, rusty hardware, mining picks, bedding, beds, chairs, cradles – a sorry display.

We came to the central pumping station. Water was a problem and they were only now getting it piped to this section. Women came one after another to the little window of the station, handed in a talon (a yellow slip) and set their two buckets under the pipe, while the stationmaster turned on the water. Hanging their full buckets on the ends of a pole balanced on their shoulders, they walked along the slippery street toward home. One young woman slipped on the icy incline and fell, the water spilling over her. As we watched in consternation, she rose with a stoical expression, picked up the empty buckets and returned to the water station. TD was relieved when the stationmaster, quite as a matter of course, refilled her buckets.

"There's a nice, friendly spirit here," he remarked as we walked on.

The local guide for the remainder of our stay was a young man from the Education Department. In the evening he took us by automobile to one of the workers' clubs. There was a fine exhibit prepared for the tenth anniversary, giving a history of the revolution.

The main library was in the same huge building. The librarian, a lively little fellow with an attractive, dark face and bright, black eyes, greeted us. He was not over 20 years old. He came out of the crowded delivery room and showed us around. I asked him if they had any of Theodore Dreiser's books.

"Not yet," he replied promptly, "but we have ordered copies of all his works published in Russian."

I started to explain that Land and Factory had put out some abridged paperback editions, but he interrupted eagerly, "Yes, but now Gosizdat has a contract with Drayzer to publish all his books. I read about it in the *Bibliographical Journal*."

When I translated this to TD, he was pleased and astonished. I was pleased, too, to learn that the American Dewey Decimal System of classification, now being installed in all Soviet libraries, was already in use here. The young librarian told us that this library had 20,000 volumes and 250 readers daily, and that 47 per cent of the borrowers were workers.

In the recreation room of the club library, members were listening on their earphone radio sets to broadcasts from Moscow, Leningrad, Berlin and London.

Next morning, when we came outdoors with our local guide, we found that the weather had turned colder. The melting snow had frozen, making a glassy surface. The guide had come to take us on an inspection tour of a state farm — "Sovkhoz in the Name of Trotsky" — 12 versts from Stalino. The chief agronom of the Donbas district was riding with us, a Latvian named l'Etienne.

The chauffeur drove at reckless speed across the treeless steppe, past mine shafts, each with its little cluster of dwellings. The car veered and skidded, bumping over the rough road. A bitter wind stung our faces. A carriage passed us, in which the manager of the sovkhoz was riding into town. The chief agronom stopped the carriage and asked the manager to turn back.

The sovkhoz stood on a slight hillock — a group of white-washed brick buildings. This big farm had been owned before the revolution by an American named Hughes. It had about 10,000 acres of land, 6000 of which were under cultivation.

In winter there was little to see besides the stables, livestock and dairy. The stables housed 200 workhorses, 150 yearlings, 60 draft horses and a few race horses. There was a special barn for brood mares.

TD nudged me. "Ask them if the mares get vacations of two months before and two months after childbirth."

"Of course," the agronom replied solemnly. "And since they breed only in winter, they have an extra warm place and special feed. The colts are over there."

I took TD's arm and pulled him toward the colts. "Here's one more nursery you've got to see," I said firmly.

The male and female colts were separated. They could only look at one another over a barrier at this tender age.

"I see — strictly Red morality," commented the author of *An American Tragedy*.

The cows were comfortably housed but, Dreiser remarked, they looked rather thin. The agronom explained that this was a German breed which did not give as much milk if they were fat. They fed the cows chopped beets, a vegetable grown in great quantities in the Ukraine. The sovkhoz dairy furnished milk to neighboring industries.

"And now for the pigs!" TD exclaimed.

I had to explain that Meester Drayzer had coined this phrase when visiting a village where he had expected to find pigs and other livestock living with the peasants, as he had been led to believe by Moscow correspondents. By this time our hosts were laughing heartily at their guest's dry humor. In this jovial mood, arm in arm we slipped and crawled over the icy ground to the quarters of the hogs, where we saw some fine specimens comfortably housed.

"Better than living with a peasant family," TD observed. "In fact, better than some hotels I've been in."

Adjoining these elegant quarters was a large space with a high wall around it where young male pigs were running about. This time the agronom was quick to make the first quip.

"The pig monastery," he announced with a grand gesture. "And their *banya* is in the courtyard."

From the pigs' palace we skated arm-in-arm with the big, fat Scandinavian manager to the machine sheds, where TD was amazed to see such a large number of machines—plows, harrows, cultivators, mowers—made by the International Harvester Company and Deering.

There were still the sheep to see, but by this time we were so chilled that we decided to go into the farmhouse. How delightful it was to come into the cozy living room and see a wood fire burning in the grate—and in front of it a rocking chair. Dreiser sank into it with a grateful sigh. He said he supposed the rocking chair was a legacy from the American, Hughes.

A large table was set for lunch. In the center was a pot of white chrysanthemums, which TD assumed were the paper flowers so prevalent in Russia. But he soon saw that they were growing plants. We were served a wholesome meal of home-made white bread, fresh sweet butter, headcheese, pickled cucumbers, wine and cereal coffee. I brought forth the bottle of vodka to share with our hosts. This time, the famous guest poured it into his cereal coffee thus, to the amusement of his hosts, creating another new beverage in his name: *Kaffé Drayzera.*"

Warmed and in a talkative mood, the guest started a discussion on relations between the USA and the USSR (at this time not yet recognized by the United States). As usual, when talking with Russians, the American delegate defended the policies and social conditions of his own country.

At a break in the conversation, sensing that his polite hosts were cool to his words, I interjected a few spirited remarks to impress them with his importance and the influence he could exert to improve relations between our two countries. Dr. Davidovskaya eagerly supported me.

Always suspicious of our VOKS guide, and catching his own name repeated several times in her speech, he muttered, "God knows how I'm being deceived when you're chattering away in that blasted language!"

Davi fell silent.

"Ungrateful man!" I scolded playfully. "We were telling them how important you are and what a good influence you can exert for better relations. Instead of deceiving you, we were deceiving them."

But my employer was not mollified by my explanation, nor amused by my banter. He was still a bit disgruntled when we left. There was the usual guestbook in which to write his impressions. But in spite of the warm hospitality, which he had really enjoyed, and the trouble the two sovkhoz officials had taken to answer his questions, he indicated in the guest book that his impressions were not good. They had said that their profits last year were only 3000 roubles and had explained that they had put most of the surplus back into the enterprise. He wrote that with 200 permanent workers, in his opinion the payroll was altogether too large.

Our open car was full of snow, which had to be brushed out before we could take our places. The agronom was wrapped in an enormous sheepskin *shuba* of curly black karakul. He had brought along a pair of *valenki* (felt boots), in case they were needed, but they could not be worn unless the snow was dry.

Our Stalino guide now put on a similar *shuba*. The long black hair of the collar made him look like a shaggy bison. They sat in the front seat with the driver and thus arrayed protected us from the bitter wind and sleet.

Back in Stalino, we stopped at an old-fashioned photograph gallery. In our heavy wraps and all covered with snow, we sat for a group photo. The photographer was an energetic little man, who displayed "*Amerikanski* tempo." While we waited, he quickly finished three copies and mounted them.

Dreiser was very tired now and eager to get back to the comfortable hotel. But he agreed that he must see at least one mine in Donbas, so we set off for a shaft. En route we picked up a special guide who had miner's clothing for us. Although it was only four o'clock in the afternoon, complete darkness had fallen. The wind blew sleet against the car panes. Electric lights gleamed faintly through the fog. A blast from a plant whistle sounded.

At the shaft, we went into a little *banya* to put on the special clothing—heavy oiled pants, coats and wide-brimmed hats. It was so deliciously warm in the room that we dreaded going outside. But soon the mine superintendent came, a handsome young man with a straight nose that gave his face an arrogant look. We were given carbon lamps and, looking like the miners we passed, we went out into the wild night and across the slippery ground to a stairway which led up the shaft. In the coal-car station several women were working on the tracks. We entered the dripping cage and were dropped 140 meters through the earth. We emerged into an electric-lighted cavern with tracks. But only this central station was lighted.

We had only our lanterns as we started down the tracks in the narrow corridor. Every few minutes a shrill warning whistle sounded. Our guide called sharply, "To the right!" or "To the left!" We would flatten our bodies against the prop-supported wall. A few seconds later, a horse would come running down the tracks drawing mine cars loaded with coal, the driver with his head bent to avoid the low ceiling. The air was quite fresh; a breeze blew against our faces.

When we passed through a door, the air felt warmer. There

was a pungent odor of horses. Here were the stables of the unfortunate animals working in the depths, living out their lives
in narrow stalls in the darkness and eventually going blind.
The mine superintendent told us that three times more air had
to be pumped for them than for the men.

As the odor of the poor beasts followed us, TD kept speaking about their wretched existence. I was thinking of them, too.
At last, we came out to where the coal was being mined. No
pick mining was done at all; the shaft was completely mechanized.

Dreiser wanted to see in action the invention of the young
miner whose model we had seen in the exhibit at the Workers
Club — a device for transporting coal from the narrow workings
to the cars. Several young miners gathered around us and
asked questions about mining conditions in America. TD admitted that he could tell them little. His pilgrimage to help
the coal miners in Kentucky in their strike was to come some
years later. These Soviet miners told him they were well satisfied with conditions. The actual diggers worked a six-hour
day with a month's annual vacation. The drivers of the coal
cars worked eight hours, but were looking forward to the seven-
hour day promised all workers.

It was cheering to stop on the way back at some of the attractive new stone cottages where the miners lived. One man
invited us inside. His wife was a mere girl with bare feet. They
had their own kitchen with a brick stove, a large living room
and a bedroom. The miner said he had the rent, electricity and
water free.

The new Mine Workers Club was nearby. This fine structure
contained 67 rooms and was modern throughout and well fur-
ished. There was a beautiful auditorium seating several thousand, a lecture hall and large gymnasium. The club had cost
600,000 roubles. A metal workers club was also under construction, costing two million roubles.

We had dinner in the cooperative restaurant next door to
the hotel — beer and schnitzel — and the music of a Viennese
violinist, with his wife as pianist and a youth as cellist. They

were playing a lovely Jewish piece which Davi knew, and when they saw how much we appreciated it, they played some American songs, starting with "Yankee Doodle."

Near the piano sat two heavily painted women. TD remarked sarcastically that he had been told there were no prostitutes in new Russia. This brought a retort from Davidovskaya to the effect that he was always looking for something bad rather than remembering the good things he had seen.

I reminded Sonya in Russian that we were all very tired and the beer had made us sleepy and dull-witted. When Mr. Dreiser was feeling tired and miserable, he always took a gloomier view of conditions.

Like a cross child hearing his elders discussing how to handle his bad temper, TD became more irritable.

"I'm not forgetting the good things," he began, belligerently, glaring at the well-meaning little doctor. "But I do remember a lot of things that make we doubt about this Soviet thing. I saw that most of these industries aren't new but had been running years before under the tsar—and some aren't even up to prewar production. That sovkhoz had only 3000 roubles profit. Those tractors they were turning out in such numbers in Leningrad were admitted by this agronom today to be far inferior to the American, and cost more. Then, that merchant on the train and his complaints. . . . Why, damn it, this thing won't work at that rate. The industries must show a profit."

When Dreiser thought of profits, he did not ask himself, "profits for whom?" He did not grasp the socialist idea that the workers were the owners, that the profits were theirs, that every fringe benefit for the workers was a dividend paid to the owners.

Gently poking Davi under the table to silence her, I tried to calm TD's sincere doubts.

"Why do you think they must show a profit? Isn't industry supposed to run for the benefit of all the people and haven't you seen how profits are going into improving the conditions of the masses?"

"I don't think you're much of an economist," he rejoined sulkily.

I stood up. "Let's get some sleep. Tomorrow is our last day here. We leave for Rostov in the afternoon. In this terrible weather," I added prophetically, "no telling what troubles are ahead."

But Dreiser's mood had changed. He was listening to the sweet, homesick strains of "On the Banks of the Wabash Far Away," A pensive look had come into his face, and he began singing softly the words written by his brother Paul to what became the state song of his native Indiana:

Oh, the moonlight's fair tonight along the Wabash.
From the fields there comes the breath of new-mown hay.
Thro' the sycamores the candle lights are gleaming,
On the banks of the Wabash, far away.

As he went out, he dropped a dollar bill in the violinist's lap.

5. Rostov-on-Don

At 5 p.m. the next day, the reckless chauffeur who had driven us to the sovkhoz took us to the station. We sped over the lumpy ice, arriving quite out of breath. The buffet and waiting room were packed with travelers in sheepskins. Standing in the crowd around the buffet, we had tea with surprisingly tasty bread, bologna and *pirozhnie* — my favorite pastries. When the train came in, there was a rush to the platform. Carrying our baggage, we struggled over the ice alongside the far-reaching string of coaches. Long lines of passengers were waiting at the steps of the Maxim Gorky and the third-class coaches. TD kept looking back at them, huddled together in the icy wind with their baggage, bedding and children.

"How on earth are all of them ever going to get on board?" he fretted.

The train moved as soon as we were settled. In reply to his anxious question, the *provodneek* assured TD that all had boarded safely. We dozed in our comfortable soft seats, but it was a rude awakening when we alighted at ten that night at

Konstantinov Junction to learn that the train to Rostov-on-Don was overdue and not expected before 3 a.m.

This first encounter with the hazards of travel in winter in Russia brought a violent reaction from the American delegate.

"Five hours in this hole! What a lack of system, what negligence! That half-wit official in Stalino said there would be only a 20 minute wait. . . "

"It eez snowbound," Davi explained, adding tactlessly, "You do not have snowbound trains in Amereeka?"

"Shut up!" he shouted.

But he proved that given a little cooling off with a bottle of Narzan he could adapt himself to hardships. Later, he had rolls with tea and a little vodka in his glass. Looking at his watch, he announced cheerfully: "Twelve-thirty. Only three more hours. . . "

Davi came back from the stationmaster's office to announce that he did not know how late the train would be, because of the snowstorm. This required some more adjustments. Our charge took the bad news stoically, but the native first-class passengers were upset. They gathered around our table for an impromptu conference. One well-dressed woman with painted lips began to cry. She had received a telegram that her husband was ill in Rostov. Suggestions were shouted to drown out other suggestions. Some passengers planned to wait here until five a.m. Then they could take a local train to the workers' settlement, where there were hotels, and wait for the Rostov train there. "Here there is nothing — nothing!"

At this point, the stationmaster came and stunned us with the news that the train was ten hours late. TD quietly reconciled himself to waiting in the station until morning. In the buffet, some people were already sleeping, with their heads on the tables. Several ragged children lay in a corner on the floor. Now and then the guards made their rounds, routing out the homeless children and prodding the sleeping passengers to inform them that they must go into the waiting room to sleep. But out there we could see that the floor was already covered with sleepers in dirty sheepskins, padded coats, felt boots. Whole families sat or lay on the floor in the midst of their baggage—bedding rolls, sacks of black bread, tin cups, pans and tea kettles. The children were sleeping on spread-out blanket rolls or sitting quietly munching chucks of dry bread, inured to such hardships.

We were worried about our charge. He had slumped over the table, coughing now and then into his large white hand- kerchief. Occasionally he raised his head and gazed compas- sionately at that sea of humanity tossing on the floor out- side.

I bent over him. Brooding over their wretched state, he said in his usually gentle voice, "You know, I've decided the Rus- sian people are like bears hibernating in winter. They look so big and shaggy in those sheepskins and padded clothes. . . . "

"Or like walking mattresses," I suggested, and this made him smile wryly and tuck the expression away in his capacious memory to use later. Then another coughing fit made him slump over again.

The little doctor hurried away and sought out the OGPU (security police) officer on duty. She showed him her creden- tials and explained that we had an important American dele- gate to the tenth anniversary observances who was ill and needed a place to rest. He immediately offered the American the bench in his office.

We made a pillow of his wool overcoat and covered him with his great fur coat. Settling his ponderous body on the hard bench, he was soon asleep. When we looked in later, the "Gay- Pay-Oo" officer also slept, his head on the desk.

By morning, all the other passengers had mysteriously disappeared. No doubt, with the adroitness of experienced Russian travelers, they had found means to continue on their way.

Scrubwomen were cleaning the waiting room and buffet, but not on their knees. In Russian style, they bent over and pushed the twisted wet cloth vigorously back and forth over the tiled floors. Then they scrubbed the tables, wiped the fur- niture, and even the rubber plants. Everything looked so fresh and clean it was hard to believe this had been the scene of so much mass misery the night before.

I aroused the American delegate from his couch. He had been sleeping soundly.

We all washed in the women's lavatory and then ordered breakfast from the genial buffet manager. Cheered by the astonishing cleanliness and privacy of the place, after his restful sleep, TD walked about humming softly as he arranged our chairs around the table.

"Look, he's already beginning to take an interest in the place," exclaimed Davi, really pleased.

"Why not?" he inquired, in high good humor. "Looks like I'm settled here for life."

The breakfast of fried eggs (a dozen or more, and no complaints), hot milk, rolls, bologna and apple preserves with our tea was tasty and quite homelike. We told jokes and Dreiser got going on his experiences as a reporter in Chicago.

Noon, and still no train. Quite philosophical about the delay, Dreiser took out a pack of cards and spread them on a table for a game of solitaire. He bet a bottle of Narzan that he'd win before the train came. He lost.

By early afternoon, we were seated in the comfortable coupé of an International coach. It was restful just to sit quietly and gaze out the wide window. Snow-covered steppes stretched to the horizon, broken now and then by villages and new factory towns.

"I've been thinking about how these endless plains can be developed," Dreiser mused in his soft, pleasant voice, "and an idea is forming: it seems to me that the government should undertake to cultivate the land just as it is running the industries, organize big farm units and hire the peasants at wages, just as it hires the workers in factories. This would eliminate many of the insoluble problems which not only Russia but every country has to face in regard to the farming class."

I suggested that the sovkhoz was a beginning. Actually, in July of the following year (1928) the Central Committee resolved to push the organizing of huge grain farms.

Darkness came soon and blotted out the steppes. There was nothing to do but lower the shades and rest until 7 p.m., when we arrived in Rostov-on-Don.

At the Hotel San Remo the rooms were large and quaintly furnished. One room had a grand piano and antique furniture. We could find only one good room, which we took for all of us. It had several windows overlooking the street. The fireplace had cherubs holding garlands over the cold grate.

We went rather dubiously to a bar in the basement for dinner. An orchestra was playing and the place looked inviting. The *shashlik*, served with green onions and French-fried potatoes was savory. "No complaints this time."

We retired early and slept until eight next morning. TD and I walked down to the postal-telegraph office in the bright sunshine. An answer to his telegram to someone he was arranging to meet abroad was waiting. At a cooperative bank he changed another hundred of his thousand dollars, received 194 roubles and grumbled at the exchange rate. (The rouble was valued at 50c.)

We ate breakfast in one of a chain of cooperative restaurants which reminded TD of an American lunchroom. He liked the appearance of this city of 220,000 population. Twenty-five miles from the Don River's mouth, Rostov was the administrative center of the North Caucasus, a rich farming and tobacco-growing region.

On the bright morning we walked to the "Don State Tobacco Factory in the name of Rosa Luxemburg," the largest in Russia. Most of the buildings had been erected 75 years ago. Although we were not accompanied by our official VOKS guide (Davi had gone to the Rostov Soviet to apprize the city council of the America delegate's arrival); the director greeted us cordially and answered the usual questions.

Michael Ivanovitch Petrov was a fine-looking young man, 29 years old, by profession an electromechanic. He had been elected to his post by the workers. He received the party maximum for this district of 210 roubles per month, of which he paid 35 roubles rent for a furnished apartment.

The director claimed that as far as tempo was concerned the factory could compare favorably with America, but the equipment and buildings were old.

"Are you acquainted with the latest methods in New Salem of turning out the boxed cigarettes in one process?" TD asked.

"Yes, but we heard of the process from France. It would be difficult to introduce it here because the new process would necessitate laying off a great many workers. In our new society, this must be done carefully and gradually."

Petrov added that the seven-hour day had been in operation since 1922, "and we find that the factory works better under it."

"Would you gain even more with a six-hour day?"

"We are already considering that."

"And five hours?"

"We don't consider fantastic dreams."

"But," insisted his inquisitor, "Bukharin included such a thing in his program for the future."

"Yes, but we don't plan so far ahead. Our workers are quite satisfied as it is. They have a month's vacation, special living quarters, a club, a day nursery, a night sanitarium where those with weak lungs stay for a period.Seventy-one per cent of our workers are women. They have three days a month off during their menstrual period because the industry is especially injurious to mucuous membranes. Also, nursing mothers have a special room where their babies are brought to them from the adjoining day nursery for nursing.

"Before the revolution," the director continued, "conditions in this factory were terrible—no ventilating system, a 12- and 14-hour day. The tsar had always hampered the growth of Rostov because it was traditionally a city of revolutionary workers. There have been great hardships in building up the city to its present state."

"What are your wages?"

"Wages are low, although our worker benefits, working conditions and machines are exceptionally good. There is poverty here," Petrov admitted frankly. "But another help is the building cooperatives in which many of our workers participated this year, and some are building for themselves."

"How much money do you actually spend for workers' wel-

fare?" Dreiser still pursued his main contention that in spite
of all the benefits both profits and wages were low.

"Since 1921 we have spent five million roubles on ventilation, sanitation, nurseries, clubs, plus our contribution to
the city Construction Department for new housing. Ten per
cent of the income of every enterprise goes for building."

By this time the tireless reporter had run out of questions.
The director rose and offered to take us through the plant. In
the first room, tobacco leaves were being sorted. The ventilating system was new and the air was changed completely every
hour. There were several veteran workers among the women
who were picking over the leaves; one had worked in the factory for 54 years, another 37 years, and they still looked quite
hardy. They told us conditions were much better than before
the revolution. New machines for pressing and cutting can do
twice as much as the old. A mechanic had invented an ap-
pliance on an old feeding machine which had increased their
output 50 per cent.

A pretty young girl with a fresh complexion came up and
addressed the American in English. She said she was from
Edinburgh, Scotland, and had lived in Russia for six years.
Her father worked in Odessa. She explained that she spoke
English so seldom that she was forgetting it. She was an ardent
Komsomolka (Young Communist).

She asked Dreiser what he thought of the Trotsky-Zinoviev
opposition. He confessed that he knew very little about it.

"It is a shame for you," she declared severely.

When we went on, TD told me that he felt properly repri-
manded and he guessed he'd better bone up on this thing. "But
the more I hear the more confused I get," he added.

Back in the office, he got another reproof. Before he could
start firing a fresh volley of questions, the director asked him
one:

"What about the Sacco and Vanzetti case?"

Now definitely on the defensive, the American delegate tried
to explain the attitude of the American public toward foreigners who had not been naturalized.

"What would be the attitude of the Russians toward a foreigner suspected of a crime?" he asked.

"In the case of foreigners, they are deported."

"But Sacco and Vanzetti did not want to be deported to Italy.... "

"That is because the fascist government would imprison them for their radical social views. But they could have been deported to Soviet Russia. We would have welcomed them."

Unable to comment on this point, the guest cut short the discussion and the tea was brought in. Everyone relaxed. The guest was presented with a wooden cigarette case and several packages of cigarettes, although neither he nor his ladies-in-waiting smoked.

We visited the night sanitarium. It was so cozy, with comfortable sleeping rooms, a homelike dining room and well-equipped kitchen, that Dreiser, suffering from chronic bronchitis, said he would like to stay there himself.

From there, I led him up the stairs. Halfway up, he halted and looked at me suspiciously. "I wouldn't be surprised if you were trying to slip another nursery over on me," he declared.

Caught in the act, I took his arm and promised, if he would come along peacefully, to find him a nice toilet. He eagerly accepted the offer and went on docilely.

"I must say," he admitted to the pleased nurse, "this one is especially fine, even better than the model nursery in Moscow."

I failed, however, to keep my promise. A nice public toilet simply did not exist in the country.

It was foggy and snowing again when we went outside. We joined Dr. Davidovskaya and, tired, chilled and unwashed, we welcomed her suggestion to go to the public bathhouse.

"I've reconciled myself to going unwashed," our charge had observed, after examining the facilities provided in hotels — a tank hanging over the washstand. When you pushed up the stopper in the underside of the tank with your palm, water leaked out in drops. Davi and I, being Russianized, made the best of the available facilities.

The central *banya* looked like a Samarkand mosque. The imposing vestibule was covered with tiles on floor, walls and ceiling. Beggars hung around the fountain in the center, as though the spouting water could make them clean. TD was nervous about leaving us to go into the men's section. He was carrying a large roll of greenbacks which he had not yet changed into roubles. This roll he entrusted to my care when we parted at the marble stairway leading down to the men's section. He looked back at me helplessly as he descended. But this was one time I could not go with him.

My bosom bulging with the bankroll, I joined Sonya, and we entered the women's section. It was beautifully tiled from floor to ceiling. In the middle of the first chamber on a dais stood a queen-size bathtub with an attendant standing guard. The tub could be used only after one had a thorough scrubbing and steaming in the steam-room. We undressed in the ante-room and entered a long tiled hall, carrying our wooden tubs. These we filled under the hot water faucets and poured the contents over our well-soaped bodies. After we had scrubbed and rinsed several times, we were ready for the steamroom. Carrying tubs of cold water and washclothes, we mounted the steps. The higher we went, the hotter the temperature. We wet the cloths in cold water and put them on our heads. I could not stand this very long. Descending in a hurry, I dashed a tub of ice-cold water over my perspiring body. It felt delicious. Davi came down, too, and we let the attendant give us a rub-down.

I worried about our charge. How was the novice taking his first Russian steam bath? Were there women attendants, as sometimes happened in these baths? As we hurried out into the vestibule, there he was waiting for us, his face pink, his soft white hair still damp and curling slighty—as sweet and shining as a baby after its bath.

The bankroll was transferred safely to his overcoat pocket, and we emerged into the icy air of the winter night. With all of us so radiantly clean and refreshed, dinner at the hotel restaurant was truly festive—*shashlik* again, with green onions, fried potatoes and beer. I disliked beer, but drank it to be sociable. Thus, washed and fed, we returned to our room to pack, hoping there would be an International coach on the train to Mineralni Vodi (Mineral Waters).

6. Mountain Resorts

When we boarded the train, we found that there were only second-and third-class coaches — no International coach — and no bedding. At least the *provodneek* did not put another passenger in our four-place coupé and he gave our charge a small pillow. We lay down on the hard shelves in morose silence.

Next morning there were still the snowy steppes, with no hint yet of the warmer weather we had expected in Mineralni Vodi. It was getting dark at half-past three when we arrived at "the gateway to the Caucasus." Mineralni Vodi was a terminal where we had to change trains for Kislovodsk, one of the famous health resorts that were built around numerous mineral springs in the mountains. There was plenty of snow here but the temperature was milder.

The train for Kislovodsk was scheduled to leave in an hour. We had tea in the buffet and listened the the complaints of a poor woman with two children. She was on her way to Grosny in Transcaucasia on the road to Baku. She said she had been waiting three days for a place on a train. The trains were so crowded that she could not get a place card in third class, for which she had a ticket. She had now spent all her money and had no food left.

Dreiser felt very sorry for the woman. He suggested we turn over our large accumulation of food — bread, butter, apples, cheese, bologna, granulated sugar (which had been leaking out of the bag along the way). The mother accepted the food with tears of gratitude. He enjoyed watching the children ravenously eating everything at once. . . .

When we alighted from the train in Kislovodsk, he breathed deeply and cried out in wonder, "We are in a different world!"

We were at one of the most beautiful of the watering places grouped around mineral springs possessing valuable medicinal properties. Although there was snow on the ground, the air had a soft, exhilarating quality. Already we felt the restful atmosphere. The hotel was so near that our porter carried our baggage. Following him, we could see, even in the darkness, the cultivated beauty around us — soothing after the cold, harsh world we had left behind. At one side of the winding street there was a high stone wall, and towering above it a magnificent building, which, the porter said, was an amusement palace connected with the railroad.

At the fine government hotel we chose a very large room on the second floor, with windows and a balcony over the street. Our official guide held the purse strings of the dwindling VOKS funds. TD did not object — he wanted to save the dollars he spent on my expenses. In summer the price was 12 roubles, but only six roubles in the winter season.

So here we were, the three of us, in this beautiful room, with private bath. There was one wide couch besides the bed. Another couch was brought in and placed beside it at one end of the room, with a Caucasian silk screen around our section.

"God, wouldn't it be wonderful if we could just unpack our bags and stay here all winter!" TD said fervently.

Supper in the charming dining room pleased him, too. "Best cooking I've tasted in Russia," he declared. In family style, we divided our portions and had a variety of delicious dishes. There were beets with *smetana* (sour cream), stuffed cabbage, baked veal and spaghetti with cheese — and good Georgian wine and the cost was only three roubles. . . .

We rose at seven next morning in order to see as much as possible of this paradise. Outside, we breathed deeply of the cold, invigorating air. The streets ran up into the foothills, on which were magnificent sanitariums, pretty cottages and rest homes. We decided to walk up to a large white building with graceful columns. Davi stayed behind to plan our day at the tourist bureau. She warned us to come back soon, since we had a full day of sightseeing ahead.

My companion was in no hurry to return. This kind of winter weather he enjoyed. The air was so bracing and everything looked so entrancing in the snow. We wandered up the winding street until we came to a market where rosy-cheeked peasant women were selling their produce. We bought glasses of hot milk, which TD found soothing to his throat. As we went on, we passed the charming rest home of the Art Workers Union. Stone steps led to cottages above, all closed for the winter.

Crossing a bridge, we entered a park and came to a clear stream ending in a waterfull. A slight steam rose from the surface. I thought it might be Narzan and took some in the palm of my hand.

"Um-m, tastes like perfume—and smells like perfume!" I held it up for him to smell.

"Well, I'll be damned it does smell like perfume. But I'd not be surprised at anything in this wonderland."

I laughed, suddenly remembering I had put scented cream on my hands. But soon we traced the health-giving water to its source. At the end of the park stood the stately Narzan Gallery, enclosed in glass. Inside was a plant conservatory and a fountain spouting the precious mineral water which had refreshed us on our journey.

TD drank his fill, reminding me between gulps that we had paid 40 kopecks a bottle for this in Moscow and more than that on the trip.

From there we went to the Jurzal, the big amusement pavilion operated by the railroad which we had noticed when we arrived. The vast building contained a summer theater, a concert hall, billiard room and museum. In the gardens we found a concert pavilion and two lovely, honey-colored Russian bears in a cage, also eagles, owls, foxes and peacocks.

We sat on a bench in the warm sunshine and gazed at the superb panorama of the main range of the Greater Caucasus with the mighty Elbrus, whose volcanic peak towered 18,000 feet above the pateau. Dreiser sat in rapt silence. I hesitated to disturb him, for he was like a man worshipping before the holy images in a cathedral.

Presently, however, he rose, turned reluctantly from the awesome panorama and lumbered after me. Davi was waiting impatiently to take us on a tour of the sanitariums, and her indignant words of reproach shattered his mood for the day.

She was armed with a typewritten introduction and had an *izvozchik* waiting. It was a handsome droshky on wheels, drawn by two sleek horses. Dreiser had seen the last of the little one-horse sleighs.

We visited a number of beautiful sanitariums. There was one for peasants from all parts of the USSR. A very clean, attractive place with a fine dining room and social hall, it accommodated 65 patients at one time, for five-week periods. There were four beds in each sleeping room. The peasant guests in their white linen costumes looked happy. Their local health department sent them free of all costs. One of the eight women guests was Ivanova Michaelova Borisova, an old Bolshevik, age sixty. We found her studying in her room. She said she was a member of her local Soviet, and was very active in public speaking but was only now learning to read and write.

Another sanitarium we visited was "in the name of Lenin." It was a scientific institute for the study of diseases of the heart. Its location on a hill commanded a wonderful view.

In the office, the manager answered Dreiser's well-chosen questions. Practically all buildings had been privately owned hotels and cottages. This particular sanitarium still rented rooms to private patients who took treatments. During the Civil War, the buildings were used as quarters for the White Guards. Their horses were stabled in the central bathroom.

"Now these once fashionable health resorts have been made available to the masses," the manager concluded.

When we came out into the frosty air, our driver was trotting his spirited horses up and down the road to warm them. The tour of the sanitariums had tired TD, as walking or looking at beautiful scenery never did. Besides, he was still a bit disgruntled at being dragged away from doing what he wanted to do.

Yet now, of all times, he must stop to send a telegram to his niece whom he was to meet in Constantinople. The clerk in the little telegraph office could not find the "LCD" or deferred rate in his book, which would have given the customer a 37-kopeck reduction. I reported this to my employer, who was waiting, chilled and weary and hungry, in the carriage with Davi.

"Oh, what a lousy country," he burst out. "These dubs couldn't run a peanut stand. Go back and tell him he's got to find it."

Another search failed to reveal an LCD rate.

"Damn fools, nincompoops. . . "

I could bear no more of this. To spoil the day over a few kopecks!

"You make me tired," I scolded. "You're the typical American tourist, always expecting to find everything just like at home. If you can't exist for a few weeks without your comforts and your LCD's, you should have skipped this tour, as VOKS advised."

In chill silence we rode back to the hotel. I blessed Sonya for her restraint, and was already repenting my outburst. As we went downstairs to the dining room, he strode ahead, ignoring me. Never before had he treated me this way. I ran past him to the door and barred the way.

"Please, TD," I pleaded, holding out my hand, "won't you make up?" My voice broke, tears came to my eyes. "It's Christmas Eve!"

He looked at me like a hurt child and started to brush me aside. But in my expression he must have discerned my longing for companionship with someone who shared my memories of Christmas Eve at home. Into his face came a softness which made it almost beautiful.

"Oh, all right, Ruthie, let's have dinner."

We ate the delicious meal in a relaxed mood. Davi was more considerate toward her charge than ever before—and he toward her. I thought hopefully that their relations might improve from now on. . . .

The manager of Kurzal, the big amusement palace, and his wife, whom I had met in Moscow, invited us to a concert and movie that evening. After listening to the music for a while, we went with them to their pretty cottage in the park. Although he managed the big concern which had put Kurzal in repair after the revolution and Civil War and had netted a 200,000 rouble profit in the last year, he had only three rooms in the cottage. However, comparatively speaking, they lived quite comfortably.

His wife served tea with jam and pastries, candy and apples, while Dreiser and her husband engaged in a heated discussion of communism. This devoted party man was a mechanic before the revolution. He now received the party maximum for this district of 190 roubles, on which he had to support his wife and three children. He was enthusiastic about the country's development, predicting that in time, *barring another military invasion*, the people would have everything. Dreiser argued that the thriving population would outgrow its productive power and there would again be scarcity and want.

Our host disagreed with this theory. A more cultured people would practice birth control. He also defended the period of war communism as a measure of the new revolutionary government, in a time of great want, to commandeer all supplies and ration them equally. The New Economic Policy had been an easing up of wartime restrictions and was on its way out. He cautiously refused to commit himself on the current party conflict regarding the next step. . . .

The manager's wife was, as TD said afterward, "a silly woman," too talkative, too heavily made up (most "nice" women didn't "paint" in those days). "She evidently has ambitions for better things," he continued. She had told us the workers were very critical of them when they tried to fix up their home.

They walked back to the hotel with us. The stars were shining, the air was clear and sparkling, the mountains rose protectively around us.

"This is a wonderful winter resort," TD told our host when we parted. "You should divide the workers' yearly vacations so there wouldn't be such a crowd in summer."

How soon he had forgotten the hardships of winter travel!

Like children who believe in Santa Claus, we were up very early on Christmas morning. It was only 4 o'clock, but we wanted to take the earliest train to Mineralni Vodi in order to catch the fast express to Baku at 7:25. TD sat in the candlelight of the coach talking of home.

"New York on Christmas morning," he mused. "Holly wreaths in the windows, children out with their new sleds, people calling Merry Christmas under my window. . . . How festive it was, how gay. . . "

"On the East Side, too?" Davi inquired.

I was annoyed at her. I had been hoping for better relations between the two clashing personalities. "Mr. Dreiser knows all sides of New York, Sonya. He finds color and human warmth as well as misery everywhere. Have you read his *Color of a Great City*?"

"I've never read anything of his," she retorted, her tone implying that she never intended to do it, either.

"Gosizdat has published some of the sketches in a small book called *New York*. . . . "

"I didn't give them permission to get out that abridged edition," the perverse author grumbled.

"That was before you signed the contract – remember? You agreed to accept a thousand dollars for the two abridged editions of *New York* and *Twelve Men*."

"Practically gave them away," he muttered, gazing morosely out the window. It was getting light outside.

"I know they are publishing an unabridged edition of *Color of a Great City* because Sergey wants me to write the preface," I went on cheerily. "But 'Christmas in the Tenements' is in the abridged edition. You should read it, Sonya, then you'd see that Mr. Dreiser wrote about Christmas on the East Side, too."

"Look here, conditions have improved a lot since I wrote that sketch," the author protested. He evidently was annoyed that "this little dub" should know that he had painted a sordid picture of life in his beloved New York.

"Yes, you explained that in your foreword to the last edition, which Gosizdat is using for the translation. You mentioned especially the sketches, 'Christmas in the Tenements' and 'The Bread Lines,' which you explained were long since abolished."

He glanced at me challengingly. "Well, that's so, isn't it?"

"I hope so," I said.

7. Baku at Last

The 7:25 train to Baku was late. We sat in the buffet at
Mineralni Vodi and prepared ourselves for a siege. We drank
tea, with a dash of vodka in TD's, then milk a little later. Still
later he felt hungry for something solid and had a festive idea.
It was Christmas Day and even if it had started out badly, we
would celebrate by ordering slices of the cold turkey displayed
in the glass case at the counter for a Yuletide breakfast. Davi,
however, preferred an ancient-looking smoked fish. The waiter
also brought what TD described as "half a pood" of thick-sliced
white bread.

"This turkey," TD declared after the first eager bite, "has
been cold a long time."

Davi ate her smoked fish with irritating relish.

Gloomily, our charge resorted to solitaire. Playing this
lone game in a crowded railway station under the gaze of a
circle of interested spectators soothed his frayed nerves. He
already had begun to feel at home when the train arrived
at 12:30. We joyfully rolled away in an International coach.

We thought we had said farewell to the steppes when we
went up into the mountains but here they were again, snow-
covered, absolutely flat. But we were happy. There was a
dining car on this train, the first Dreiser had seen in Russia.
It was wider and more spacious than an American diner. Now
we had a real Christmas dinner — borsch, fish with horseradish,
roast duck, baked apple with rice, cereal coffee and *pirozhni*.
Dreiser cheerfully paid the bill, which was five roubles.

We retired early in our comfortable beds made up by the
provodneek on three of the four upholstered berths, an upper
and a lower on either side of the compartment. We were
awakened when the lulling motion of the train ceased. The
train stood still for a long time. We could hear our neighbors
talking about the wreck of a freight train ahead of us — a split
rail, a car overturned and the others piling on top. Four crewmen had been killed.

We slept fitfully after that. It was 8:00 a.m. before the train began to move slowly. Reaching the wreck, we saw beside our tracks twisted freight cars, grain, paper and packing boxes scattered about, and soldiers guarding the bodies.

"It could have been our train," TD said.

"Picture *The New York Times* headline," I suggested lightly. "DREISER IN RUSSIAN TRAIN WRECK ON CHRISTMAS DAY."

"She's getting such a kick out of it," he told Davi, "I bet she almost wishes it had happened to me."

"But it would have happened to us, too!" she protested.

Now the country was changing to frozen marshes of tall brown grass, wild ducks flying, small clumps of trees in the distance. Then a range of snow-covered mountains came in view. Little villages were near the tracks, a cluster of clay huts with thatched roofs on piles. There were pigs and cows in the mud of the dooryard and in the doorway a woman in a red kerchief sifted grain in a round sieve.

By noon all the snow on the steppes had disappeared and was visible only on the distant mountains. Herdsmen in picturesque caracul cloaks with broad, straight shoulders, and high fur hats watched their sheep and cattle. Out of Petrovsk Port we passed a row of dugouts which were carved out of the high embankment along the tracks.

In our car there were a group of responsible party workers returning to Tiflis and Baku from a conference in Moscow. Among them were Armenians, an old Georgian who had worked with Stalin, a White Russian, a Siberian and a Jew. One young Armenian from the Tiflis Soviet was most hospitable. He urged the American delegate to drink Caucasian cognac, Tiflis champagne and all-Russian vodka. He had dinner with us in the dining car and afterward sat in our coupé and sang Armenian and Georgian songs. An exuberant, crazy fellow was this Elchegaikov ("Gaika"). Before he left us to change trains for Tiflis, he made a solemn promise to show us the sights when we arrived in the Georgian capital.

It was 10:00 p.m. when our train came into Baku, capital of the Azerbaidjan Republic on the Caspian Sea. It seemed a wild kind of station. Crowds were surging back and forth, the people jabbering in a strange tongue, the porter running ahead of us with our baggage. The official language was a Turki dialect. The swelling population had reached 447,000. Their manners and customs were Persian, but we soon perceived that they were now adapting to the new ways.

Our porter dashed up to the line of swarthy *izvozchiki*. Their two-horse carriages were the finest yet. The drivers' costumes were long bright-blue coats tied with red sashes. Big fur hats perched rakishly on their black hair.

We rode through the dark yet lively streets to the new seven-story hotel Novaya Evropa (New Europe). An open elevator, about which the tiers of floors circled, carried us to the sixth floor. We took a two-room suite for eight roubles, filled out forms, showed travel documents, and finally, after an unusual amount of red tape, we settled for the night in quarters that were poorly heated even for this mild climate. The windows were sealed and there was no ventilation.

We ate breakfast in the hotel dining room. The food was very expensive, 1.60 R. for a pot of coffee – but it was *real* coffee at last. While Davi looked up the local Soviet, we went walking and were soon at the wharf. A fresh breeze off the sea was blowing, reminding me pleasantly of the San Francisco waterfront. The area was swarming with the swarthy, husky carriers typical of Baku. Their clothing was ragged; they were either bent double under the weight of their loaded racks or, with wooden shoulder pieces slung over one arm, looking for customers. There were also odd little wagons on two wheels, decorated in bright colors, the horse's harness beaded with silver. One cart carried a long plank, half its length hanging over the horse's head. Numerous old ships and the rusty remains of others were in the harbor.

Dreiser stopped to talk with a young woman in the courtyard of a large new apartment house facing the water. She said it was for shipworkers. Her husband had been lost at sea two months ago. She was left with two children to support on a pension of 26 R. a month from the government shipping company and she paid 50 kopecks a month rent for one room in a two-room flat – with a kitchen and toilet for two families.

We took one of the gorgeous droshkies back to the hotel. Our faithful VOKS guide was impatiently waiting for us. She reported that the Baku authorities were not very cordial and had not even furnished a guide.

"Evidently, my fame has not spread to the shores of the Caspian Sea," Dreiser remarked.

"Oh, but the woman in the office claimed to know all about you. She said she had read all your works – you are her favorite poet." There was veiled sarcasm in Davi's tone.

"Splendid!" exclaimed the celebrated novelist. "It is gratifying to find here in Transcaucasia, the most ancient abode of the human race, now occupied by 40 or 50 races, each speaking its own language, someone who appreciates my poetry."

"Oh, then you do write poetry," Davi exclaimed. "Now I'll take you to the Musselman Working Women's Club."

"Fine," he agreed, enjoying himself at her expense. "I'm sure I'll be appreciated there, too. You doubtless know, Davi, that women are my specialty."

The Musselman Women's Club "in the name of Ali Bairomova" was a very large building, formerly the residence of a rich Armenian merchant. Here were clubrooms containing a reading room, theater, the usual Lenin Corner built like a mosque – a bust of Lenin on one side, a portrait of him on the other and, above the dome, the hammer and sickle. The little woman who led us around was herself a Musselman; she was tiny, with a pretty face, large dark eyes and black hair. She said that the club had grown from 550 members in 1924 to several thousand. A large percentage of these women were still illiterate, wore veils and had no training for work. The club held classes in sewing, embroidery, rug-weaving, midwifery, music and dancing. They were also involved in a campaign against illiteracy.

Before he suspected what was heppening, Dreiser found himself in the nursery that kept the children of the members during the day. A parents' meeting was in progress, and the children greeted us with "*salome malekov*" (how do you do). Dr. Davidovskaya and I were more enthusiastic about the club than was the great specialist on women. We thought it was wonderful that the Musselman women were being emancipated, throwing off their veils and learning to read and write.

Dreiser, however, remarked that, "from the unveiled faces I have seen, I would be inclined to believe discreet covering might add to their charms."

Leaving the club, we joined the crowds on the narrow cobbled street. Most of the women were wearing veils or had large cotton shawls which enveloped them drawn discreetly over their faces. Their figures at first glance had a romantic Oriental charm—until we noticed the cheap, modern shoes and colored cotton stockings.

Many of the stalls on the street were selling *shashlik*. Mutton on sticks was being turned over glowing charcoal in an iron pot. We looked into one fascinating little place with steps leading up to it and a garden at the side. At once, the dark, sinister-looking proprietor called to us to come in. But we wanted to go up the hill to a great church looming at the end of a narrow street. The street itself was full of life and color and the romance of the East, but the church proved to be like all the other Greek churches TD had seen, except that the old priest was wailing rather than chanting.

The alluring little place had sold out all its *shashlik* when we returned, so we found a less festive one. It was just another beer hall but the proprietor was very accommodating. He suggested two portions of *shashlik* and one of beaten mutton, also cooked on a stick over the spit, a lobster and beer, all served with dried peas, green onions and radishes. There were, besides, thin loaves of white bread baked in great slabs resembling washboards. After this tasty repast, we stopped at a bakery and bought little cakes to eat with our tea in the hotel suite. We were tired and chilled, and we enjoyed the samovar before retiring. It had been a good day.

Early next morning we started out by streetcar for the oil fields. At the seashore we walked to the offices of the State Azerbeijansky Oil Industry. The weather was chilly and the fog was almost a drizzle. Ford cars were racing up and down the muddy streets. Altogether, it was not a good day. When the little doctor presented her documents at the manager's office, he ordered a Ford to take us to the oil fields.

Our guide, who was a foreman, told us that most of the wells had been sunk in the water and vast stretches had been drained. This group of wells produced 2000 tons of oil a day. There was an eight-hour day in three shifts and the average worker earned 70 R. a month.

Dwellings of the 520 workers in this field were in sight of the wells on the hills. In the tsar's time, everything had been sooty from the kerosene burned in the homes. Now they burned natural gas. Their living quarters were rent-free — two rooms for an average family.

"What about these carriers I see everywhere?" TD asked.

"They belong to a trade union, but they don't work for wages. They receive certain benefits as union members and can find other employment through their union. Their earnings amount to about 90 roubles a month."

"Well, what do you know!" exclaimed TD, "Why, that's 20 roubles more than you said the average oil worker makes. Instead of pitying the carrier, I envy the rascal his free life."

After the usual question about conditions "before and after," the foreman explained that while the cost of exploitation was higher than in the United States, the products cost less and "therefore we can compete with other countries. Production costs in Russia are higher only in the mechanical industries where machinery must be imported."

The obliging foreman told us how to get to the Chorni (Black City), where the refineries were. He put us on a streetcar which went along the wharf. Arriving at the Black City, we picked our way along the muddy roads to the main office. There we were given a permit to visit Plant No. 2.

When we went outside to wait for a guide, Davi started to explain that Black City wasn't black any more, because "conditions have improved so much since the revolution."

Dreiser walked away from her. "I'm tired of hearing about how much better conditions are since the revolution." Pausing to turn to me, he grumbled, "It's all this leveling down that worries me. I'm afraid this new order will make for drabness. Everybody having the same standard of living will lower it for all. If all the people must be provided for equally, there can never be heights of beauty and luxury."

I said he could see in Moscow that the intellectual workers already were creating a higher level for themselves, that there always would be differences of individual ability, tastes and temperaments even with equal opportunities and plenty for everyone. The leveling down was "material, not intellectual."

At this, he burst out with his favorite theory. "But, as I've said before, the increased population resulting from 'plenty for everyone' would consume the increased wealth and lower the standard of living for all."

"Don't you remember what the manager of the amusement palace in Kislovodsk said about the danger of overpopulation?" I asked. "He told you: 'The higher the culture of a society, the more it practices birth control.' "

"That's the bunk," TD declared. "The ordinary man wants children when he can afford them. . . "

"Then why is it," I interrupted, "that the poor, ignorant masses are the ones who mass-produce babies? You know as well as I do it's because they don't know how to avoid having them."

Ignoring the point I had made, he lumbered away from me with such surprising speed that I had to run to catch up. He called over his shoulder without slackening his pace, "You remind me of a little trainer running after his elephant and prodding him with a sharp stick to keep him in line."

"Wait for Davi!" I called.

"Is that little squeak still with us?" he inquired, without turning around.

"You may be interested to know you're running away from the guide the plant office sent us!" I shouted.

At that, he came to a dead stop, and we three were cozily together when the guide reached us. He began to explain the process of refining oil and pointed out the many reservoirs on the hills in which oil piped from the fields was stored. From the reservoirs the oil was piped to the batteries, where it was heated and from which kerosene, benzine and different grades of refined oil were extracted and piped out into troughs. There were 350 workers in Plant No. 2, on three shifts.

As it was the end of a shift at 3 p.m., we took leave of our guide. He kindly advised us to hail a nearby *izvozchik* who had just moved some furniture to the neighborhood, rather than ride on the crowded trams. We were glad to leave Black City, even though it was no longer black. Tired and hungry, we went to a nice little family restaurant near our hotel.

In the evening, Dr. Davidovskaya took her charge to a film she thought he should see. I concluded from the title, *A Woman's Victory*, that he would not like it. But he went with her in order to give me a free evening to type my notes. I had a steaming samovar brought up to our room for comfort and warmth when they came back.

"Just as I expected, it was rotten," TD announced irritably, but he looked pleased when he saw the samovar, tea glasses, bread and cheese on the table. Over our hot tea, he told me about the picture. "It was a story of feudal times in Russia, how a bandit-baron carries off a girl and forces her to marry him, and how she outwits him on her wedding day. . ."

"Goody, goody!" I interrupted, applauding.

"Wait till you hear the rest of it," he warned. "You won't like it. When the soldiers come to arrest the bandit-baron and he breaks down, she leads him forth as her beloved husband—and all ends happily."

"I'm surprised Mr. Dreiser didn't like it," I said to Davi.

On the following morning, we rose very early. The sun was struggling through a thick fog and it promised to be a fine day. Leaving Davi to report to the Baku Soviet again, we hired a picturesque *izvoschik*, who wore a bright blue coat, red sash, and high fur hat. His two horses were correspondingly resplendent in silver-plated harness, ribbons and bells. TD wished to visit the Moslem mosque he had seen from his window. It stood alone on a bleak hill and we drove through mud to reach it. He had expected something exotic but it was plain and shabby, serving only the poor people of the neighborhood.

Descending the hill, the *izvoschik* drove to another mosque, whose domes and minarets had been visible in the distance. It was a splendid edifice completely satisfying TD.

When we returned to our neighborhood, we met Davi. She eagerly told us that the clerk at the travel bureau had advised us to see the Old City inside a fortified wall. It was not far away and soon we had entered the old Moslem world. It seemed unreal, as though we were looking at a picture from the Arabian Nights. Through the narrow winding streets streamed carriers with packs, boxes, even bales of hay on their backs. There were also loaded donkeys, sometimes carrying grown men who looked ridiculously big sitting on the tiny beasts. Women held their shawls over their faces even when carrying buckets of water or babies. Stalls displayed porcelain, chests, rugs, shawls, and sometimes had meat cooking over little charcoal fires. Street peddlers were buying their day's stock of oranges from the merchants. Over all sounded the hubbub of voices speaking in strange tongues; everywhere there were dark, friendly faces. A strange phenomenon was the sight, now and then, of a red-bearded man, or a red-haired woman. It was a dark, unnatural-looking shade of red.

Davi was seeking the Chantsi Dvoretz, a 15th century palace to which the clerk had given her directions. We wandered in and out of the narrow streets, inquiring of passersby, but no one seemed to understand what we were looking for. Finally, a slender boy stepped out from a group, pointing and gesticulating in an effort to make us understand that he would guide us there. We nodded, assuming that he did not speak Russian, and he went on ahead, looking back whenever he turned a corner in a timid, questioning way, to be sure we were following. In and out we went, climbing up broken stone steps, through dirty courtyards and narrow passages until we came to a high stone wall with parapets.

"I'm sure this is it," said Sonya.

The wooden gates in this ancient wall were closed. The aged keeper came out of a little niche to tell us the castle would be open to visitors tomorrow. He shook his head when our evidently tongue-tied guide asked if we might look inside, and answered irritably in his native tongue.

I took out our guide book and read aloud that these ruins were those of a fortress of Arabian architecture built in the ninth century. The castle had 68 rooms and the throne room was still intact. We peered through the crevices in the wall and could see the castle, a small, gray stone building, which had been standing since the 15th century.

"After all," Dreiser said philosophically, "I came to see the oil fields, not ruins."

But I knew he really found these Arabic ruins more fascinating.

Another boy had joined us. When he learned that two of us were from America, he and the first boy looked at us wonderingly. The tongue-tied lad made a clicking sound and tried to repeat "Amereeka!" The one who had just arrived said, "He wants you to take him to America where they can cure his tongue."

Dreiser remarked that to us this place held some of the magic of the Arabian Nights, while for these boys America was the land of enchantment. He gave the handicapped boy a crisp dollar bill for his help and we left him staring after us.

We returned to the hotel and packed, then went through the red tape of departure—tips for everyone, taxes on our passports, which, as usual, had been held at the desk during our stay. We expected to catch the 1:40 p.m. mail train to Tiflis. But when Davi went to the station window to get the place cards, all places were taken. So there we were, sitting in the crowded buffet on our baggage. Waiters dodged around us with trays loaded with soup and meats.

Such incidents on the tour too often spoiled the American delegate's pleasant memories. He refused to eat. Even to see the food nauseated him, he said.

Davi sighed resignedly. "There is nothing to do but return to the hotel. . . . "

"No, I won't go through all that damned red tape again!"

She suggested that the Hotel Bristol was much nearer to the station. Glad to economize on transportation, she fetched a carrier to take our baggage, and we walked. But the Bristol was much farther than she had thought. In spite of his heavy load, which included TD's suitcase, bag and fur coat, the carrier started out at a run.

"STOP! STOP!" she yelled, running after him.

TD sat down on a park bench. He was overcome with mirth at the ludicrous chase.

"Oh, oh, oh," he gasped. "That little dub will be the death of me yet!" Suddenly sobering when he remembered the carrier had *his* luggage, he exclaimed, "Hey, maybe she won't catch him!" and jumping up, he strode after her.

It was my turn to sink down and laugh helplessly. Really, those two would be the death of me! I could laugh—I was carrying my bags.

"Yes, indeed," Davi told us later, "I caught the rascal right at the hotel door and I gave him only 50 kopecks for running away from me like that."

We went to bed very early, for Davi's latest information was that our train would leave at about 4:30 a.m. A cold wind whistled around the sealed windows and rattled the frames. We heard TD coughing and wheezing. I threw his fur overcoat over him and the little doctor offered to rub liniment on his chest, but he would have none of that. Some time later, we heard the noise of a fire being made in the stove through the hall opening, so the room was warm when we rose at 4 a.m. We had slept without undressing and were soon on the street. A chill wind was still blowing, the stars were gone and wet snowflakes were flying.

At the station, we learned that our train was three hours late. Checking our baggage, we returned to the Bristol Hotel, where we were permitted to occupy our room until 7 a.m. After fitful sleep, we were back at the station. The corridors and waiting room were packed with the familiar restless throngs. We claimed our baggage, piled it in a clearing and sat down on the pieces, watching the ebb and flow of the human tide.

"Never in my life have I seen such wretched people," muttered the American delegate, already forgetting his night in the Donbas station.

Here were the remnants of the *bezprizornie*, children made homeless by revolution and civil war. There were old men scratching themselves beneath their tatters, poor mothers sitting patiently on their blanket rolls, holding their sleeping children. . . . One of the homeless children, barefooted, his hair matted, rags and tatters hanging from his bare shoulders, approached us. Extending a dirty hand, he begged, "A little kopeck, Uncle."

Dreiser's only response was to hold on to his bags and turn his head away from the revolting sight. He was not really so callous, but kind, compassionate Dr. Davidovskaya had advised him not to give alms to the waifs. "You will bring the whole pack. There are homes in every city for them. But they run away, the ones who are so wild. Some are lost forever."

Two more hours passed. By this time, TD was cheerfully adjusted to the situation. He told anecdotes to cheer us.

8. New Year's Eve in Tiflis

At last, we were seated in an International coach en route to Tiflis. The railway followed the Caspian Sea for several miles. The land side of the tracks was a brown waste with low, bare hills, flocks of sheep and clusters of shepherds' dugouts.

"I bet there's no Lenin Corner here," TD remarked.

"Don't be so sure," I retorted.

We were coming to wilder and more desolate stretches. Camels grazed and caravans moved across the plains. The camels wore faded striped covers and carried packs on their backs. Now we had left the sea behind. The railroad veered to the north through level grazing country. The villages were somewhat less primitive, with new clay houses that had thatched roofs. A red-tiled roof marked a new building in the center, which TD guessed would be the village Soviet.

Against a background of clay houses, a woman's motionless figure stood out, as she watched the train. A gray veil enveloped her face and form, "like a symbolic figure on a stage," Dreiser observed.

Farther on, another woman in bright red garments carried an earthen jar on her head. Here, the houses were on high poles. A caravan of oxen moved along beside the tracks. There was a tractor in the field. The country gradually became more

civilized and prosperous; there was much new building, a new
bridge over a river, new tracks under construction.

We were arriving in Tiflis, capital of the Republic of Georgia,
a fine, modern city. This station had the same wild appearance
as Baku. Our porter raced madly into the street, but this time
Davi wisely refrained from following him. He found a dilapi-
dated automobile, and we had to bargain with the driver above
the roar of his engine.

"Five roubles to the Hotel Orient," was the offer we had to
accept, as the hour was close to midnight and there were few
conveyances in sight. We rattled along through the darkened
streets. The air was not balmy but at any rate there was no
snow. At the hotel, the fat driver demanded two more roubles
for the baggage. Dreiser protested. The driver bellowed and the
case was referred to the hotel manager, who came out to see
what the rumpus was about. We won.

We were delighted when we came into the charming Turk-
ish-style lobby of the Hotel Orient. Our rooms were less attractive, but at least this was a two-sheet hostelry.

Our windows looked out on the main street, and in the morning we were astonished at the beautiful view. Across the street
stood a great church of cream-and-brown stone, the brown running in bands around the walls. With its large central dome
and four cupolas, the whole was perfect in symmetry, like the
Cathedral of the Redeemer in Moscow. It towered against a
background of mountains. In the foreground, the foothills were
verdant with gardens, and the streets were lined by tall cypress trees. A railway ran straight up to the top of Mount
David – a part of the mighty Caucasus – which rose directly
above Tiflis to a height of 2500 feet.

In the street below, automobiles were spinning by; the main
thoroughfare swarmed with well-dressed people. Dreiser was
eager to go outside and see more of this modern, prosperous
city. But wet snow was falling when we started out, quickly
dampening TD's enthusiasm. We walked through slush in
the damp, chill air to the postoffice. There was only a package
of Soviet production charts from Sergey.

It was the last day of the old year and the shops were crowded with customers buying New Year's gifts. In a Caucasian silk shop, Dreiser bought several pieces of richly colored silk in variegated patterns. He gave me one of these and two gossamer, handloomed gold and brown scarves. These New Year's gifts were the only presents Dreiser ever gave me and I still have them.

This New Year's Eve was much more festive than the Christmas Eve we spent in Kislovodsk. But the weather was far from festive in its effect on TD—the dampness and cold had affected his chest. When we returned to the hotel, he felt miserable. Nevertheless, since we had tickets for the opera, he insisted upon going. The opera house, he said, was as fine as those in Moscow and other cities. He enjoyed the new comic opera, *Life and Joy*, written by a Georgian, and especially appropriate for New Year's. The music, TD said, was good, the costumes colorful, but the plot was hackneyed, and Dreiser found more interest in watching the audience. The Georgians have very marked racial characteristics, and he pronounced them a strong, virile people. The men were tall, handsome, dashing; the women proud of bearing in their silk gowns, although "the dark, heavy features which make for masculine beauty are too hard in a woman," he commented.

When we came out of the theater, Tiflis was meeting the New Year on the streets and in the cafés and also in our hotel restaurant. *S'Novom Godom* (to the New Year) was heard on all sides.

Gaika, the Armenian Communist, member of the Tiflis Soviet who had been so attentive on the train, had found us after telephoning the hotel for two days.

But Dreiser did not feel in a sociable mood. "We no sooner hit a town," he grumbled, "than the young men come running, presumably to show *me* the sights. Well, I'm going to bed. I feel rotten."

"*S'Novom Godom!*" the young man called gaily.

Sonya, who was in a sociable mood, bought a bottle of Georgian wine at the hotel bar and invited Gaika to our room.

Strains of the orchestra downstairs came up clearly, so that the undignified Tiflis council member could whirl me around (my head was whirling already from a glass of wine). I sank down on the Turkish divan, gasping that it was Tovarisch Davidovskaya's turn. Gaika whirled her around more sedately.

TD commented next morning that we must have had a gay celebration. He himself was quite chipper on this sunny New Year's Day. The snow-covered mountains dazzled the eyes in the sunshine.

It was still early in the morning when Councilman Gaika arrived to take us sightseeing. We all went to the café Germania for breakfast. From the restaurant, we strolled through the gardens across from the Hotel Orient. "Sovnarkom," the headquarters of the Soviet of People's Commissars of Tiflis, was located here. The garden was lovely — formal beds of flowering plants, cypress trees, flowering vines, red gravel on the paths, down which fine-looking young soldiers from the nearby barracks were strolling. A lone swan glided majestically over the pond.

Dreiser wanted to look into the church he had admired from his window. But Gaika said it was now a Young Pioneer Club. In the courtyard there was a sports field.

Annoyed, the American delegate remarked that this was "an incongrous use for such a noble edifice." The Communist official said that an earlier proposal was to tear down the church and erect a new building on the site, but the church was spared.

"I think a better use would be to turn the church into a mausoleum for the country's distinguished dead," TD rejoined testily. Gaika glanced knowingly at Davi and me, as if to say, "What a reactionary old bourgeois!"

At the nearby government garage, our influential friend was furnished a car. He drove us to the old section of crooked streets, old houses with flat roofs and balconies, and open-air markets. On the hills above stood a medieval fortress. Only one wall and a tower remained of Metekh Castle, a gloomy prison in which, before the revolution, political prisoners were confined. But it was closed now, of course, Gaika added.

Dreiser's interest in churches led our guide to speak of the Communist party's leader, Josef Stalin. "This country is his birthplace," he said proudly. "Tovarish Stalin was reared in the church and educated for the priesthood."

We rode more than halfway to the summit of Mount David. At each bend in the road the view became more wonderful. At a considerable height, we looked down on the city, and TD said he could make out his church. At 2000 feet there was a colony of cottages for delicate or tubercular children, called "The Children's City."

The American author was moved to find in the churchyard of the small sixth-century Church of David the grave of Griboyedev, whose comedy *Gorye ot Uma* (The Misfortune of Being Clever) he had read in English. Here, too, were the graves of the famous Georgian poets Ilya Chavchavadze and Akakia Tsereteli.

Gaika told us that Tiflis was the ancient capital of the Georgian kingdom dating back to the seventh century, and was now not only the capital of the Georgian Soviet Socialist Republic but also of the Transcaucasian Federation. It had an extraordinarily mixed population. Georgians were the majority race, but there were almost as many Armenians and many Persians and Jews.

On the way back, we stopped at a pretty central park and went into a picture gallery. TD liked the collection of Georgian paintings. Two large oils of streets in Samarkand pleased him. He had expected to visit that enchanting central Asian city, and now he gazed at the pictures of street bazaars in the shadow of ruined mosques. He turned to me. "Those domes and towers remind me of that mosque in Leningrad with that exquisite blue mosaic work," he said.

Gaika showed us the sulphur springs and the fine bathhouses built over them. He said the name Tiflis was derived from the ancient Georgian word *tbilisi* (warm springs). He regretted that we would not have time to visit some of the many cultural and educational institutions. The Georgian State University had more than 7000 students, he said.

9. Voyage to the Black Sea Ports

Our friend saw us off on the night train to Batum. There was only one *myaki vagon* (soft car) on this train and it seemed a thousand people were trying to get places on it. However, Gaika took Davi to the OGPU officer, one of whom was always on duty at stations. He waved his magic wand and soon we were settled in a four-place coupé, with a young Red Army officer occupying the fourth place. He proved to be very helpful.

In the morning, a real winter scene met our eyes. Even now, en route to the Black Sea resorts, relentless winter had pursued us. We saw a white landscape, a stream running through snowy banks and falling snowflakes.

Lying on an upper shelf, I was reading the description of Batum in my Russian guidebook and translating aloud:

"The Russian Tropics: The warm, humid climate makes Batum a splendid winter resort... The rains are tropical. Temperature in winter is mild. It never snows. The best months of the year are October, November, December...."

"We're two days late," TD interrupted grimly from his place below. However, as we traveled on, the snow disappeared gradually and a heavy fog and drizzle took its place. TD gazed moodily out at the dreary landscape, folding and unfolding his large white handkerchief, as was his habit when bored or in deep meditation. What he saw were marshes, lush foliage, harvested crops hanging on trees to protect them from the dampness, houses built on piles, succulent green grass. The men we saw along the way wore turbans. Their villages were primitive. The better houses were on brick piers, to raise them above the marshes. In the background there were low mountains.

Belatedly, TD thought about interviewing the Red Army commander. "Lord, this is my first chance to talk to an army man." he exclaimed. The commander was quite willing, so I took out my notebook.

Answering the first question, he said there were 450 men in his regiment.

"Do you make social distinctions in rank?"

"In battle, the commanders are at the very front. Off duty, they eat and sleep with the men."

"Do the new labor laws apply in military ranks?"

"Yes, the eight-hour day applies to soldiers also. In fact, they often work less than eight hours. Much of their time is given to education, and the eight-hour day is in force there, too."

"How does army life today compare with conditions before the revolution?"

"Before, under the tsar, the soldier was severely restricted and abused. There were signs on the boulevards and street cars and other public places: 'SOLDIERS AND DOGS NOT ALLOWED,'" (Dreiser remarked, "Like Kipling's Tommy Atkins.") "Now, under the dictatorship of the proletariat, the soldier gets a month's vacation every year and everything is free to him."

"Are you on socially equal terms with your higher officers?"

"Off duty, yes. On duty, of course, I am a subordinate." He gave more details of existing relations between officers and men. "The officer cannot discipline the men harshly, can never scold nor yell at them."

"Doesn't this make for lax discipline?"

"No, discipline is maintained more through instruction and training than through punishments, which are now abolished. In tsarist times, punishments were terribly severe." He added, "Illiteracy is being abolished through the army much faster than in civilian life." He claimed that living conditions of the soldiers were very good and they did not complain. "If a relative comes to visit a soldier, he is given a room. At all times, relatives may come to entertainments in the army camps."

Our train was already three hours late. Now it stood still at a desolate station and the Red commander went out to get news. There had been a wreck ahead, he reported, and our train was waiting for orders concerning the relief train which would come from Batum to pick the passengers up on the other side of the wreckage. It was an hour before our train moved on slowly for a few miles, then stopped in a wild spot.

The passengers alighted, carrying their baggage. We had to circle around the wreck down a muddy hollow alongside the tracks for half a mile. Natives, clad in ragged clothing and with cloths wrapped around their heads turban-fashion, ran up to the passengers, begging to carry the baggage. We hired two young fellows and a girl to carry some of our heaviest pieces as we struggled along in the mud.

Presently, along came a cart drawn by two oxen and driven by a merry-faced girl. The heaviest pieces were piled on the cart and the Red commander sat on top to escort the baggage.

By this time, we had reached the wreck. Several overturned oil cars were scattered over the tracks. It was a freak accident. The brakeman had slipped in the mud, smashing his lantern against an oil car. The oil had caught fire and the brakeman was burned to death. The chief conductor, farther back, quickly uncoupled the other cars and saved 26 of them. The guard who related the story to us declared solemnly that the engineer's black hair had turned white from fright.

Dreiser was dumbfounded when he heard this.

"Lord, hold me, I feel my head spinning around!" he groaned. "To think of that old superstition turning up out here in the wilds of Russia!"

He plodded on in the mud carrying his heavy fur coat and growing more disgusted with every soggy step.

"What a lousy country! Wrecks, wrecks, wrecks. . . ."

"You do not have wrecks in Amereeka?" Davi asked.

What he muttered was inaudible as he lumbered on, which was just as well.

In gloomy silence we reached the relief train and climbed on board. Soon we were running close to the shore of the Black Sea—dark sand and tangled underbrush on the shore side and wooded mountains on the other side. Already we were passing several sanitariums in the foothills for patients suffering from lung trouble, rheumatism and heart disease. In view also were orchards producing tangerines and oranges, and a big tea plantation. In the subtropical botanical gardens outside Batum

there were eucalyptus trees, palms, mimosa and other luxuri-
ant vegetation. In the background rose the evergreen mountains, the snowy summits of the giants of the Caucasus towering behind them.

"Tropical beauty," TD commented skeptically, "but will it
be warm in Batum?"

He had his answer soon. It was gray and chilly when we arrived in Batum at 5 p.m. An *izvozchik* took us to the pier. In
the waiting room of "Sovtorgflot" (Soviet Trading Fleet) we
heard the discouraging news that we could not buy tickets until 9 o'clock for the steamer *Pestel*, sailing at midnight. Davi
went to the bank to draw money while we sat waiting in the
buffet, where a rare assortment of human driftwood huddled
around the iron stove.

Our spirits were at low ebb, yet we had to face a new problem. The cable on my portable typewriter had snapped, and
it was absolutely necessary for me to finish typing my daily
notes in order to hand over the complete diary of the tour to
my employer at the border.

As soon as Davi had returned, we left her to watch the baggage and went into town. TD carried my typewriter. In the
nearest restaurant, we ate a cheerless dinner which cost the
comparatively exorbitant sum of 4.20 R. We asked the waiter
about the possibility of getting the machine repaired before
our steamer sailed. Fortunately he knew the repair shop proprietor and offered to take us to his home.

He led us a wild chase down dark, deserted streets, turning
corners so fast it was hard to keep him in sight. I ran breath-
lessly after TD, who strode along at a rapid pace in spite of
being burdened by the typewriter. At last we came to the mechanic's house. He readily agreed to repair the machine and deliver it to the steamer before sailing time. We went back to the
restaurant with the waiter, TD gave him a tip (I hope, a generous one), and we trudged wearily to the wharf without seeing
the resort town which the guidebook said was lovely. Or, as
Sherlock Holmes told Dr. Watson, we saw but we did not observe.

In fact, Dreiser was too ill to notice anything. He complained of chest pains and we watched him anxiously. He sat by the waiting-room stove with his head hanging down, racked by coughing and constantly wiping his mouth with what I feared was his last clean handkerchief. Those soiled handkerchiefs had been a chore for me along the way. I had to find a hotel maid who would get a bagful laundered in time for our departure (as always, stressing that they must be boiled).

How pitifully altered was the American delegate! His smart light-gray topcoat was grimy, his scarf bedraggled, his suit untidy, his bow tie missing, and he himself was unwashed. There was something touching in the spectacle of America's foremost novelist at the age of 56 braving the Russian winter to examine the workings of a new social system which was at variance with his own theories.

At last the gangplank was lowered and we boarded the *Pestel*. TD and I remained on the crowded deck watching for the repairman. What if he didn't arrive in time? I could not possibly complete the diary by hand — and have a copy for myself, as my employer wished, so that I could continue to help him from Moscow.

Now we heard the equivalent of "All ashore who's going ashore!" No repairman. Crewmen were standing by to raise the gangplank. I covered my eyes in despair.

"Here he comes!" shouted Dreiser.

There he was running from the shore, the Corona case in one hand, waving frantically with the other. The charge was 15 roubles, exorbitant in those days, especially when paid in dollars — but for once TD did not haggle about price.

He was pathetically glad to be on the last lap of his tour. But his stateroom below deck was dismal and dank, with five bunks. The sea was rough, the waves dashed over his porthole. But one thought cheered him: "If this were summer, I'd have four roommates."

The women's cabins were on the upper deck and much more comfortable. But this was a one-sheet boat, blanket on request, washing facilities the usual washbowl with tank above.

At seven in the morning we reached a small port named Poti. I walked with TD on deck in snow, rain and cold wind.

"The Russian subtropics," he growled, turning up his fur collar. "God, I hope I can get to Constantinople!"

We went down to the dining salon, which looked very comfortable. We were hungry, having eaten nothing since last evening in that dreary Batum restaurant. But the ship's food was unappetizing: cereal coffee with watered condensed milk, greasy fried eggs, thick slices of white bread.

We were cheered at the sight of our young Red Army commander approaching our table. He sat down for a chat. He was getting off at Sochi, he said. Sochi! I exclaimed. Why, only last September I was there on vacation at the Railway Workers sanitarium. I was quite excited at the thought of seeing the beautiful resort from a steamer.

"Do you belong to the Railway Workers Union?" the commander asked in surprise.

"Oh, no," I explained. I had met the group of railway workers — an engine driver, a mechanic, an office worker and a young scrubwoman — in my coach on the train. When they found I had no reservations at any resort, they adopted me and took me with them. I described the restful beauty of Sochi, medical care, sulphur baths. The commander was keenly interested, but my employer changed the subject. All he could think of was getting out of this lousy country to Constantinople to meet the niece, then to Paris — and New York!

He passed the morning playing solitaire in the lounge or gazing somberly out at the slow loading at the port of Poti, all the while folding and unfolding his big white handkerchief. (Fortunately, his supply of clean ones would last until we reached Odessa.)

A bookstand in the lounge displayed several paperback editions in Russian of Teodor Drayzer: *Sister Carrie*, *Free and Other Stories*, *Lynch Court and Other Stories*, put out by a Leningrad concern. I read the titles to the author.

"Well, what do you know," he commented. "We should have asked for an accounting from these enterprising comrades when we were in Leningrad."

We went on deck when the steamer left Poti at 1 a.m. The clouds were breaking to the south, revealing the mountain range on the opposite shore. TD pointed. Across the water lay Constantinople, his current dream city. He watched in delight the clouds of gulls, silver in the sunlight as we put out to sea.

Nearby, he noticed a group of jolly young sailors. Our friend, the Red commander, said they were on their way to Sevastopol to attend naval school. One of them, a tall, ungainly youth with a Slavic face, followed us with his eyes. Presently, he approached and asked shyly if this was the author of books he had seen on a rack in the lounge.

"The photo on the cover looked like him."

I explained about the author's presence here and presented him. Dreiser shook hands with the boy reservedly. He always seemed reluctant to bring his own personal life and profession into his objective investigations.

In the evening we arrived in Sukhum but remained some distance from the shore. The famous resort looked alluring in the twilight with its lights reflected in the water — "one of the best for sufferers from chest troubles," according to the guidebook. It was cloudy, the breeze was cool but the air was mild.

We walked on deck in a calmer sea the next morning. The sun came out, the air was still and warm. TD watched the dolphins leaping out of the water as we steamed west. He said it made him happy just to see them so joyous and free. He excitedly pointed out the flocks of wild ducks, mud hens and northern loons.

He was still in high spirits when we reached Gagri at noon. It was called the loveliest of the Black Sea resorts. The mountains were a towering background for its fine hotels, sanitariums, rest homes and baths. We did not dock, so the unloading was done in small boats.

Now, once again, just when the spirits of our temperamental charge were beginning to rise, in more beautiful surroundings and a milder climate, something happened to spoil his mood. He turned his eyes away from the restful beauty to watch the third-class passengers climbing into the boats.

"As Asiatic and dreadful as ever," he muttered. "The huddled masses of them nauseate me."

I tried to comfort him. "You mean the centuries of oppression which created these huddled masses nauseate you, don't you?"

But he clung to his mood of revulsion. "Russia is permanently spoiled for me by the cold and the dirt and the lack of creature comforts," he burst out petulantly. "Bukharin talked of building a paradise. But when? In 50 or 100 years? I will seek mine while I am still alive."

The *Pestel* sailed on along the shore which still lay at the base of the great mountains. They rose ever higher as we neared Sochi, among them three lofty snow-covered peaks of the Greater Caucasus. There were very large and handsome buildings along the beach, former mansions or palaces now used as rest homes. Near Sochi were the famous Matsessa sulphur baths, which I had enjoyed during my stay.

It was 4 p.m. when we slipped into the quiet harbor. The sun was setting, making streaks of red and gold upon the dark sea. The higher peaks had turned rosy in the reflected glow of the sunset, their clearcut profiles like pink cameos. Sochi! I could see the sanitarium of the Northern Railroad Workers at the top of those long wooden stairs. I called excitedly to TD, who was gazing out to sea. But even as he turned to look, the glory faded, the mountain peaks were cold-white again, twilight hid my precious landmarks.

Early on a frosty morning, we docked at Novorossisk, a leading Black Sea port of 62,000 inhabitants. It was our first opportunity to disembark. When we walked off the boat, there was a line of *izvozchiki* with a different type of droshky. We sat on a folded carpet, our feet hanging over the sides. The seats ran lengthwise as they do on a San Francisco cable car. Alighting at the center of the new, drab town, we searched for a restaurant, hoping to find relief from the ship's food. But none was open.

Soldiers were drilling on a hill; on the street level there was a bazaar. We wandered about still looking for food. Peasants were selling their products, but what TD wanted was a glass of hot milk and some plain cookies. We ate standing at the counter in melting snow and mud. . . .

Returning to the main street, we saw that a restaurant was open. But the odor inside was so sickening that we ordered only tea — TD's spiked, of course. I opened my handbag to comb my bobbed hair. The little mirrow showed a pale face with dark circles under the eyes, and a fever blister on the lower lip.

TD's omnipresent handkerchief fell on the floor and he bent to pick it up.

"Hey, what's this under the table?" he asked, holding up a small, shiny tube.

To my embarrassment, I recognized my lipstick, the first I had ever owned. I had bought it at the GOOM department store in Moscow for the trip and had been applying it cautiously, fearful that the "paint" might be detected.

"What do you know? — it's a lipstick," he went on unsuspectingly. "Somebody dropped it." He appraised me. "Why don't you keep it? You could use a little lipstick."

"Thanks," I murmured, returning it to my handbag.

TD noticed people carrying little fir trees. "How come Christmas trees in January?" he inquired.

I reminded him of the difference between the Julian and Gregorian calendars. "Tomorrow, January 6, is Christmas Eve by the old calendar."

"And just look at all the stouthearted believers!" he marveled.

On the way back to the boat, he opened the subject of my continuing to live in this damned uncomfortable country. I explained that I planned to join my husband and child in England when I had finished my work in Moscow — "including writing prefaces for your books."

At the same time, having a "contentious" mind, I pointed out some advantages in living in the Soviet Union. Moscow was not like these provincial towns, any more than New York was like Terre Haute, Indiana. The capital was a great cultural center, in spite of its present low living standard. I loved the stimulating intellectual life, the absence of dog-eat-dog competitive free enterprise, and the personal freedom-especially from the strain of keeping up appearances. Although my salary was low, there were workers' benefits such as free medical care, rent according to income. . . .

He was not listening. He kept scratching himself as we neared the dock. "I think I've got lice," he growled. (He had not bathed since Kislovodsk.)

I saw Davi approaching with our cabin mate. "I've found a good restaurant!" she called triumphantly.

Dreiser complained bitterly afterward that "it turned out to be the same old layout—potted rubber plants, buffet with cold cuts, cabbage soup, and the same old smells. A flop as usual," he concluded, glaring at the well-meaning little doctor.

The sea was very rough when the steamer continued on its course again. At 7 a.m. it docked at Feodosia (Theodosia) on the east shore of the Crimean peninsula. Sonya wanted to see the town but I stayed behind to wait for our charge, who had not yet come up from his cabin. I feared he might be ill. I stayed on deck, gazing at the historic walls and towers crowning the surrounding heights of this noted resort. I looked it up in the guidebook.

The quiet little town had lived through three brilliant epochs—under Greek, Genoese and Tartar-Turk rule. I felt sure that Theodore Dreiser, who often held forth on the superiority of Greek civilization, would want to see the town.

Presently he appeared looking so depressed that I hastened to tell him all I knew about this famous port. It was our first stop on the Crimean coast where remains of ancient culture still survived. "I know you'll want to go ashore."

"That last stop cured me of taking shore leave."

I persisted. I told him that many great writers had found inspiration in this place. "Homer, Euripides, Racine, Goethe, Pushkin, Mark Twain. . . . "

"So what? I'm not looking for inspiration. I'm looking for facts about this much-touted communistic system. To tell the truth," he went on, "I'm getting fed up with this harping on the bright communistic picture as opposed to the dark capitalist world. . . "

"That's precisely why I thought you'd find relief in seeing these relics of ancient cultures. Besides," I added brightly, "this town is your namesake."

"How come?"

"It's Theodosia in English."

"Not really. It used to be called Kaffa under Genoese rule," he retorted. At this moment our faithful VOKS guide came running on board. "Oh, why didn't you go ashore?" she cried. "It's a wonderful historic spot. I even saw an art gallery."

I assured her we were just going and took our charge firmly by the arm.

The street facing the sea was lined with beautiful buildings, formerly residences of the rich, and now clubs, rest homes and sanitariums for the workers. TD stopped to admire a palace of gray stone with exquisite mosaic work. I said it had been built by a tobacco magnate who had left it unfinished when he fled to Europe after the revolution. I read the sign over the front portal: "SANITARIUM OF THE SOVIET COMMERCIAL EMPLOYEES UNION."

"How inspiring," he remarked, and walked on, adding bitingly, "In this communist paradise, the workers even rest together."

But he soon began to appreciate Theodosia. The great moat around the town had changed little since the Genoese period. In one old Armenian church, "Archangel Michael," we found in the yard the grave of the painter Aivazovski, who was called the "Raphael of the Seas." On a side street we found the Historical-Archaeological Museum, where an art gallery housed the work of Aivazovski and of Bogayevski, who was still living.

Dreiser had seen their paintings of the Crimean coast in European galleries, he said. Aivazovski was the founder of the Russian-Cimmerian School of painting. In this art gallery, Dreiser loved Aivazovski's collection of marine paintings. One canvas occupied a whole wall.

Noting the American author's interest in the artist, the guard told him Aivasovsky loved Theodosia the best of all places. He had lived here as a boy and used to go down on the wharf to sketch. Trespassing was forbidden; he would be driven away, punished by his mother, or even arrested but nothing could keep him from the seashore.

The museum also contained many priceless objects out of the 2500 years of Theodosia's past. Dreiser lingered beside the ancient relics, musing over their historical significance. He was in an exalted mood when we returned to the ship.

As we steamed toward Yalta, the sea was quite heavy. Davi and I took to our berths but our charge, a stout sailor, walked on the rain-drenched deck, preferring this, no doubt, to his dank cabin below.

It was nighttime when we docked at Yalta, described in the guidebook as comparable to the French and Italian Rivieras. The captain told us that the recent earthquakes in the Crimea had been most severe here. TD was brooding again and did not want to go ashore.

"Wouldn't be able to see anything but a few lights in the shops."

Nevertheless, Davi and I were determined to have a look. Before we took off, I made one last effort to impress our author with the information that Mark Twain had visited Yalta in the 1860's and had described it in *Innocents Abroad* as a "splendid spot."

"So what? I'm not competing with fellow-worker Clemens," he retorted and continued to pace the deck.

We saw little but the lights of the magnificent sanitariums and palaces, the grandest of which was destined to be the meeting place of the history-making Yalta Conference at the end of World War II.

The black shapes of the sheltering mountains rose in the background. The air was delightfully warm. In the darkness we stumbled over the stone foundation of a ruined building, which reminded us sharply that there had been a devastating earthquake here recently. We decided not to risk going any farther.

When we returned to the boat, Dreiser was missing. We could not find him in his cabin, in the lounge or on the decks. None of the crew had seen him. Alarmed, we concluded that he must have gone ashore after all. We were running down the gangplank when we saw him coming toward us with that hulking gait of his. I rushed down to meet him and was aghast at what I saw. There was a cut above one eye and blood was trickling down his face.

"Where have you been? What happened?"

He appeared quite calm. "After you left, I decided I'd better see the place Clemens thought so splendid. I walked along a dimly lighted street past some new frame shelters. Not very inspiring. But a dark street drew me. I was walking past a walled garden where tall cypresses stood, when, all at once, a section of the brick wall crashed down to the sidewalk right in front of me. I yelled and jumped into the street. People came running, calling and gesticulating, but I didn't know a single word to say. I just walked away — and here I am."

"You are bleeding, Mister Drayzer," our little doctor cried. "Let me look at your face!"

"Never mind, just a scratch. I'll wash it off. I'm going to bed. The walk made me sleepy."

Next morning, we looked at him anxiously when he came to breakfast. I examined the cut over his eye and a bump on his forehead which was turning blue. Theodore Dreiser was a casualty of the Crimean earthquake.

We docked early that morning, at Sevastopol, the historic port in which many bloody battles had been fought. It also was the center of the revolutionary movement on the Black Sea coast. The town was razed by the Allies during the Crimean War in 1854. Count Leo Tolstoy was an army officer during the seige of Sevastopol. In 1905, it drew world attention to the revolt of the sailors on the battleship *Potemkin*, made immortal by Eisenstein's film.

Dreiser was keenly interested in seeing the town. We hired an *izvozchik,* but all the old fellow wanted to do was to jog along the main street and down to the sea again. With its boulevards, wide streets and fine homes, Sevastopol looked peaceful enough despite its bloody history. Since there were Naval academies on the outskirts, many sailors and marines were to be seen.

At the Marine Parade there was a monument to an admiral who saved the port from the Turks in 1853. From here we had a view of the North Anchorage, where there was a vast common grave of 127,000 men — brave defenders in the Crimean War. It was saddening, TD remarked, to realize that there was hardly a street without its historic association with some battle fought there, that every inch we trod had been soaked with blood of Russian defenders.

At this point, our driver started to turn back to the sea. "Drive on!" Dreiser commanded.

"There are two streets in town, *barin*, and we've already been on both." And he continued in the same direction. At the corner he began helpfully to point out places of interest. "There's the streetcar to the railroad station."

"Wonderful," said TD.

"And over there is the bazaar."

"Fine, we'll get out here." He paid the lazy driver only half the sum agreed upon for a tour.

We gave up on sightseeing and, ever in search of palatable food, walked over to the open market. We found a kind of dairy lunch and bought hot milk, omelette, white bread and butter. This was wholesome food after the ship's fare.

We returned to the boat just in time to bid farewell to the sailors, who were leaving to go to the naval academy on the hills above Sevastapol. Dreiser belatedly went into the lounge, bought copies of his books, autographed them and gave them to the tall fellow who had admired him from afar. He was surprised and grateful.

"It will be a great memory," he said shyly.

Toward evening the steamer anchored at a small landing point off shore to discharge passengers. The sea was very high. TD stood on deck and watched a tug trying to come close enough to take off passengers. It bobbed about and any moment might have struck our side. It was a wild scene and TD loved it — darkness, high wind, human peril — but finally the passengers were off and our ship was on its way again.

Our last night on board was the roughest of the seven-day voyage. Before Sonya and I retired, we managed to get down to TD's cabin to make sure he was all right. I dropped down on the side of a berth and fought seasickness. He lay staring at the five life belts on the wall.

"Probably all rotten," he muttered. "I'll bet if a fellow put one on, he'd sink right to the bottom."

His words, his tone, his hopeless expression struck me as ludicrous. I burst out laughing and at once he joined in. The tears rolled down our cheeks. Paroxysms of mirth relieved my nausea, and the terrible tension. Now we could face with more courage the last lap of our tour.

10. Odessa, Last Stop

At eight o'clock of a cold, foggy morning, our good ship *Pestel* sailed into the fine harbor of Odessa. We disembarked, bag and baggage, and gazed about us at a city in decay and ruin. The hotel auto took us to the Passage, which stood on the main square facing a great cathedral. TD admitted that his room in this very old hostelry was not bad. He rather liked the old black furniture and mahogany wardrobe. But the bed had a straw mattress – and it was a no-sheet hotel.

"Most people bring their own," the maid said stiffly. "It's extra for the linen and blankets."

But TD did not complain. He liked the view of the square and the cathedral from his windows.

Davi went to Derutra, the tourist agency, to make inquiries about procedures for the American delegate's exit. TD and I spent the afternoon riding to the end and back on several streetcar lines. It was a raw, foggy day, not conducive to admiring the scenery.

Odessa had been a beautiful city, the finest on the Black Sea coast, but the grand old buildings were smoky gray and in need of repairs. It had suffered greatly during the Civil War and occupation by the Allies. But, with a population of 430,000, Odessa was recovering. It had many banks, trusts, cooperatives and trade union organizations, and a number of newspapers and magazines were published here. The official language was Ukrainian but public notices were printed in Russian.

When we returned from sightseeing, we picked up Davi and went to a family restaurant for dinner. The proprietor gave a homey atmosphere to the place by playing the violin to his wife's piano accompaniment, but the food was not home cooking.

Dreiser groaned. "Same old borsch, same old schnitzel,*cutletti, pirozhki* – and Hungarian goulash that would make Bela Kun start another revolution – oh, my God!"

On Monday we all went to Derutra to make the final preparations for departure. This was the beginning of the end of Dreiser's ordeal. I should have warned him beforehand that everyone, even an important American delegate, had to go through a certain amount of red tape to leave Russia. In any case, our VOKS guide should have explained this to him earlier. However, his antagonism toward Dr. Davidovskaya discouraged any efforts on her part to explain anything to him.

To begin with, he learned to his consternation that there would be no steamer to Constantinople before January 18. He could not bear the thought of waiting that long and decided at once to cancel the voyage and take the train to Paris via Poland. He had made arrangements to meet his niece in Constantinople, and I knew this was causing him worry.

Nor was it so simple to arrange the trip to Paris. The clerk examined his passport and said he would need a Polish visa, as well as a renewal of his Russian visa. Next, we learned that he had no exit visa at all. He would need to make application and pay 21 roubles.

The delegate began to protest loudly. He was inclined to put the blame on Davi, but she tried to explain that since he was a guest of VOKS, the Moscow office should have attended to the matter. The clerk finally agreed to write a request to the visa department not to charge for the exit visa.

"It will be ready in two days," he promised.

After this upsetting business. I took the irate traveler for a long walk in the late afternoon sunshine. We went up and down the 200 historic steps which had been shelled from the battleship *Potemkin* in 1905 (TD had seen this portrayed in Eisenstein's film).

The red tape was gradually unwinding at the tourist bureau, with the American delegate cursing each inch. Then, as an anticlimax he learned that he could not take manuscripts and printed matter out without a special permit. This would mean minute examination by the customs authorities of all his papers and notes — including, heaven forbid, the original typed copy of my diary! This last indignity aroused his most explosive wrath. Here was another example of communist suppression of individual freedom.

Davi heaped fuel on his righteous indignation by adding, "It is also necessary, Mister Drayzer, to get written permission to take out sums of money exceeding 300 roubles." Some of his personal funds from the thousand dollars cabled him from New York still remained, thanks to his thrift.

"It's an outrage for soviet bureaucrats to question my right to take out American money I brought in! I'll telegraph VOKS about this."

Returning to his hotel room in this mood of mounting resentment, he began collecting his papers, notes, Russian books (some autographed) and letters. They quite filled the bag. I told him I would not have the diary completed until he was leaving. He could carry it in his overcoat pocket.

"I suppose the customs people will hold me up while they read it," he commented bitterly.

At this inopportune moment a young reporter from the *Odessa News* came to interview him. He spoke English, so TD expressed himself freely. What did he think of Russia? was the reporter's first question.

At this point what he thought of Russia was unprintable. But he did show some restraint. In a long speech about conditions, he conceded cautiously that it was "an interesting experiment. . . but you have a long way to go before you should try to put the system in other countries. I have no objection to your trying it here, but you should not try to change other governments until you have proved that the system is workable here." He went on tartly: "Before you send any more money abroad for strikers, you should take the homeless orphans off the streets."

The reporter answered politely that only a hundred remained in Odessa of the many hundreds of children of civil war and famine. He suggested that some older boys and girls became so wild that it would be hard to catch and hold them.

After this trying interview, we hurried down to Derutra with the bag of papers. The Intourist official at once took possession of it and began to examine and list the contents. This made Dreiser boiling mad, and the discussion about his cash on hand even madder.

"Give me that paper from VOKS stating that I am a guest of the Soviet Government!" he demanded of Dr. Davidovskaya. "Maybe it will help me get over the border without all this red tape and inspection of my private property!"

Davi, of course, refused to give him the document which, at the moment, she held in her hand. Denouncing "your incompetence, this lousy organization, and the whole damn business," the American delegate snatched the document and strode out into the street.

I ran after him. "Give me that paper!" I said.

He stared at me in hurt surprise—"the only person he could trust in Russia, the only person who could get him out of this country alive."

"Don't you see, TD, Davi is our official guide, the document was given to her and she must show it to Derutra in order for them to issue the papers you need to get out?"

He meekly handed it over.

This was his final break with his VOKS guide.

He had calmed down by evening. We had dinner at the Bristol Hotel where the breakfast that morning of pancakes, ham and eggs, and cereal coffee had been satisfying. TD said he "had no kick coming." Now, he was tempted by the "wild duck" on the menu.

"I think I'll try it. Sounds good. I've seen plenty of ducks flying around this part of the world."

He even ordered stuffed cabbage. The duck was worse than the Christmas turkey, the cabbage was even worse than that, and he was in a bad mood again.

He walked his mood off. We went along the waterfront past fine old homes. "Probably 60 families in there now," he muttered. But he enjoyed watching a division of soldiers marching and singing.

I suggested we go to the opera that evening. I felt sad that Sonya would not be with us, not only because her charge could no longer bear the sight of her but also because she was packing to leave.

The Grand Opera House impressed Dreiser as one of the most beautiful he had seen anywhere in America or on the

Continent. The splendid structure stood in a park setting. Rimsky-Korsakov's *Sadko* was being performed. The first act was so badly done that TD wanted to leave. Since he had never seen *Sadko*, I urged him to stay for the second act in order to hear "The Song of India." He was glad he had stayed. The scene in the marketplace at the wharf, where a crowd had gathered to see Sadko off, was colorful. When the envoy from India, clad in brilliant raiment, stood with folded arms and sang the "Song of India," TD shared my rapture. But he still insisted upon leaving at the end of the second act.

"I want to remember that song. The next act might spoil it."

All things come to him who waits — "if he yells loud enough," TD added. On the following day he was granted permission to take out his papers without customs inspection, and his money, too. But he was unrelenting in his unreasonable hostility to Davidovskaya and in his resolve never to see "that little nincompoop" again.

Back in the hotel, I took a copy of the *Odessa Izvestia* containing the interview and the author's photo to Dreiser's room to translate. It was a nice article, considering the material the reporter had to work on. But TD made little response when I read it to him. He was feeling ill and the room was cold. So he lay down in his fur coat, fur gloves, fur hat and even overshoes. He looked so comical lying there in his winter wraps on the sagging bed, a sullen expression on his face, that I could hardly refrain from bursting into hysterical laughter. But I knew that this time he would not respond as he had done at the station when we were leaving Moscow and on our last night on the steamer. He would not in this final stage of his long journey, when all he wanted to do was escape, give up his mood of disgust and disillusionment.

It was at this inauspicious moment that he decided he wanted to dictate a farewell letter to the Russians. In dismay, I suggested that he should rest, he was in no mood for it. This brought an indignant denial.

"Look here," he protested, "I love these Russians. I don't intend to soft-soap them, but I admire the tremendous fight they're making for a better life and I'll tell them so."

Somewhat skeptical, I brought my Corona. With the little portable on my knees, I perched at the foot of his bed. "I am an individualist and shall die one!" he proclaimed. The tone was fatherly and affectionate, but he gave plenty of blunt advice to his hosts on their shortcomings, especially plumbing.

"The Russian house, the Russian yard, the Russian street, the Russian toilet, the Russian hotel, the individual Russian's attitude toward his own personal appearance. . . cannot possibly be excused on the grounds of poverty. There are as many poor people in Holland, Germany, France and England, but you would never find them tolerating the conditions which in Russia seem to be accepted as matter of course. . . "

"But TD," I protested, "they haven't developed the means and equipment of those Western European countries yet."

"It will not do, as some insist," he went on firmly, "to say that this is a matter of prosperity and equipment. It is not, I insist it is not. . . "

Then, with special emphasis: "Your hotels, trains, railway stations and restaurants are too dirty and poorly equipped. You do not let in enough air. . . . You live too many in one room and are even lunatic enough to identify it with a communistic spirit. . . "

I stopped typing. "Klimokon, head of the cooperatives, told you poor people don't live that way from choice. 'Now we are poor,' he said. 'We are supplying only 75 per cent of the people's needs. . . "

"I rise to complain," he continued in a louder voice, sitting up in bed. "And I suggest in this connection that more individualism and less communism would be to the great advantage of this mighty country. . . . "

I typed without further protest, and the five legalsize pages were finished, in three carbon copies. He signed and dated the letter: January 13, 1928. (Full text in Appendix.) He instructed me to deliver one copy to VOKS, another to Junius Wood, Chicago *Daily News* correspondent in Moscow.

"I like Wood," he said. "I want him to have the scoop." He added, "Thank Reswick of AP, too, for all his kindness. And tell Dinamov I'll keep in touch with him."

After this ordeal, another awaited me. I had to say goodbye to Sonya. She was packing when I entered our room and greeted me coldly. I told her I was very sorry that her relations with Mr. Dreiser had been so difficult.

"He is a terrible man!" she burst out. "All the time it's swine this and lice that, and yet you lick his boots!"

"Can't you see that my first duty is to my employer, Sonya — as yours is to VOKS? We both only tried to do our duty. I tried to help him see everything, favorable and unfavorable because an honest writer like Dreiser will tell the truth as he sees it. I'm sure he will be a friend of the Soviet Union, and isn't this terribly important if we are to have peace in the world?"

Her face was set in hard lines, for she had suffered much. I went on to remind her that he was a sick man, yet he was determined to finish this tour he had taken at the urging of American friends of Soviet Russia. "Don't you think we should be more understanding of his irritable moods?"

Her face softened. She agreed to report nothing derogatory about me, and I promised to speak no ill of her. I really felt that she had done a wonderful job under most difficult circumstances.

After that was over, I returned to the business of getting my charge across the border. There were still delays, frustrations. Derutra reported that the Polish visa had not come. TD still had not located his niece, and had anxiously sent a telegram to Constantinople to trace her.

He was feeling thwarted when we went to breakfast in the Hotel Bristol. We sat in a deserted corner by an aquarium of goldfish. No sooner had we finished our pancakes and fried eggs than he opened the old debate on socialism vs. individualism. I had the feeling always that he was arguing with himself, not me. He reiterated his theory that "the strong must rule the weak; the big brain, the little one," a phrase which he had used in *Hoosier Holiday* (for which I was writing the preface to the Russian edition).

"Eliminating sharp contrasts will take the color and variety out of life," he repeated.

Knowing that he expected me to disagree with him, I obligingly declared that the leveling process was wholesome; it was necessary to lower the living standards of the few at the top in order to eliminate the poverty of the many down below.

My statement provoked an eloquent response.

"This system will mean the death of creative art, the crushing of the individual, the triumph of mediocrity, of dubs like Davi over me. . . "

"See," I interrupted rudely, quite fed up with his contemptuous attitude toward poor Sonya even after she was gone. I pointed to the goldfish which kept coming to the surface and opening their mouths, "They're saying blah, blah, blah."

Dreiser stood up. He was angry at me for the second time since we met.

"Very well, you can have your communism. We'll part good friends and go our separate ways."

I sprang up, too, fighting back the tears. Was our close companionship of the past 11 weeks, when I had tried to be a good secretary and an impartial guide, to end in a parting of the minds? A sob escaped me.

He turned around and his face softened. "Look here, Ruthie, if you're going to cry let's get out of this depressing place." He took my arm. "Maybe a trip somewhere would cheer us up."

We rather aimlessly took a streetcar to a summer resort called Fontan Village. It was dreary weather to match our dejected mood. A thick fog hung over the city so that only objects in the foreground could be seen from the car window. But what a view it was! Mile after mile of ruined buildings, and fragments of stone walls standing on the wasteland.

"My God, it's as if a marching army had battered down everything in its path!" TD exclaimed.

I started to remind him that the Allied armies of intervention during the Civil War had done just that. Foreign troops supported by the Anglo-French entente had ravaged this region in 1918-1920.

But I remained silent. There must be no more arguments. All he thought of now was escaping to the fleshpots.

Fontan, on the seashore, was no doubt a pleasant spot in summer, but now it looked forlorn in the chill fog. There were small cottages of white plaster and ruins of handsome homes on the slopes. Boys were coasting down to the beach, where there were large fishing boats and nets drying.

We walked into a gully, past a white clay cottage with a brush fence. A little old woman sitting on the porch called to us. She wore a rusty black skirt and a man's vest over a worn sweater. She had a sweet face, and I sensed that here was material to feed the insatiable curiosity of the famous chronicler of little people. I told her my companion was an American delegate to the tenth anniversary celebration. Not visibly impressed but hospitable, she invited us into the three-room cottage. The living room had the usual wall stove, religious pictures on the whitewashed walls and an altar. In the second room was a wooden bed covered with sheepskins. It was cold in the third room, where they kept the cans of milk which they sold to the townspeople.

When we sat down in the living room, I asked her to heat milk for us, which she was glad to do, after adding peat to the fire. Her husband came in, a pathetic little man. He said he had been a gardener before the revolution for the rich who lived up the slope. There was no work for him now. His house was exempt from taxes, and he could get a government pension but it was too small to bother applying for. His wife cut slices of white bread for us and the cat, while we drank the hot milk. They had income from the milk and in summer they moved out into the yard and rented their house for the season. They had lived in this gully unmolested all through the Great War, the Civil War and famine. Even their cat survived the famine. "Yes, of course, people ate cats," the wife said.

"What about the ruined buildings we saw?" TD asked.

They said many of them had been destroyed in the fighting against the White Russian forces and the Allies. But some of the residents tore down the deserted homes of the rich and traded the materials in Odessa for food.

How did the people in America live? the old couple asked us. Did they have the Soviet system there?

For once, the loyal American was restrained in his description of the wonders of his native land. In his compassion for the dreary lot of the old couple, perhaps he did not wish to paint in glittering contrast a land they could never hope to see. He did tell them that America might one day try the Soviet system.

When we had finished the hot milk, which TD said was very good (it was his favorite beverage next to vodka), he paid her with one of his remaining dollar bills. A gold piece could not have delighted her more.

We looked back at the little cottage when we were out on the road. I said it reminded me of the old couple's fairy tale hut in "The Three Wishes." But I hoped the dollar bill wouldn't bring them such bad luck.

TD liked the analogy and he pursued it further while we waited for the streetcar. After a meditative silence, he said: "I like to take a more pleasant tale for comparison than the cruel, moral lesson of 'The Three Wishes' while we're standing here in the cold waiting for that blasted streetcar. How about that Greek legend, 'The Miraculous Pitcher,' retold in the school readers?"

I agreed it was much pleasanter, and we certainly needed cheering up. When we arrived at the hotel, TD's room was cold; he was chilled and feeling ill again. I found the maid and asked her to prepare a hot bath for him. I was determined to get him across the border in an ambulatory condition—and washed. This would cost extra, for it meant bringing wood and building a fire in the metal stove in the big bathroom down the hall. I waited until the tank felt hot, ran the steaming water into the big bathtub and tapped on his door to tell him his bath was ready. I knew the maid would not give him this service.

By morning of the next day, everything was ready for our departure. The Polish visa had come; our tickets were in order for the 5:40 train. Although the day was foggy and cold, Dreiser was in a relaxed mood. He wanted to walk up and down the famous stairway again. Not far from there, by way of the 200 steps, was the State Historical Museum. It contained a large collection of remains from the Greek occupation of the Black Sea coast several centuries before Christ. Anything about the culture of ancient Greece fascinated TD.

An artist named Chernyavski showed us a collection of his pottery and paintings, chiefly of Bessarabia. He looked like a wandering priest. His black robe was tattered; his scraggly hair, framing a sallow face, fell from under a fur hat. The times were hard for him, he said — not even enough money to buy paints. "We are not needed anymore. . . "

Dreiser asked me to tell him that his paintings of local scenes were charming, especially an old fortress near Odessa. "I like his sense of color and his skies."

The artist was moved by the American's words of praise. "No one here is interested in the old art forms. We simply exist."

Returning to the hotel in the chill fog, we longed for hot tea, but the maid announced stiffly that there would be no *kipyatok* until after six. She was unresponsive to my announcement that our train would leave at 5:40. We finished packing.

I was to accompany my employer to a station near the Polish border where the train would divide and my International coach go on to Moscow. Derutra had arranged for their agent to meet him at Shepatkova on the border, and also at Warsaw. He remarked that we seemed to have found some efficiency, now that the trip was ending. "Of course, they charged me enough for the services."

He added, "Well, at last I'm going to leave, yes, literally crawl across the border. Why, I'd rather die in the United States than live here!"

This Dreiserian outburst at the end of a hard journey reminded me of a similar outcry from Charles Dickens at the end of his American tour in 1842. There are other similarities in the lives of the two giants of English and American literature. Dreiser was born the year following the sudden death of Dickens. Both grew up in impoverished and insecure homes, due to the misfortunes as well as the weaknesses of their middle-class fathers. The two men were alike in their irrepressible spirit of protest. They were men of compassion, deeply moved by social injustice, and were hated by the Establishment.

In "The Life of Charles Dickens" (*Charles Dickens*, Vol.XX, Books Inc., 1936, p. 32), Everett H. Rupert writes of the Dickens tour:

"... At this period the country west of the Alleghenies was still a howling wilderness. ... The inhabitants were illiterate, crude in their manners, lawless, and, in the eyes of Dickens, a thoroughly bad lot. Methods of travel by horseback, coach and canal boat were slow and uncertain, utterly lacking in convenience or comfort. ... Charles was fighting a heavy cold. But he had come to see America, and. . . was determined to see it through. . .

"The last letter he wrote before his departure was the yearning cry of a lost spirit whose prayer was:

"'Oh, God, take me home — home — HOME!' "

He was playing solitaire while we waited for train time. For the first time on the tour, he won.

"Your luck is changing," I said, happy for him. "Perhaps you'll leave with kinder thoughts about us."

"About you, yes — always. If it hadn't been for you, I'd never escape alive."

At 5 o'clock a Derutra man came to take us to the station, and the manager was there to see us off. But for all their belated solicitude, the accommodations for the *Amerikanski delegat* were far from comfortable. Half the coach had soft compartments, the other half hard — he was assigned to a hard one. It was lighted by a candle in a glass case over the door.

The stupid little *provodneek* had been led to conclude by the presence of the Derutra officials that he was carrying an important American, "personally conducted." He hung around, watching us expectantly. Was there something we wanted? he kept asking.

"I know what *he* wants," muttered TD, "he thinks we are made of money."

After the train had started, he brought us *kipyatok* in a white enamel pot, tea leaves and glasses. I said when the tea had brewed that a Russian would pronounce this excellent *kipyatok.* I laid out our stock of food on the folding table under the window — bread sticks, cheese, cake and a lemon for our tea, and we had a delightful lunch. TD was cheered, even though this last time I had put lemon juice, not vodka, in his tea.

By now it was quite dark and the flickering candle filled the coupé with soft shadows. Every few minutes the car porter shuffled in to ask if we wanted something. Was the *barin* ready to have his bed made up? He was afraid the *barin* would find the bedding uncouth. TD had me tell him half a dozen times that he did not want his bed made up until we had reached the junction. Just ahead was my International car bound for Moscow and TD had asked me to sit with him until the coaches were divided. After this had been explained to him, the pest kept asking if the *barishna* was ready to go into the International car now?

We talked quietly between the solicitous visits of the *provodneek.* TD grew pensive as he gazed out at the snowy plains and frosty woods in the moonlight. That museum of Greek remains we visited yesterday, he said, had impressed him with the enduring perfection of Greek civilization, which, in his opinion, had never been surpassed.

"And those Greek traders brought it to the Black Sea coast for me to see! Maybe I was destined to come and find them. Who knows? I wonder. . . "

For all his realism, there was a mystic streak in Theodore Dreiser.

Our tipsy *provodneek* appeared. Did the young lady wish to go into her car now? I asked how long it would be until we reached the junction. An hour and a half. "Then I'll wait here."

TD talked of his youth. He had always wanted to be close to nature, to all animal life, but he hadn't much chance as a boy to get out into the country. Some time, when he was back home and had all those writing commitments out of the way, he wanted to do a book on Thoreau. I said he should do that. I was born on a farm; I, too, loved life in the country.

The *provodneek* was back again. I decided to transfer to my train. There would be no rest for TD until I did. He went with me, not trusting the drunken porter. We crossed over a precarious connection between our cars. The International was clean, bright and warm. Why couldn't he have had this bit of traveling comfort on his last night in Russia? We bade a faltering farewell.

I had just settled down in the comparatively luxurious compartment when the little porter appeared again. He said he had borrowed the tea service from this car and had forgotten to remove it from the gentleman's compartment — but he couldn't make him understand. I returned with him and tapped on the closed door.

A voice roared inside: "You fool, what do you want now?"

"It's *me*!" I shouted above the roar of the train. Almost unbelievingly, he opened the door.

"Oh, it's you," he exclaimed softly, and somehow the tone took me back to that evening eleven weeks ago when I had tapped on his door in the Grand Hotel.

I explained that the porter had to return the tea things to the International coach.

"Tell him to take it and get out. I probably would have killed him if you hadn't come back. Why don't you stay with me until we reach the junction?"

We sat in silence, quite content to be together for this short while longer. All too soon the little man was back again. We were nearing the junction. Again, farewell.

The author in Red Square, Moscow, at the time of Dreiser's visit. The Church of St. Basil is in background.

PART TWO

Long-range Influence of the Tour

January 1928-December 1945

GRAND
HÔTEL TERMINUS
RUE St LAZARE
PARIS (VIIIᵉ Arᵗ)

Société Anonyme de l'Hôtel Terminus
Capital 7.000.000 de Francs

R C SEINE 217.603

TÉLÉPHONE
LOUVRE 59-70 - 59-71
59-72 - 59-73

PROVINCE 430 Inter

ADR. TÉLÉGR. TERMINUS-PARIS

Paris, le Jan 17 1928

Just to make good
for once.

Dear Ruth:

I got through safely. At that
station - after you left - tho car
stood still for 3 hours. Then it

~~~~~~~~~~~~~~~~

All very nicest thought.

But Russia -

heaven in any world

St Theodore, the Indian.

And not a smell anywhere, since Paris

Part of Dreiser's letter from Paris on his way home from the Soviet
Union

First Reactions to the 77 Days

1. Correspondence and Newspaper Comment, 1928-1929

In Moscow, I picked up my work where I had left off so abruptly 11 weeks before. I was eager to complete my commitments and join my family, who were snugly settled in a seaside cottage on the coast of Kent. The name of the cottage, The Nest, appealed to me. My husband's account of the English fireplace, tea on the hob, Jimmie's little private school on a quiet street of Dymchurch, behind the ancient Roman seawall, made me long for the change after five and a half years in Russia.

At the same time, I was uneasy about the permanent reactions Dreiser might have to his tour. His first letter, written in Paris, added to my uneasiness:

Paris, le Jan. 17 1928
Just to make good
for once.

Dear Ruth:

I got through safely. At that station—after you left—the car stood still for 3 hours. Then it was hooked to something and walked until 3 p.m. when it landed 30 miles from the border. There I waited until 6:30 for a car that was to do the remaining 30 miles. We did that in 2 hours. Then the Poles—thank God—and another wait of 2 hours before their train started. But a nice clean International with a French porter and clean sheets 8 feet long. And they ran to Warsaw by 8 a.m. The change in atmosphere revived me beyond measure. And Warsaw—after Russia—you should try it. I had to wait there from 8 a.m. to 8 p.m. but enjoyed every hour. And now Paris—warm and bright.

Come out into the sunlight. Only Russians can solve that mess
if they ever do.

All my nicest thought.

But Russia —

Never in any world

St Theodore, the Nubian

And not a smell anywhere, since leaving.

The tone of the letter depressed but did not surprise me. Illness and discomforts had brought out the sensual side of his
complex nature. It was probably only a temporary reaction
which had made him gloat over "a French porter and clean
sheets eight feet long" and had made him exclaim exultantly:
"And now Paris — warm and bright."

However, his individualistic social theories went much
deeper than physical discomforts. At the time his Paris letter
came, I was working on the preface to the unabridged Russian
edition of *Color of a Great City*. In these sketches of New York,
I had again noted that the author drew literary inspiration out
of the great city's social contrasts. In his opinion, they lent
color to life.

He had missed these color contrasts on the tour, save in the
exterior grandeur of old mansions and palaces converted not
only into art museums but also into living quarters for the
masses, or into clubs, schools and sanitariums for the workers.
The aesthetic side of his nature revolted at the sight of the
uniform drabness, ugliness and meanness of "all this leveling
down under the new regime."

It was unlikely that 77 days in the USSR under difficult
conditions had given him a sympathetic understanding of New
Russia's social system, its problems and dreams.

A month after his departure a letter arrived in Moscow
from Dreiser. He enclosed a sheaf of press clippings.

New York, Feb. 24, 1928

Dear Ruth: It was fine to hear from you here today. I didn't expect
so interesting a letter so soon. Yes, I'm back — and in the ring, as
these clippings show. There were a lot of others in the afternoon
papers. Being back among, to me, more agreeable conditions even
in Europe, led me to much quiet thought. I felt that I should not

confuse my personal discomforts and temperamental reactions to a changed world with the actual Russian approach. Most of all I decided that, however little I might, I should not seriously try to injure an idealistic effort. Besides, learning that there were bread lines here — the first since 1910 — I became furious because there is too much wealth wasted here to endure it. Hence, while I am going to stick to what I saw favorable and unfavorable I am going to contrast it with the waste and extravagance and social indifference here. I may find myself in another storm. If so, well and good. . . .

He went on to write about more personal things:

I'm glad your working for Wood. I like him. He's a fine fellow. And so is Reswick. Tell them both that they are bright spots in my Russian days. . . .

And as for data over there — send me rough mental sketches of these things — from your own point of view: 1. The New Bolshevik Art. 2. Theatrical conditions — old and new. 3. The Woman question (that is, morals, marriage, divorce). 4. The condition of the Peasant as you see him — and lastly that contrast you suggestested between Siberian and Russian peasant. Think these things out in extended letter form. . . .

You know I always think the very finest things of you. In fact, if it hadn't been for you where would I have been. . .

The clippings enclosed in Dreiser's letter told of his arrival in New York on the Hamburg-American line January 22. "On the same steamer was the Soviet shipment of ten million gold roubles consigned to Chase-National. However, the American novelist was of more interest to the waiting line of newspaper reporters than the twenty crimson Soviet-sealed caskets of gold. . . . Dreiser talked at length about his impressions of Soviet Russia."

The New York Times quoted him as saying: "I cannot understand why there should be bread lines in a nation as rich as America. . . . Nowhere in Russia will you find men without overcoats standing in breadlines waiting for a handout."

The Chicago Daily News: "Contrasting the free and uncontrolled grafting we face here with the regulated accumulation centered in the Soviet government, I much prefer the Russian system."

Other papers quoted Dreiser as saying that the so-called capitalist countries would have to meet the Russian plan halfway in order to avoid a cataclysm such as upset the old Russian regime. In a conversation, Winston Churchill had agreed with him about the influence of the Soviet Union on other nations and, according to Dreiser, favored spending half the British treasury on humanitarian projects such as those initiated by the Russians — in order to prevent the overthrow of the British Government.

"About art and literature, the novelist said there is 'no sincere cultivation of the arts in Russia. Unless artists turn their talents to propaganda for communism there is little hope of recognition. The authorities there want cheerful things — a reaction to Russian literature of the last century. They are writing as a result of what they have been through. . . . ' "

All the newspapers printed his comments on art collectors in Russia: "There are none, nor should there be. . . . Art and books belong where everyone can have them, and that is what has happened in Russia with all private collections of art and libraries."

On the following day, *The New York Times* (January 24, 1928) quoted an American Legion orator as saying, in an address on "The Ideals of Washington as Opposed to the Ideals of Karl Marx," — the first of a series in answer to Theodore Dreiser — that Dreiser's visit to Russia was "one of those personally conducted investigations we all know about."

Here, then, so boldly castigating his own country and praising a new form of government which was ostracized by patriotic Americans, was Theodore Dreiser — the same incorrigible individualist who had loyally defended the American way of life to Soviet officials.

Evidently, he had displayed the same loyalty to his native land when he stopped in England on his way home from the Soviet Union. In *T. P.'s Weekly* (June 9, 1928), Thomas Burke in an article, "Talks with Theodore Dreiser," praised this loyalty in him:

"Dreiser is a complete American. Unlike the shallow intellectuals of his country, he does not sneer at America or turn his back on it and seek sham culture in the cafés of Paris. He is proud of being an American, and he is as American as Mark Twain."

The English essayist's impressions of Dreiser when he interviewed him after his Russian tour are worth quoting further at this point:

"Theodore Dreiser, whose powerful work, *The Genius*, will next be added to Constable's collected edition of his novels... is an author whose appearance matches his work. Indeed, his figure is one of his books given human shape—large, deliberate, and loose, without fire and without fatigue. He walks with the ponderous pace of the books, and his slouch is expressive of his own prose.... On his third visit he is only now beginning to 'feel' London.... This time its unobtrusive majesty has captured him. The South of England, too. 'I know now... those Southern landscapes are the very soul of English poetry.' But our slums appalled him, and he could not understand how so wealthy a country could tolerate them. In America, he said, the rich men would be called upon, for the honour of their city, to come forward with the money necessary to clean them up....' There is nothing here of querulousness or self-concern. He is a looker-on at the human comedy, interested in everything and caring for nothing."

This brilliant portrait of Dreiser on his way home from a tour of the Soviet Union depicted essentially the same Dreiser who had accepted the invitation to visit new Russia, on his own terms. The acceptance was a symptom of an awakening concern about social conditions, which grew stronger in him during the tour. But the struggle between the idealistic side of his nature and his materialistic realism—as well as his loyalty to the American system—began to show itself at every challenge to his preconceived convictions. When he argued with Bukharin or Zhanen, he was defending those convictions. When he argued with me, he was really arguing with himself.

His NANA (North American Newspaper Association) articles, which began to appear in March in leading American and European newspapers, showed his awakening social concern, although his ideas were still confused and contradictory.

I first came across these articles after I left Moscow on my way to England, in April. After I arrived in Dymchurch, I wrote TD:

"I am most awfully proud of your NANA articles, which I ran into along the way. In Amersfoort, Holland, where I stopped overnight with neighbors of S. J. Rutgers, friends showed me the Amsterdam papers with your articles. In London (visiting O'C), I received the first five articles clipped from the *Buffalo News* and forwarded to me by Junius Wood. And down here at 'The Nest,' my family had received the whole series of 11 articles clipped from the *Morning Oregonian* and sent by my husband's aunt. We read them aloud, sitting around the grate fire. Of course, there are some errors, misstatements, omissions, etc., but I think you got in an enormous amount of information and drew a good bird's-eye picture."

In the first of the series, Dreiser wrote: "I feel the Soviet form of government is likely to endure in Russia, perhaps with modifications, and... spread to or markedly affect politically all other nations. ... I think our own country will eventually be sovietized. It is not a very great step from a nation of chain stores, railways, hotels, newspapers, and chain industrial establishments... to a chain Soviet system."

This reckless prophecy, which he had made also to Zhanen in Leningrad, indicated that the novelist had a long way to go to understand the economic base of the Soviet system, i.e., public ownership of the means of production and distribution, with private profits eliminated.

His confusion at this stage was understandable. He had a vast amount of firsthand experiences and notes to sift and digest, and a deadline to meet on the syndicated articles. This confusion resulted in views expressed in one article that contradicted those in another.

For example, in the first article he extolled the system in which the "superstate controls everything" and "does not permit any individual accumulation of wealth, as individual wealth on the one hand can only spell individual poverty and want on the other."

Yet, in the third article he reverts to his original defense of the capitalist system: "I was inclined to decide that a little too much is being done for labor, too little for the brains necessary to direct it... that the elimination of the old-time creative businessman... was likely to result in slowness or seeming indifference in a society from which the urge and tang of competition has been removed... 'From each according to his ability, to each according to his need'. But that is madness," Dreiser adds. "Is Edison to receive the same as a swineherd? Rockefeller no more than a steel-puddler?"

"They insist," he continued in the same vein in article No. 9, "now it is the workers who rule them (the Party), but that is a pleasant theory only. The government directed by this Communist Party employs labor just as might a capitalist trust.

"Man there in Russia is taught that... he must not flaunt his strength or victories or use them to oppress others. He may use them for the general good or not at all. And in the closing paragraph: "There is no sly or grafting adulteration of anything you buy, because there is no commercial or predatory reason therefor."

I chanced upon the NANA series again in the *Daily Oklahoman* when I visited my mother on my stepfather's farm in May 1928. There had been a brief meeting with Dreiser in New York. He came to my hotel and took my little son and me to lunch in a smart restaurant. In this elegant setting, with fashionably dressed diners staring curiously at our table, I felt self-conscious and ill at ease in the company of the man with whom I had been perfectly at home for 11 weeks. Although we corresponded regularly for the remaining 17 years of his life, I saw TD not more than half a dozen times after that, and never in his social circles.

We, Jimmie and I, traveled by "slow train" to the land of my birth. I wrote (with malice aforethought) a detailed description of that journey to Dreiser, dated June 1, 1928:

"It is all very well for you writers in New York to tell about the hardships of travel in Russia, but just try going by train southwest of Kansas City. I never in all my Russian experiences went through such an ordeal... sitting long hours on sooty plush seats and in prairie dust in terrible heat... long, senseless stops at little stations, throat sore, head aching.... I infinitely prefer the Russian third-class sections of wooden seats on which you can lie down to an American day coach....

An hour and a half to cover the last 20 miles. Before we reached our destination, the little town of Hobart had grown to be
life's goal. Oh, to see Hobart and die! Half-dead, I dropped
off the steps into my mother's arms. . . . "

TD's unaccustomed delay in replying (June 20) showed
some irritation at my derogatory comparisons of American
and Russian travel.

"Dear Ruth, Both letters are full of just the sort of details I
like to read—the hard colors of my native land. I notice for all
your knocking you indicate prosperity en route. All the females
are well dressed. After Stalino and vicinity you should not
complain too loudly, Besides, you chose a most indirect
route." (Exactly as he had insisted upon doing on the tour.)

My stepfather, an old cotton farmer, (who was interested in
politics and had run for Congress), liked Dreiser's NANA
articles in the *Daily Oklahoman*. He showed me the March
21st issue, with a front-page headline:

"TRODDEN MASS STIRS TO CALL OF NEW IDEAL AU-
THOR SEES GROWING CONCERN ATTEMPTING TO
PROMOTE WELFARE FOR ALL) . . . It may be down at the
heel and out at the elbows in spots, but it is active and determined. . . . On the other hand, consider the condition of these
people in the days of the czars and, worse yet, since the close of
World War I and revolution. Hunger, death for millions by
starvation, no housing or lighting system worthy of the name,
no roads, telephone or telegraph communication beyond those
fixed by czarist military and commercial regime, no educational and social program worthy of the name. Oppression,
high taxes, lords and slaves. . . . Already very much has been
accomplished."

Then followed a paragraph which showed his efforts to be
an honest reporter:

"And yet by turns, and according to what one is looking at
or thinking about at the time, one can become either abnor-
mally optimistic or deeply depressed. . . . But don't forget that
only a mile from here is a government agricultural station
with a tractor and electric engine and cream separator, com-
bination reaper and thresher. . . and the latest theories and

ideas on farming—intensive large-scale farming—directed by earnest young communists trained in the dreams and theories of Party leaders in Moscow."

Then came a piece of almost poetic prose:

"And that here in this down-and-out village of huts in the midst of a vast field of snow were classes for political and economic education, agricultural, industrial, idealogical. And that here was stirring a movement intended to teach these people to lift up their heads, not to be afraid, not to submit to wrongs but to fight, to demand and achieve a fair reward for their efforts. . . . As you looked at the little huts in the snow, and the vast and virtually uncultivated fields and forests, and the thousands of gilded churches with their ikons and gold, and thought of the comfortable mentors of an earlier day teaching these people tame and unthinking submission to an indifferent, parasitic aristocracy, you said, 'All hail to the communistic dreams of a better day!'"

However, this emotional outburst did not end the article in the *Daily Oklahoman*. For several hundred more words (at a dollar a word) Dreiser lapsed into contradictory statements. He attributed the contrasts and contradictions which confused him to the "semi-Asiatic temperament so different from the European and American." As an example, he cited the big apartment house for workers we visited in Leningrad where he found people "living half-a-dozen to ten in a single room, a single toilet and bathtub on each floor, communal kitchens for several apartments."

His conclusion was that they liked living together, they liked cooking together, and "who wants a bath in Russia more than once a week anyhow?"

But Dreiser repented of his peevish, unreasonable carping in the very next paragraph of his NANA article and earnestly demanded of his readers: "But do you think I am quarreling with them? I was never further from quarreling with any people in the world. I like them."

Nevertheless, he went on in this article to analyze these Russians, whom he found so congenial, as having temperaments different from our own. After this labored effort, he concluded,

"But as I say... I could keep on and offer a thousand contrasts and yet, not a city or village in Russia today is not feeling the thrill of the new intellectual and social life emanating from the leaders in Moscow."

I arrived with my mother and little Jimmie at her Palo Alto home just in time to receive the proofs of *Dreiser Looks at Russia* to correct and revise. TD's telegram (August 14, 1928) indicated that it must be a rush job. His letter of August 18 explained the delay in asking for my help:

"What threw me off in connection with the Russian book was your saying that Wood wanted you to do one with him. At the time, because of a request from Boni & Liveright, as well as Covici-Friede, I was busy laying out various chapters and collecting material from my book of notes. But I thought if you and Wood were planning a book you should be allowed to go ahead.... I would have been delighted to have your aid— but you weren't here." He then informed me that he was mailing the complete set of proofs for me to go over.

I could see at a glance that it would be a difficult task. It seemed a hodgepodge, a carelessly thrown together conglomeration of impressions, facts and evaluations. Much of the text of his NANA articles was used here, with some alterations. Apparently, he had not followed the diary nor used its chronological form. Instead, he had arranged his material by subject in chapters.

For example, having restricted himself to a serious consideration of the subject of Chapter III: "Russia's Post-Revolutionary Political and General Achievements," he had to philosophize and speculate, since his impressions and recollections alone could not furnish him the necessary facts and figures. Much of importance in his own observations, which I had recorded, had been omitted, and his many fine, prophetic comments were sunk in a quagmire of contradictions and confused thinking.

He was unable to cope with such subjects as "Communism— Theory and Practice," the title of Chapter VI, and "The Present-Day Russian Peasant Problem," Chapter X. On the other hand, in "Random Reflections on Russia" he could ramble on, drawing on his own personal observations and just being himself. This was the form and style which had made *Hoosier Holiday* and *Color of a Great City* good reading. Fortunately, he followed the advice I gave in the corrected proofs and put this chapter last. He wrote in the published text of *Dreiser Looks at Russia:*

"Now that I am closing this book, do permit me to ramble a little. I saw so much. I have really suggested so little of a very, very great thing that is happening in the world. One thing I learned there in Russia, that I [never] so much as questioned in America, was that it is a mistake to imagine that any true distinction for man is to be derived from material possessions. There is really nothing to that. Man's true distinction is mental."

I mailed the galley sheets, lavishly embellished with marginal notes, along with a letter dated August 25:

"I am returning the book proofs, corrected, criticized and amplified, all in the margins." I took a deep breath and went on: "I suppose in a way the book is a bit of realism, for its contradictions and various moods are just what any thoughtful person goes through when he looks at Russia. My main worry is: Will it be read?—some of your chapters are pretty heavy.

"Below, as a supplement to my notes on the proofs," I concluded, "I am setting down some general ideas, suggestions, and criticisms."

Dreiser's reply upon receipt of the corrected proofs confirmed my suspicion that he had put the book together hastily to meet his publisher's dateline.

"Thanks for that very severe Dutch-Unklish letter," he wrote (September 5, 1928). "I went through it with the greatest care and reverence and made almost all of the changes you suggested. For instance, I reversed chapters 17 and 18. Then I took Captain Lenin out and put him last. I meditated on all your side corrections and where these were sound (nearly all were) I incorporated them. In one or two places you failed to get my meaning. For instance, philosophically and practically there is a vast difference between *religion* and *dogmatic religion.*" He went on to explain this at some length.

"There is, for instance, the religion which is a response to as well as an awe or reverence before the beauty and wisdom of creative energy. Many people — free of dogma — enjoy it. Then there are the dogmatized religions of the world. I think many people are likely to approve of the differentiation. . . .

"As for the 'bad construction of sentences' etc., " TD continued with characteristic good-humored humility, "guilty. I have been so offending all my life. All my books are full of them. You should have started with *Sister Carrie*. But there is one chapter that is satisfactorily done, I am sure," he added waggishly, "the state of the ladies in Russia. I am supposed to be at my best in this field, am I not?". . .

"What I really fear, though," he added seriously, "is that my writing the book has crossed you in some way. If so, I'm sorry. But I could scarcely escape doing it. The international newspaper syndicate that first bought the series wished to issue the newspaper stuff in paper form at a dollar. Liveright, who has a contract with me, objected and claimed the stuff as a book. Covici Friede and Simon & Schuster both urged me to print and Constable wanted it for England.

"Finally, therefore," Dreiser went on, "I took out my book of notes and went to work. The sad mess which now troubles you is the result. But I'm doing my best to improve it and regardless of these few counter squeaks I'm honestly grateful to you for pointing out the bad as well as the good. I know you wish me only good and if I can be of service to you, you have only to call on me. Appreciatively, very, T. D. "

In September of the same year (1928), when I was busy correcting the book proofs, I had received a letter from Tom Mooney in San Quentin prison. He had been trying to reach Theodore Dreiser, he wrote, in order to give him material on his case. I replied that I would come to the prison and get the material. On October 8th, I wrote TD about my visit.

The last paragraph of my letter read: "All the people working for his release — the judge in the case pleading for him, the captain of police writing that he thinks Tom innocent, one of the victims of the bombing stating that he believes Mooney is the victim of a frame-up. Mooney has the idea that you can have great influence. He and his cellmate are reading *The American Tragedy*. I said they didn't need that kind of book, but Mooney replied, 'We don't find it depressing.' They liked to read the writings of one who understands so well their sufferings. Tom read me three letters from Clarence Darrow, who is working for his release. I think a letter from you to the governor would have great weight."

Dreiser responded in a letter (October 28, 1928):

"The Mooney data interests me very much — particularly the letters of Governor Young and Paul Scharrenberg and Chester H. Rowell. In the former (Sept. 19) the Governor says, 'I have never been able to bring myself to a belief in the innocence of the accused.' Therefore, he must have in mind facts which warrant this statement. And if so, and in the face of all this contra-evidence, he should most earnestly set these forth and so rid the American mind of a sense of injustice and persecution in this case — or release Mooney. Worse, he wrote Scharrenberg he has not had time to go over all the evidence. But he should take time. The matter is too vital, yet instead of doing this he writes Mr. Rowell that he cannot grant a pardon — and this before re-examining the evidence.... I shall be writing him and Mooney...."

Earlier, I had written to Dreiser that my friend of Moscow and London, May O'Callaghan, whom he had met in Moscow, was coming to New York, hoping to get work in the editorial field. Anything he could do to help her get her bearings I would greatly appreciate. His reply (dated October 18th) came promptly:

"You may be sure that when 'O'C' — as you call her — shows up I will do what I can." He added, "The Russian book will be distributed to the dealers this coming week. I'll send you a copy." He did, and wrote across the title page: "To Ruth Kennell who was a part of this in Russia, from T. D."

2. Dorothy Thompson Sues TD for Plagiarism

Meanwhile, unexpected trouble had appeared in connection
with the publication of *Dreiser Looks at Russia* by Liveright
(November 11, 1928). The first I heard about it was in a letter
from the author (dated November 15), which began cheerfully without any warning of what was ahead:

"Here is the letter just sent to Governor Young. I have also
mailed a copy to Mooney. If I do get an answer I'll send you
a copy. If not I'll write Young something different and then
give the correspondence, unless it is favorable, to the papers.
How are you? I wonder much how you are getting along and
think of you a great deal. Unless you are really successfully
writing out there it does seem as though you would do better
here. Your friend O'C agrees with that." (So she had arrived!)

The letter continued in the same pleasant vein. "Glorious
weather here. Perfect. And I write and dream the days away.
Just now a large bunch of Russian clippings came from Sergey — all Greek to me.

"I'm in the papers for plagiarism," he suddenly announced,
"but if ever anything was the bunk this is."

I anxiously looked over the clippings he had enclosed. They
carried sensational headlines. Upon its publication *Dreiser
Looks at Russia* was met with a suit filed by Dorothy Thompson, correspondent for the New York *Evening Post,* who had
recently married Sinclair Lewis. The suit charged that "it
appropriates many and substantial portions of her material."

Naturally, the New York *Evening Post,* championing the
cause of Miss Thompson, scooped the story in its November
13th and 14th issues. The columnist, Percy Winner, proclaimed "a startling similarity in much of the material, language and selection of material." As examples he prints two
narrow columns of "deadly parallels," a few passages from
Chapter II, "The Capital of Bolshevia" descriptions of streets,
night spots, the Kremlin:

"The streets are cobblestoned," writes Dreiser, "and if the snow has melted, are muddy."

"The streets are cobble-stoned," writes Dorothy Thompson, "and if the snow has melted, swimming in mud."

There are other passages just as trivial — "women peddling everything from apples to brassieres"; "the primus, the one-burner oil stove"; "the famous Tverskaya, through which the Czar used to enter the city" from St. Petersburg. . . . Such descriptions were to be found in every guidebook used by writers as well as tourists. Dreiser's explanation (quoted in the *Post* article November 13) that both he and Miss Thompson had received the *Weekly News Bulletin* published in Moscow by VOKS sounded credible.

Having built up his case on these trivialities, Mr. Winner goes further, pointing out that this is not the first time the famous author has stolen material: "In October, 1926, a remarkable similarity in subject, language and treatment was discovered between passages in Mr. Dreiser's 'Dark Laughter' and a section from Sherwood Anderson's story, 'Tandy' in his 'Winesburg, Ohio.' " More careful attention to facts would have disclosed to Mr. Winner that *Dark Laughter* is a novel by Sherwood Anderson, not Theodore Dreiser.

I wrote to TD, expressing my indignation and sympathy. He replied at once (December 2, 1928).

"You are a sport and a darling and no mistake. The warm, determined way in which you hurry to the rescue, regardless of how much or little evidence you have. . . . But don't worry about this case. It is a petty fake strike for publicity. She took three separate pieces of stuff I gathered — the Russian Peasant Hotel, my trip in Moscow. . . and my interpretation of the intellectual base of the public schools — all of which I talked over with her and when I didn't know she was rushing off daily letters to N. Y. or contemplating a book, and then when she gets back here and sees that my book is likely to catch on, starts a publicity rush for herself (she and Lewis). If you were here I could tell you some things. But don't worry. I have good lawyers and she and Lewis will know something more about plagiarism than they do now before its all over." He concluded warmly, "I love your mind, your spirit, your downright honesty and I treasure your affection.

"Never got an answer from Young. But please tell Mooney I am organizing a committee. I propose to print this record he sent me and some additional things and send it to people who count. Maybe we can make a little uproar. I hope so. Love, T. D. If anything develops I'll send you all the data."

Later, he sent me a copy of a letter from Sergey Dinamov: "Moscow,12.12.28 — There was published here a news item about you and Dorothy Thompson. What a strange incident! She knows only the vicinities of the Grand Hotel — and you know the real Russia! Your answer to her is very good. One of my friends wrote me about it. — Yours affectionately, Sergei."

Dreiser wrote me a final word on the suit (February 11, 1929): "As you see by the legal exchange of letters, of which I enclose copies, Dorothy decided not to come into court. It took nearly one month to get a bill of particulars to which a legal replay could be made. Meantime, my attorneys, Hume and Cameron, examined Dorothy's 'The New Russia' and Anne O'Hara McCormick's 'The Hammer and the Scythe'. I have a copy of their 14 page comparison of the two books. Sometime when you are East you may see that. Both the *Times* and the *World* referred to their similarity but no word from either lady. The McCormick book was published 6 months before Dorothy's. Please send the *World* column back to me for my files. There will be no suit here or anywhere for the simple reason that the first question Mr. Hume would ask Dorothy would be: 'Is this work of yours wholly original with you?' If she said yes the McCormick book marked with hers also for comparison would be given her for explanation. Apparently, there is some other work which both read and profited by. Despite or because of all this, the Russian book (*Dreiser Looks at Russia*) is now being printed without change in England, Germany and Scandanavia. Draw your own conclusions."

Although the plagiarism suit was withdrawn, there is little doubt that its accompanying notoriety cost the Father of American Realism the Nobel Prize in 1930. Who, in the long run, was the winner? Theodore Dreiser and Sinclair Lewis were the two American candidates. The Nobel Prize for Literature went to Sinclair Lewis.

Incidentally, Gosizdat, in publishing the Soviet edition of *Dreiser Looks at Russia*, ignored the plagiarism charge.

In my preface to the Russian edition, published in Moscow in 1930, I quoted a few passages which I thought Russian readers would appreciate:

"The Communist code: If it has lessened the glitter and show, it has at any rate taken the heartache and material tragedies out of millions of lives. . . . Where are the rich? Where are the groveling, feverish poor?" (p. 253-54).

I also quoted a suggestion in the book which the United States Government would have been wise to follow at that stage of postrevolutionary construction:

"I would like to see Russia, as it is now, recognized and aided financially in order that this great impetus to something better may be strengthened. . . . Is it not common sense to aid it to do the best it can?"

From what I know of Theodore Dreiser's activities during the year 1928, they were not those of an ivory-tower literary pundit but of a man of the people who, after his return from a body and mind-shaking 66 day-tour accomplished the following tasks (and more): wrote 13 newspaper articles, several magazine features, met the deadline on a book (surviving with dignity the ordeal of a resulting plagiarism suit), took on the internationally notorious Mooney case and launched an ambitious project to bring the Russian ballet to America.

Moreover, he spent several weeks with Helen at the Marine Biological Laboratory at Woods Hole, Mass. He wrote me from there on July 27:

"H and I have been here since July 1st. I have been digging into biology and getting a strange new light on life. I know of nothing that will do so much for your mind as biology. . . the one thing that will remove all your moralistic or semidogmatic inhibitions and let you set up a decent social code for yourself. Turn to biology."

Ignoring the personal references in his glorification of science, I replied with news of Sergey Dinamov:

"Our mutual 'young, tired friend' writes me that he has attended to your 'businesses'. Among a bundle of papers he sent is the Russian edition of your *Free and Other Stories*, published by ZEF and edited by Dinamov. I noticed on the back of the paperbound book a list of your collected works, including *Chains* with preface by Ruth Kennell, and *A Gallery of Women*, preface by Ruth Kennell. The first I admit, but the second is news to me... how speedy the Russians are getting. Already listing the book before it is out."

On top of all his other work during 1928, Dreiser had written a poem! In December he sent me this prose poem, " *My City.*" I acknowledged its receipt on December 29:

"I have read it several times and each time I like the poem better. The first time... I was inclined to wish you'd stick to plain prose and a little afraid you had reached Sherwood Anderson's stage. But at the last reading I got the whole feel of it and it is beautiful and meaningful... you very much put you heart in this. New York can't mean so much to everyone, but it means a great deal to you. You've put all of that meaning into these frugal — yes, really! — words. I could read Anderson's prose poems over and get less meaning each time, for he writes for the sake of words. You are a mystic, too — a big bunch of contradictions. So this is what you were doing when you wrote me last July that you were 'writing and dreaming the days away'."

I sent the copy of Dreiser's poem on to Sergey, hoping he would try to get it published. So far as I know, it has not been published in the United States. Sergey responded (February 13, 1929):

"No, Dreiser's poem 'My City' is not interesting for the Russian reader — it is too individualistic."

Apparently the editor of the Moscow weekly *Krasnaya Nyeva* did not agree with him, for it was published in the No. 22 (May 1929) issue, alongside a panel photograph of Manhattan skyscrapers.

How skillfully the translator put the difficult English lines of the prose poem into beautiful Russian! Since I do not have a copy of the original English, I have made a labored translation from the Russian back into English, including only the first paragraph of the long first part which is straight prose:

NEW YORK

Nowhere is there anything like it. My city. Not London. Not Paris. Not Moscow. No one has ever seen a city like mine. Immeasurable. Proud.

It captivates. It makes the blood run faster in the veins. It makes one sing, hate, or faint and die. And even in defeat, in loneliness, in despair, when the limbs fail from lack of will-power-how strengthening, how good the day! How full of meaning! Days of hunger, of loneliness, of hopelessness, cannot overcome that meaning, that enchantment for me. . . .

High towers —
Clustering spires —
Carved flowers of steel and stone,
They crowd out the air,
They rise above the fogs and storms.
Steadfast —
Haughty —
Somber —
Menacing —
Shoulder to shoulder in jutting canyons:
They draw together in close rows.
Dreams —
Ambitions —
Illusions —
Moods —
The architect drew a building,
The poet — a tower.
High towers raised by ants,
Built by beetles and midges,
Clusters of spires —
You pierce the wind and the sky,
Protect the crowds of swarming ants,
Shelter the world of moles.
But at your feet flows the unforgettable river;
Around you the scornful,
The unforgettable land;

And before your power — the countless years.
High towers —
Clustering spires —
Defiant spears of steel and stone.
Yes, but inevitable winds undermine your strength!
Yes, but the inevitable days approach, lie in wait!

3. Dreiser Undertakes to Bring the Russian Ballet

Meanwhile, the novelist, poet, social and economic theorist, and devotee of the arts had been working zealously in the last-named sphere. Through Reswick of the Associated Press in Moscow, Dreiser was endeavoring to bring the Russian ballet to America.

In March 1929, he sent me copies of his file of articles, letters, cables, even a schedule for the proposed tour. I marveled at his enthusiasm, the magnitude of his undertaking and the tremendous progress he had made. I was touched by his confidence in my ability to help him in this project, but felt utterly incompetent to do more than encourage him in his praiseworthy ambition.

His letter accompanying the papers was almost jubilant in tone:

Dear Ruth: I thought you might like to see this material. The ballet is actually coming. Today, a rich woman here, Mrs. Christian Holmes, contributed $25,000. Otto Kahn gave $25,000, Condé Nast $5000, J. D. Mooney $2000, Arthur Sachs (Banker) $1000, Reeve Sibley (Banker) $1000. Ray Long, editor Cosmopolitan, $1000. A $32,000 deposit required by Russia was furnished by three bankers whose names as yet I may not use. All this is private and personal and not for publication yet. I thought you would be interested. I have been exchanging cables with Russia since last September. T. D.

Included in the copies of papers he sent me was a typed statement marked "Not for publication" and headed in his handwriting: "The All-Russian Ballet in America." The statement explains the author's reasons for entering upon this prodigious undertaking:

"On my recent visit to Russia, the keenest artistic impression that remained with me was that of the new Russian Ballet in Moscow. . . .My enthusiasm prompted me to make immediate inquiries as to the possibility of bringing this organization intact to America. . . . At first the Soviet officials were disinclined to any such proposal for fear that they would lose these artists, but after assurance that they would be returned intact, they gave me their tentative consent. For six month I have carried on a cable correspondence with the highest authorities. . . .

"My own interest is strictly an artistic one. I hold no financial interest and shall derive no profit other than that of the pleasure of introducing to America a new and triumphant form of artistic expression."

Dreiser went on to explain that in order to raise money for this undertaking, he had organized an American corporation and proposed to issue $100,000 worth of preferred stock. A small group of art patrons would underwrite a guarantee in the form of a bond in the hands of the Moscow State Theater. Mr. H. S. Kraft, an impressario of standing, had been secured as the business manager. Among the supporters not already mentioned were Frank Crowninshield; Mrs. Louise Campbell, secretary of the Art Alliance of Philadelphia; Ralph Holmes, *Detroit Times*; Fremont Older, *San Francisco Post*; George Douglas, *San Francisco Examiner*; Abraham Cahan, *Jewish Daily Forward;* Edward Ziegler of the Metropolitan Opera Company.

In one of several letters to Theodore Dreiser offering assistance, Leopold Stokowski, Director of the Philadelphia Orchestra, wrote that "artistically it will be a most important event."

Vice-President of General Motors, J. D. Mooney wrote that he was "heartily in sympathy with a thing which will, as this visit should, tend to accelerate acquaintanceship between the United States and Russia. . . . An excellent opportunity exists, in the medium of this ballet, to dramatize the beginning of an international relationship on a scale which is adequate to possess real significance."

This "magnificent enterprise," as Ray Long called it in his letter offering support, ultimately failed because of insufficient financial backing. It was nevertheless a dedicated effort on Theodore Dreiser's part to bring a rare artistic contribution from Soviet Russia to his own country. The failure of his pioneering effort must have been a great disappointment to the man who had suffered so many disappointments.

Deems Taylor had been so impressed by Dreiser's efforts on behalf of the Russian ballet that he published in the *Musical America* (February 25, 1929) a delightful interview with the author by R. H. Wollstein, "The American Tragedian Turns his Freudian Eyes on Music." I have before me the marked copy which TD sent me. I quote some of Dreiser's remarks in the closing paragraphs of the lengthy interview:

"Of the moderns I like the Russian school best. . . . There is no distinctly radical music movement. . . . The one musical form that they are working out in a new way is the ballet or pantomine. And that is gorgeous!

" 'I got the greatest kick out of that. There you have mass movement — mass color — mass spirit, and the most stirring effect of concerted and unified action. They have the National Soviet Ballet School, accommodating some fifteen hundred pupils, ranging in age from three to eighteen. They pay almost nothing for their tuition, and get the best to be had in actual instruction, as well as the richest scenic materials with which to practice their art. This new ballet form is tremendously interesting. I don't say there is any definite political connection between communism in government and mass spectacles on the stage; the two seem to have come into a tremendous being together. All the ballets produced seem in some way to glorify the people, or the spirit of humanity, rather than the kings or princelings of orthodox operatic lore.

" 'Free of all religion as they are, ' " Dreiser went on, 'these Russians put on Hugo's *Notre Dame* (*Esmeralda*) exactly as it is written. They leave out nothing as another country would have to do, because it might offend priests or zealots. They give it like *Coq d'Or* — pantomine, accompanied by voices off stage — and I tell you it was like getting to Heaven to sit there and witness that magnificent, moving mass spectacle. I forgot the cold outside — I forgot I was lonely and in a strange land.

There was nothing to do but glory in the ecstasy of it. Nowhere but in Russia could they put on such vivid mass spectacles. . . .

" 'They haven't any too much money there, but they're able to produce the finest things. It is part of the Russian make-up to venerate art. I know for a fact that men like Stalin — people who actually bear the burden of running the government (Communist Party members) — are content to work hard for as little as a hundred and twelve dollars a month. They ask no better. But a man who is recognized as an artist — as a potent factor in building up the country's artistic life, is feted the way royalty used to be, and is paid, proportionately speaking, a higher salary than he would be paid here. I wish we might learn a little of Soviet Russia's reverence for art.' "

Dreiser had marked another article in the same issue by Ivan Narodny, "The Musical Ax in Russia," which tells of the part music played in the Russian Revolution. "It was greatly inspired and sustained by music. Lenin knew the psychological value of melody and rhythm and felt the need of a new musical literature that should express the communistic spirit; yet he feared the effect proletarian control of industry might have on music."

Narodny goes on to tell about the Bolshevik Congress in Tammerfors, Finland, in December 1905, at which Lenin presided. Narodny attended as a delegate of the revolutionary Soviet of Narva, Esthonia. Rimsky-Korsakov, who was a friend of the Bolshevik party, was staying at the Hotel Bauer, where the meeting was held. He was working on his *Coq d'Or* at the time.

"Comrades," Narodny quotes Rimsky-Korsakov as saying, "you must not forget music in your conspiracy to overthrow the Czar."

Lenin is quoted as saying his only objection to operatic music is that "it has been composed with ears tuned to bourgeois pleasures. It lacks the vitalizing, heroic spark and is empty of inspiring images. It turns around the leisured life of nobles, royalty, gamblers, and so forth — a rich man's lullaby!"

Rimsky-Korsakov, according to Narodny, admitted that

this was true. "That's the reason I am seriously considering the writing of a musical play on the theme of Stenka Razin, which could be performed by amateur companies, student societies and in small-town theaters—only if the censor will not suppress it. There is no doubt that music has a great influence on the public."

Lenin is quoted as saying at this point: "Music has a peculiar psychic effect on the human mind. Bakunin called it the poor man's aural tonic. But it must have melody and rhythm, as had the old ritual chants, and not be like the modern unmelodic and unrhythmic compositions of Debussy and others."

In reading the two articles TD had sent me, I was struck by a certain similarity between the musical tastes of Lenin and Dreiser, especially regarding the limitations of the operatic form. Both stressed the ballet and other pantomine forms in mass spectacles for a socialist Russia. . . .

Here, in the realm of music and the ballet, the best side of Dreiser's complicated nature was displayed, the side which drew many intellectuals to him. But there was also the gross side of his nature which repelled them. Perhaps this was not inborn, but developed in his struggle against sordid poverty and environment. Perhaps, in order to gain recognition in his literary work, he had become ruthless and sometimes coarse in his approach.

4. American Tragedy *Banned in Boston*

Early in 1929, Dreiser was again the victim of a silly legal attack. It did not disturb or damage him as had the plagiarism suit. In fact, it was the type of publicity which some authors welcome today to promote the sale of their books. TD sent me the clippings and other data:

"*New York Times,* Apr. 18, 1929—BOSTON JURY CONVICTS NEW YORK PUBLISHER FOR SELLING DREISER'S 'AMERICAN TRAGEDY.' A Boston jury has again upheld the 'obscene book' law, under which many recent novels have been barred from this city. Donald S. Friede, a N.Y. publisher, being found guilty today of violating that statute in the sale two years ago of Theodore Dreiser's 'An American Tragedy'. The case was brought as a test. . . . Judge Hays in his charge warned the jury:

" 'The only question before you is, Are the pages read to you . . . impure, indecent, and obscene and manifestly tending toward the corruption of youth? . . . You must determine if the thoughts aroused by those words are offensive to morality and to chastity and manifestly tend to corrupt youth."

In a letter to Dreiser (April 20, 1929), Arthur Garfield Hays, defense attorney together with Clarence Darrow, wrote: "Isn't it preposterous to think of literature being passed upon by a jury composed of one automobile washer, two janitors, one hatter, one treasurer and four clerks? The chief argument of the district attorney referred to the paragraph where you said that Clyde and Roberta were so unsophisticated and inexperienced that they knew nothing of contraceptive measures. 'Good God,' he said, 'doesn't this teach immorality, that youth should interfere with the way of nature?' "

In my reply to TD (May 2), I commented on the Boston trial as being "incredible, yet in our double-faced civilization, quite possible." I went on to explain the enclosures in my letter: "I am enclosing my translation of an article in the Moscow journal *The Needleworker* (January 1, 1929), by A. Olenin. Its title, 'Dreiser, Exposer of the American Bourgeoisie' would be even more shocking to the Boston judge than your reference to contraceptives in *American Tragedy*. The social viewpoint is the same as that expressed in the review I sent you of *The Financier* — how refreshing in our sordid, hypocritical world!"

I thought the article about him in *The Needleworker,* addressed as it was to the workers of Moscow, would be quite diverting to the author of the Cowperwood novels.

Here are some extracts:

Among foreign authors, particular attention of working-class readers is attracted recently to Theodore Dreiser. He should be very interesting to the wide reading circle of needleworkers. Dreiser, in fact, deserves the close attention of the reading masses. . . . By his creative power, his deep penetration into the mighty and wonderful

machine of American capitalism . . . Dreiser stands out as an artist
of world significance. . . . His achievement is the triumph of realism,
the accurate portrayal of things as they are. . . . Certainly such an
important representative of American social-historical novelists
has for us the greatest interest.

Observing the spectacle and the complicated process of social
life in America, Dreiser records it with minute detail, with docu-
mentary accuracy, with deep scientific observation. . . . The result
is that his novels are historic documents of the whole epoch of
bourgeois America. In his novels (for which he repeatedly suffered
consequences) he comes out against many bourgeois standards,
many family morals of the American middle class, against the contradictions of that society. But he does not recognize the inevita-
bility of the one escape from these tragic situations: the social
revolution. He remains a part of the radical intelligentsia. But as
an artist he is powerful; from his pictures the reader can form his
own conclusions. . . .

Earlier in 1929, I had received clippings from TD of articles
in the *Forum* and the *New Yorker*. I wrote him that I had sent
them on to Sergey. In the *New Yorker* there was a biting satiri-
cal attack by G.K. Chesterton on Dreiser; in the *Forum* a reply
from Dreiser himself.

Among the clippings TD sent was an editorial in the *Chattanooga News* (October 30, 1929) commenting on his article in
the *Forum*:

"Theodore Dreiser presents his philosophy of life and of living. . . . He does not desire immortality, and certainly doesn't
believe in it: 'I really view myself as an atom in a greater
machine, just as is the cell in the greater body of which it
finds itself a part. But as for myself being a free and independent mechanism with a separate soul or spirit of its own? —
Nonsense! Science knows nothing of a soul or spirit. . . . When
I am dead, as I see it, I shall be dissolved into my lesser con-
stituents; I shall then be, if anything, a part of universal force,
but merged and gone forever."

The editor comments: "We could quote Bryan's confession
of faith that would answer it, but . . . Dreiser would not want to
live into eternity. . . . Here is his view of life:

"'I see life as a very grim and dangerous contest. . . . The
human mind thus far developed is at best a petty piece of

machinery. . . . What we plainly see is birth and death . . . murder, the chase, life living on life, the individual sustaining himself at the expense of every other, and wishing not to die. And then beauty, beauty, beauty . . . beauty no less in fire and flowers, in Shelley and Christ.'"

The editor concludes, "Dreiser's philosophy is that of one who has been seeking to solve problems beyond his depth. There is a remedy — Faith."

It appears evident from his *Forum* article that Dreiser's stay at the Woods Hole Marine Biological Laboratory had affected his thinking profoundly. However, it proved to be only one facet of his complicated mind. He still had the ability to see beauty in a force he termed so ruthlessly mechanistic; and not only that, still to feel that the life of another individual was worth saving, that the American principles of justice were still worth fighting for.

For example, his interest in the Mooney case did not falter. In the *American Mercury* (May 1929), I read Travers Clement's article on the Mooney case. He quoted from Dreiser's letter to Governor Young, who had declared, "While I have been dissatisfied with some aspects of the trial, I have never been able to bring myself to the belief in the innocence of the accused." Dreiser replied: "In view of the apparently conclusive character of the evidence of Mooney's innocence submitted to you, does it not seem proper for anyone to ask for a statement of what facts, known to you and not in the evidence given you, warrants such a declaration?"

The governor did not give Dreiser a direct reply. He merely sent him a copy of his letter to Judge Griffin, who had asked the same question: "This question on your part is of course a purely rhetorical one."

"And so," Travers Clement concluded in the *Mercury* article, "the case rests, with Mooney beginning his 13th year in San Quentin."

Theodore Dreiser was already being recognized as a fighter in the organized struggle for social justice.

5. A Temporary Coolness Between Ruth and TD

Unfortunately, at this time, when we should have been working closely together in the social causes we both felt were important, a coolness developed between us. I was entirely responsible for this. Upon reading the first installment of his serial novel in the slick magazine *Cosmopolitan* (January-February 1929), I waxed indignant.... Here he was retrogressing to something worse than his writings in the *Vanity Fair* years!

The serial, entitled "This Madness," was described editorially as "a series of self-admitted romances of his life in his first novel since *The American Tragedy* in 1925."

This a *novel* – after *American Tragedy*?

The editor quoted Dreiser as saying: "You people may not realize it, but in *This Madness* you are publishing the most intimate and important work so far achieved by me."

The editor replied, "We do realize it, Mr. Dreiser. We realize that no man, certainly no American, has written so honestly about the part love plays in the life of a great artist."

I dashed off to the author what I considered a brilliant piece of literary criticism:

"In this novel the Father of American Realism writes pseudobiography with the unreality and romanticism of a schoolboy, and the social snobbery of Robert W. Chambers.... Certainly, Chesterton would withhold his choice invectives from this – it throws a silken veil over ugly reality ... on a par with Jack London's last novel, *The Little Lady of the Big House,* after he had sold his soul to Hearst. He had got the 'luxury lust' which you speak of in the fine article on Hollywood you sent me."

He replied to my first blast with a mildness which reproached me:

"As for your opinion of my *Cosmopolitan* material – allow me to most cordially blow you a kiss from the tips of my fingers. You are one who do not get it." He doubted that I had read one-sixth of it.

I retorted (March 19, 1929) that I had read one-third of it, and now, with the April installment, "The Book of Elizabeth," half of it. "The same millions of eyes which peruse 'Mr. Coolidge's Own Story: The Price in Heartaches of Being President' — after swimming through the full-page ads for sanitary napkins, deodorants, creams, make-up . . . will at last come to the third installment of *This Madness*. . . . It is just this sort of stories which encourages the 'luxury lust' in America which, as you wrote in your Hollywood article, was stifling art."

TD made no attempt to reply to my criticisms but in a letter (dated February 11) he lectured me somewhat irrelevantly:

"And now in regard to your literary future. Let me give you a last straight word. It is what you do in writing — your *thought contribution* and nothing less that makes or breaks you. What people charge you with is always completely overcome by what they can get from you intellectually."

Finally, on March 20, Dreiser curtly closed the one-sided debate on his latest novel:

"Sorry you are leaving for Russia. Evidently, your friend desires to stay, as she is extending her passport. As for *This Madness*, I am sorry that I cannot alter my experiences and reactions to suit you. This situation appears to be my literary fate. T.D."

Notwithstanding my carping criticism of his writings, TD was being very helpful to O'C who was now in New York, as he had promised me. In fact, Miss O'Callaghan already had seen him more often than I had since we parted at the Polish border. She wrote me (March 21, 1929):

"Theodore Dreiser has been kind enough to allow me to use his name in applying for an extension of visa. By the way," she continued, "T.D. has sent me an invitation to a party at his place on March 27th . . . He behaves rather decently on the whole, as does Helen whom I rather like."

Her letter of April 5 told of the big party at his home.

"The party was a crush. I am sure there were between 100 and 200 people there. There was Russian singing and African Negroes presented some exotic dances. Old D. was in great form. In speaking of you, he said: 'you know if I don't do things the way Ruth wants them, then it's all up.' He was referring to your criticism about his *Cosmopolitan* story. . . ."

At this time, when I felt that I was being rebuffed because of my unkind criticism of Dreiser's novel, and particularly his attitude toward women, Dinamov sent me a review of *The American Tragedy*. The review was by the literary critic U. Aksinin, in the Moscow newspaper *Nasha Gazeta* (August 28, 1928), which Dinamov had delayed in sending me.

"At the center of the novel is the problem of abortion. Abortions, as is known, are severely dealt with by the American shopkeeper-lawmakers, especially if a member of the poorer classes is involved."

In Aksinin's review there is a reference to *Chains*, the Soviet edition of which had been published earlier.

"The predominant theme of the collection of short stories is sexual. In his preference for this theme, in showing the dark and great power of sex, and in general the biochemical interpretation of man, Dreiser shows his petty-bourgeois nature. The sex philosophy of Dreiser is explained in the preface by Ruth Kennell."

Excerpts are given from my preface to illustrate Aksinin's analysis:

> The story, from which the title *Chains* was taken, again uses the soliloquy to record the brooding, introspective thoughts of a rich man, hurrying by train to his faithless wife . . . the petty bourgeois situation of the young woman who has sold her beauty and youth for wealth. . . . Dreiser has never gone beyond a primitive attitude toward women. . . . Practically no woman in his writings functions in any other way than through her sex life. . . . The man, of course, is meanwhile engaged in doing the world's work, creating, building—always having in the background a beautiful creature to entertain and stimulate him. . . . To Dreiser this is simply the eternal law of life. He sees sex as the strongest force . . . but he makes an unequal appraisal of the roles men and women play . . . ignoring the possibility of the woman also playing her part in the world's work. . . . An honest person must admit that women in bourgeois society have deserved such an appraisal.
>
> Another story in the collection, "Typhoon," is *An American Tragedy* in short form. . . . No writer has so understandingly portrayed

the common tragedy of the unmarried girl about to become a mother. Dreiser has a profound interest in individuals . . . which can, as in this instance, make the secret mental agony of a girl in trouble the most important thing in the world. . . . His stories with this theme stand in silent condemnation of American society, which so cruelly punishes the unmarried mother.

Hauling sledge, of the type Dreiser rode in from Yasnaya Polyana station

CHAPTER II

The Stock Market Crash

1. Dreiser Crusades for Mooney, the Harlem Miners, the Scottsboro Boys

Suddenly, on October 28, 1929, the stock market crashed. In Bronxville, New York, where my husband was teaching, stock-market speculators were still elated over the election of Herbert Hoover. They had taken the train to Grand Central that morning dreaming of adding to their fortunes. That night many of them returned to their suburban homes bankrupt.

Friends had persuaded Dreiser to invest in the stock market and he had suffered a substantial loss. Fortunately, he had followed Helen's advice and invested in his 35-acre country estate. He also had some income from his writings. But this was a jolt to his remaining illusions about capitalist America, although he did not realize that it was only the prelude to more than a decade of economic depression.

At the same time, he was keenly aware of the economic distress of the whole population. Fourteen million people were out of work. Hundreds of thousands of teen-age boys and young men roamed the country as hoboes. Characteristically, Dreiser wanted to see for himself what the conditions really were. He went with Helen on a long automobile tour through the South and up the Pacific Coast, then by the northern route across country to New York.

While in San Francisco, he paid his first visit to Tom Mooney in San Quentin Prison. He was so emotionally aroused by Tom's continued imprisonment that he went to see Fremont Older, editor of the *Call*, to get the latest news. Then he drove down to San Simeon for a meeting with William Randolph Hearst.

I have in my files a clipping from the *San Francisco News* (November 3, 1930):

DREISER BLAMES MOONEY'S PLIGHT ON APATHY OF U.S. TO VICTIMS OF INJUSTICE.... Novelist Claims Billings and comrade are Examples of Tragic Social Condition Toward Which Voters of Country Are Drifting.

Theodore Dreiser blames the plight of Thomas Mooney and Warren Billings on the 'voiceless indifference' with which the American people stand by while others suffer. The famous writer gives his reasons in an article in the winter issue of *Hesperian,* published in Carmel:

"I am not at all interested in re-stating the Mooney-Billings case.... The facts have been so freely rehearsed in the past ten years that at least in one sense they constitute a chestnut. What really does interest me is the indifference—the really Imperial Roman indifference—of almost the entire body of American citizens to any and every type of ill that befalls any and every other than themselves—the voiceless indifference with which they stand by while others fail or fall, so long as they themselves are comfortable or being entertained in some ridiculous or inane way....

"Consider the case of the Minnesota Gag Law—a state statute recently enacted which declared that any paper on publication which regularly publishes malicious, scandalous and defamatory matter is a nuisance and may be suppressed by application of the induction process; and already one newspaper is restrained from publication...affirmed by the State Supreme Court...Or let us take the case of Yetta Stromberg, a former University of California student, sentenced to 10 years in San Quentin for having raised a red flag over a camp of workers' children in the San Bernardino Mountains last summer. And the state Supreme Court has now refused even to hear the appeal of her case! Or that of William Z. Foster, Robert Minor, Harry Raymond and Israel Amter, suffering indeterminate sentences...for heading a protest march down Broadway without a permit...Not even thinking on such matters....

"And yet, as I say, the vast mass of Americans, the unions, the white collar brigade, the jobless clerks and office help...all standing by, either indifferent or fearfully or wilfully silent.... Yet this is a government whose welfare, as well as existence, as a valuable economic and sociologic experiment demands that people do think—that they be not indifferent to the power-seeking of a selfish few; that they avoid, if possible, the chains of a financial autocracy already too anxious to enslave them.

"Mooney? To be sure, Mooney. But he and Billings are but two other illustrations of a tragic drift toward which almost the entire voting body of America is indifferent. Mooney. Oh, yes. Yetta Stromberg? Oh, yes. The Minnesota Press? Oh, yes.

"Well. Must I plead for Mooney? Let me rather plead for my entire land – a social dream that was and is now nearing its close. And for what reasons? Ignorant and selfish and brutal individualism on the part of a few."

Thus, three years after he went to Moscow, proclaiming himself an "incorrigible individualist," Theodore Dreiser renounced individualism.

Back in 1923, he was quoted as saying to a reporter in Los Angeles: "I don't care a damn about the masses. It is the individual that concerns me" (*American Radicals* Monthly Review Press, 1957).

But in 1930, amid the mass misery of the Great Depression, he was zealously writing and lecturing and joining with organized groups who were fighting against what he termed the inequities of the American social system. He had come to believe that a financial autocracy was destroying the social and economic democracy which he had loyally defended on his Russian tour.

The following year (1931), while still working for the release of Tom Mooney, Dreiser led a group of writers to the Harlan coal-mining district in southeastern Kentucky to observe the National Mine Workers Union struggle for decent wages and working conditions. Conditions there were a public scandal. A five-page report by John Dos Passos on the Writers' Committee investigation (New Republic, December 2, 1931) gave a detailed, factual account of the unspeakable living and working conditions of the miners. The sex incident involving Dreiser on which the mine owners attempted to focus public attention received a contemptuous passing reference in the last sentence of the report.

Beatings, shootings and arrests by union-hating cops followed the pattern so similar to that of racist police in the Black ghettoes today. Since Communists and Wobblies were active organizers for the National Miners Union, the standard thought control device, a criminal syndicalism law, was added to the arsenal of the defenders of law and order. The International Labor Defense bore the burden of the legal defense of arrested workers.

Dos Passos commented: "The thing is that the miners felt they were fighting for their lives and were ready to join any organization that would give them back solidarity and support them in their struggle against intolerable conditions."

Dreiser asked Molly Jackson, one of the leaders, about "the condition of the people." Aunt Molly let him have it:

"We have buried four to seven babies a week . . . on account of cholera, flux, famine and stomach trouble brought on by undernourishment. Their food is very bad, such as beans and harsh foods fried in this lard which is so hard to digest. . . . I talked to the Red Cross lady over in Pineville. I said there's a lot of little children in destitution. . . . They are going to get pneumonia and flu this winter that will kill them off. . . . They said, 'We are not responsible for those men out on strike. They should go back to work and work for any price they will take them for.'"

Theodore Dreiser was indicted for adultery and the mine owners tried to hide behind the scandal. Fortunately they overplayed their hand. The case was dropped, but the glare of publicity revealed something so rotten in the State of Kentucky it no longer could be ignored.

"The point at issue in Harlan County," The *Christian Century* (November 18, 1931) wrote, "is not Mr. Dreiser's conduct but Judge Jones's conduct; not the moral standards of a visiting novelist but the legal standards of a circuit court. It has been the course pursued by Judge Jones that has brought the conditions in Harlan County under scrutiny by the rest of the country."

The Dreiser Committee returned to New York and kept up pressure for justice in Harlan County. Dreiser published his report under the title *Harlan Miners Speak.*

At the same time, he was participating in other struggles for justice, including his efforts to free Mooney and Billings. On November 5, 1932, he went again to San Francisco and had a second meeting with Tom Mooney at San Quentin, at which he expressed deep emotion over Tom's continued imprisonment.

As the main speaker, he addressed an audience of 15,000 in the Civic Auditorium in San Francisco. Leo Gallagher was chairman and Lincoln Steffens was one of the speakers.

Outside, 5,000 people paraded with banners, chanting, "Free Mooney." However, despite many such demonstrations and protests as these on an international scale, Tom Mooney was not freed until January 7, 1939. During his brief period of freedom, he worked unceasingly until he had obtained the release of Warren K. Billings. His health broken by prison life, Tom Mooney died three years after his release, on March 6, 1942.

Meanwhile, Dreiser joined in the efforts of civil rights groups to free the Scottsboro boys and other victims of political persecution. Race hatred in its most violent and cruel form was manifested throughout the case of these nine black youths. They were taken from a freight car on March 25, 1931. Two white girls from Chattanooga's "Hobo Jungle" charged them with rape during the journey. All were indicted by a grand jury on March 31.

Their trials began on April 6 in Scottsboro, Alabama. On April 9 all but one of them, a 13-year-old boy, were sentenced to die in the electric chair. On the same day, the International Labor Defense entered the case, with identical telegrams to the trial judge and the governor. On April 24, a telegram of protest was received from the chairman of the Transport Workers of Berlin.

Dreiser was soon in the midst of the worldwide uproar. He wrote articles and letters of protest, and spoke at meetings. On June 20 he demanded a new trial. The pages of the *Daily Worker, New Masses* and other publications of the radical left carried news of his activities on behalf of the condemned black youths. Timid liberals were quick to predict that such immoderate protests "drive away more effective support." Actually, there followed one retreat after another by the racist authorities in Alabama.

The Scottsboro case continued for many tragic years. In the book *Scottsboro Boy* (Doubleday, 1950), Haywood Patterson tells about the horrors of life for Negroes in Kilby Prison. He concludes his autobiographical account with a warm tribute to the tireless efforts of concerned persons like Dreiser:

"I guess my people gained more off the Scottsboro case than any of us boys did. It led to putting Negroes on juries in the South. It made the whole country, in fact the whole world, talk about how the Negro people live in the South. Maybe that was the biggest thing of all. Our case opened up a lot of politics in the country. People said more about lynching, the poll tax, and a black man's rights from then on."

I am reminded that Dreiser's moving short story, "Lynch Court" (also the title of a Russian collection of his short stories) has been published in several editions in the Soviet Union. The story is based on a lynching he had covered as a young reporter.

For the remainder of his life, Dreiser was interested in the struggle for Negro rights. In his will, he specified that his widow, Helen, was to leave 20 per cent of his estate (valued at $185,000) to an orphanage for Negro children. (Helen died September 22, 1955.)

On August 27, 1931, on the occasion of Dreiser's 60th birthday, the International Union of Revolutionary Writers sent him greetings from Moscow. Addressing him "Dear Comrade," they expressed their deep appreciation of his association with them, "and trust that we will struggle together for a peaceful world. We are happy to be able to call you our comrade. We wish you a long, full life of creative work so valuable to the world proletariat."

This message was printed in the Moscow newspaper *Literaturnaya Gazeta* on the same page with a four-column glowing tribute by Sergey Dinamov headed: "Greetings to Our American Friend!" The article dwelt on the development, after his visit to the Soviet Union, of Dreiser's understanding of social conditions in America which he had not seen clearly before. In the last paragraph, Dinamov declared:

"A new Theodore Dreiser is born. The American working-class has won a new friend. . . . Our country has gained a strong supporter. . . . Theodore Dreiser is on the right path. Onward and upward, Dreiser!"

Hugo Gellert's sketch of Dreiser's head embellishes the article.

An important factor in Dreiser's changing social viewpoint was the Great Depression of the 1930s, which had a devastating effect upon his faith in rugged individualism. He saw men suddenly reduced from riches to bankruptcy by forces completely beyond their control. He heard President Hoover assuring them futilely that "prosperity is just around the corner." He saw the big brains of America offering apple-selling as a program for starving men. And he saw the "little brains" turning more and more to the radical left for meaningful answers to questions which the "big brains" could not or would not provide.

During this period of Dreiser's change from a realistic novelist viewing men and society from an impersonal height to a social crusader, he had the bright idea of joining the Communist party, as did other liberals at that time. It seems the party leaders did not encourage him, aware that he had no basic knowledge of scientific socialism. Nevertheless, while literary critics awaited a new novel to follow his first great success, and his publishers reminded him that *The Bulwark* had to be finished, the author was zealously dashing off a treatise on "Tragic America." He was becoming a pamphleteer of the radical left.

Meanwhile, I was back in the United States after a year in Moscow as feature writer for NEA Service. Teachers' salaries in Bridgeport had been arbitrarily cut, and I was busy writing stories for young people about Russia to add to the family income.

Dreiser was the first to break the long silence between us: "You can still write brilliant (if excoriating) letters. Ruth, dear, please don't be mad at me. I care for you. I really do. I'd use the word *like* if that covered it, but it doesn't: Your (*sic*) human, and tenderhearted and loyal and efficient and brave." Then he added, "In addition to that I still think your fussy and quarrelsome, always watching the other fellow intensely to see whether he's toeing the mark as you feel that he *should* be toeing it. Its the damned New England in you. The everlasting, indestructible American school marm. But people aren't just always valuable or lovable or worthwhile because they can toe marks. Sometimes they're damned well worthwhile as a relief from the toe-markers — without them where would the moralist be? ... Ruth dear, please don't quarrel with me. I want to remain near you. . . . But write me anyhow. With love, T.D."

I replied quite casually.

"Dear TD: Sergey sent me a lot of clippings the other day. Among them were some reviews of *The Titan* and a newspaper article on a lecture by V.N. Maksimovsky for the Society of Historian-Marxists, 'The Riddle of Machiavellism.' On this one Sergey scribbled, 'This will be interesting for Dreiser.' If so, I'll translate it for you. Next is a pamphlet, 'The Ideology of the Scientific and Technical Intelligentsia,' by S. Dinamov, who wrote on the cover: 'It is my last article. I think it will be interesting for Dreiser to know about.' Even so," I added, "I can't promise to translate such a heavy treatise. . . . I hope you are well and happy and busy writing something really great!"

2. An Anti-Semitic Detour

Perhaps it was fortunate that Dreiser's crusading spirit soon found an outlet after the election of Franklin D. Roosevelt. Roosevelt's bold New Deal was restoring public confidence in our way of life and providing a constructive, meaningful program for the radical left.

The rise of fascism in Italy and later its twin ideology, nazism in Germany at first caused little concern except among a minority of the radical left, always the first to sense the dangers which later lead to disaster.

During these crucial months of events which were leading the peoples of the world into the catastrophic conflicts preceding World War II, I had little contact with Dreiser. Once I went into New York and had dinner with him. I had evidently written him (but do not have a copy of the letter) about my struggles to continue my literary work along with being politically active and taking care of my home and two children.

He wrote me from Mt. Kisco on April 30, 1935:

"I am sorry you are feeling so down ... but what I always feel about you is that you should be an active worker in some cause entirely apart from home and children. . . . I see all sorts of causes that need fighting for. . . . Since I saw you, I had quite a siege of illness, some mysterious change which robbed me of 22 pounds and even put me to bed for a few weeks. Because of that I gave up my apartment in the Ansonia and came up here to get on my feet. . . . I gained my 22 pounds and health again, and on Friday I am leaving for Los Angeles to do some intensive work on that book I hope to publish in the fall. However, I expect to be back here again in September and will look you up then. It seems after hearing you say that you need spiritual back up, of all the women I have known you are about as intense and mentally active individual as anybody I know. I know if I were actively campaigning for something, you would be the first one I would send for. . . . If I were you I would try to put some more work on that book of yours because I feel that if you ever carry it out the way I suggested, you might make a success of it. Let me know how you get along with it. . . . Regards, T.D."

From Bridgeport, Conn., I replied (June 5, 1935):

"Dear TD, I was shocked to hear of your illness, and felt ashamed of writing such a complaining letter about my own troubles. It was sweet of you to take time to reply, and so comfortingly, before you left. . . . You didn't tell me what the present book is about, perhaps it is still 'Moods.' If I had accomplished all you have in your lifetime, I would feel justified in resting, but I probably wouldn't either, for doing things and growing are the only justification for keeping on living, and activity prolongs life. . . .

"As for finding a cause to fight for, that would be easy, considering the rise of fascism in Germany, Italy and Japan, and the Spanish Civil War. . . .

"By the way," my letter continued, "an organization you could honestly do a lot of good in without committing yourself too far is the American League against War and Fascism. Here the lions and the lambs rise up together — it is the beginning of a united front against the things we hate and fear."

Hesitating to offend him again by hypercritical reproof, I had refrained from writing him about the heated controversy following the publication in 1933 of "Symposium on the Jews" by the editors of the *American Spectator,* including Dreiser. With his consent, the *Nation* (April 17, 1935) had published the correspondence between Hutchins Hapgood and Theodore Dreiser about the symposium. However, the scathing attack by Mike Gold in the *New Masses* (May 7) impelled me to mention it.

"I thought it was unfortunate to have your name headlined on such an issue — featured on the cover: 'THE GUN IS LOADED, DREISER!' I had to admit Mike Gold clarified the whole confusing problem. . . . I recalled that you and I had discussed the Jewish problem when I saw you last. [This referred to our meeting in New York.] I'm afraid I was not very clear in my thinking then, but Hapgood's letters and now Mike Gold's article have clarified my thoughts. I wish we might discuss it again. If you didn't read Mike's article, I urge you to do so. He has said some true things. . . . Don't overwork. Affectionately. . . ."

Dreiser did not refer to this matter in his reply nor in any subsequent letters, although I mentioned it again in a letter in June 1936:

"Frequently I have occasion to defend you in the antiSemitic scandal . . . because I don't like to see your reputation besmirched," my letter said, "and at such a time as this, when the social crisis is deepening and we must choose one side or the other."

As I saw it, he had come under the influence of wealthy Jews who were promoting Balfour's plan for a Jewish homeland in

Palestine, and had gone along with the idea. The Balfour Declaration was made November 2, 1917, and Zionists had been promoting it before World War I. Though Dreiser detested British imperialism, he failed to detect the pungent odor of Arabian oil and the defense of Britain's Suez Canal in Mr. Balfour's humanitarian interest in a Jewish homeland in Palestine.

Dreiser stated his support in the frame of reference of unconsciously anti-Semitic stereotypes which he had absorbed in the home of his fanatical German Catholic father. He attended parochial schools until he was twelve. Now, under attack, he defended his position with wild, apparently intolerant, observations, which were answered indignantly by Hutchins Hapgood and later by Michael Gold. It was not in Dreiser's nature to admit that he had made a fool of himself. But it became clear later that he learned from this unpleasant experience and accepted what he had learned.

In fact, Dreiser did write a statement which was a restrained effort to justify his position. (*New Masses* April 22, 1935.)

"Of course . . . I draw a distinction between the Jewish worker and the Jewish exploiter. . . . What you have just read by Lenin on the Jewish question meets with my full approval. And if my letters are used by the Nazis as propaganda I repudiate such use. . . . my interest in Communism is that it will equitably solve the relations of man. . . ."

Although they found this explanation insufficient, both, Mike Gold and Hutchins Hapgood came to the same conclusion. They believed that Dreiser was confused, not malicious. Some of his best friends were anti-Semitic Jews. Bitter attacks from the left no doubt stiffened his position at the time, and he attempted somewhat irrationally to justify it. Eight years after his Russian tour, he was still holding to some of his basic philosophy and holding to some of his faith in American capitalist democracy.

In *The Mike Gold Reader* (International Publishers, 1950) there is a beautiful tribute, "The Dreiser I Knew," which erased all the severe reproaches of 15 years before in "The Gun Is Loaded, Dreiser." Overlooking the impact of the Russian tour, Mike Gold dates Dreiser's beginning of understanding and active participation in the class struggle from the Great Depression. He writes:

"The years that followed demonstrated how deep were the roots of Dreiser's humanity. From then on, this great novelist became prominent as a venerated leader of American's progressive intellectuals—our Maxim Gorky, our Romain Rolland. He made mistakes; his philosophy fluctuated, and crackpots and Iagos could still confuse him. But his heart was sound. His lifelong sensitivity as an honest artist took political reality at last."

Even his subconscious prejudice against the Jewish people appears to have faded away during the earnest pamphleteering years leading up to America's entry into World War II. A paragraph in his letter to me (February 20, 1940) indicated this to my satisfaction:

"Presently, I'll send you a book called *The Socialist Sixth of the World,* by Hewlett Johnson, Dean of Canterbury. It's really wonderful. Its banned in England but is circulated privately. I've ordered ten copies from England."

He had marked two pages without comment:

"Jewish workers in factories and on the land in the Ukraine, the Crimea, Moscow, Georgia, Baku, Siberia, have proved their fitness and capacity. It is now clear that Jews can, given time and opportunity, master industrial and agricultural tasks as readily as men and women of other nationalities.

"The question of land settlements had been raised from the earliest days of the revolution. Jewish colonies had been formed in that most lovely place, the southern shore of the Crimea . . . also in the Ukraine. The two million Jews who had been drawn into agriculture had already effectually exploded the old lie that Jews by nature were unsuited to the land or factory. . . . Given a fair field, the Jew can excel in most things. . . . Jewish collective farms there are profitable and flourishing. The little artisans, shopkeepers, and small middlemen who remained have become proficient farmers."

This silent gesture closed for me an ugly episode in Dreiser's life.

3. The Pre-World-War-II Years

When, on June 18, 1936, Maxim Gorky died in Moscow, America's leading liberals paid tribute to the great revolutionary writer: Eugene O'Neill, Malcolm Cowley, Clifford Odets, Fannie Hurst, Lincoln Steffens, Carl Sandburg, Max Lerner, James Farrell, Upton Sinclair, Sherwood Anderson Corliss Lamont and Theodore Dreiser, whose tribute (*Soviet Russia Today,* July 1936) I think was one of the most eloquent:

"For me, Gorky's passing closes the golden age of Russian realism. He was among the last of that great world group of realistic thinkers who look into our present and future from that hardly achieved mental peak which gives the widest and clearest vision. Communism, mechanism, the widening doors of astronomy, physics, chemistry, sociology, economics — revealing what? A world in which is no stress, no strain, emotional or mental? Only that literature, of which Gorky was a master, acknowledging the great sorrows and illusory pleasures of our real life, arrests and holds a thinking world. Man may find ways to be economically free and at ease. But will he ever escape from the emotional restlessness and strain which comes from knowing life, as Gorky knew it? I lay my mental wreath beside the bier of this very great man."

On August 27 of the same year (1936), Dreiser observed his 65th birthday at his home in Mt. Kisco. A *New York Times* dispatch on the 29th featured the author's tribute to Roosevelt. Dreiser had interrupted "the writing of his 23rd book to give an interview in which he hailed President Roosevelt's suggested peace conference of world rulers as 'an idea worth planting.' In the interview the novelist said he was 'all for Roosevelt' because he had saved the nation in a time of crisis and established a sort of socialism in this country. Asked if he thought there could be a Socialist government in the United States, he replied: 'We already have it.'"

In this historic year, events in Europe were moving relentlessly toward fascist victories which threatened peace and freedom everywhere. On November 15, General Franco's advance troops penetrated University City in Madrid.

At the same time, the Stalin government was reacting ominously to the dangerous world situation. On November 23, eight Soviet engineers and one German were sentenced to ten years in prison for sabotage in the Kuznetsk Basin coal mines in western Siberia. The trial in Moscow of Karl Radek and other members of the Central Committee of the Communist party began in the following January. The trials of Marshall Tukhatchevsky and seven other Soviet generals ended in June; they were sentenced to be shot for treason.

A Christmas (1936) card from Dreiser expressed the wish to see me. "All good wishes. It was so satisfying to have your thoughtful letter. Winter has pushed me out of Mt. Kisco for two months or so, anyhow. I'm at the Park Plaza, 50 West 77th St., and if your down this way I'd like to have you stop in. Meantime I'll write you."

The year 1937 started threateningly, with President Roosevelt signing the resolution embargoing arms shipments to Spain. Under the nonintervention agreement, British, French, German and Italian warships began patroling the Spanish coast. President Roosevelt signed the Neutrality Act, a deathblow to the Loyalist cause. Hitler announced that Germany repudiated the war-guilt clause in the Versailles Treaty, and on January 30 Neville Chamberlain succeeded Baldwin as prime minister — thus beginning an era of British foreign policy which was to lead to international disaster. In Moscow, Bukharin and Rykov were expelled from the Central Committee of the party — a prelude to their trial for treason.

A pattern was now emerging in the crazy quilt of events taking place in trouble spots all over the world. In July, Japanese bombing planes attacked Tientsin in the first major attack in the undeclared war on China; in September, Hitler told the Nuremberg National Socialist Congress that Germany, Italy and Japan were linked to save Europe from "chaotic madness." On November 6, the three Axis powers proclaimed their solidarity in the "Anti-Comintern Pact." It was not accidental that all this happened on the eve of the 20th anniversary of the Russian Revolution.

Dreiser's message to me on his 1937 Christmas card referred to the shocking events in Moscow and expressed nostalgia on the tenth anniversary of his tour.

"This is not just one more of those things. I think of us in Russia so often. What do you think of it now?"

Perhaps he was remembering our parting ten years before at the Polish border, when he wrote me an unexpectedly beautiful and moving letter:

116 W. 11th St., N.Y.C.
Jan. 24 – '38

Dear Ruth:

I know you think I don't give you many thoughts or I'd write oftener – at least answer your letters promptly. But it's not true. I think of you much – year in and year out – because of your vivid, restless, searching, searching temperament which is never wholly absent from me. For me your mind is *right* and your emotions, too. I never forget our trip through Russia and how humanly and above all understandingly you bore with me. Out of the many who have come and gone – men and women – here you are, vital in my mind and affections. I am always hurried with a lot of things. (If you could only know the amount of self-illuminating work I have been doing!) But through it all I go back regularly to that vivid, gay, helpful experience I had with you – and am so grateful for having been so close to one who plainly has never been afraid to live and has so done. *And I've been wanting to say this to you for so long –* for it springs from a deep and enduring liking and affection compelled by your own qualities – or shall I say those qualities in you which have arrested my interest, admiration, respect *and* affection and held them.

I hope you are ok. Write me when you can. Love T.D. Do you ever hear from Sergei? I heard from him regularly up to six or eight months ago – not since.

The year 1938 had begun with Chancellor Schuschnigg of Austria conferring with Hitler and consenting to take five Nazi sympathizers into his cabinet. Foreign Minister Anthony Eden had resigned from Chamberlain's cabinet because of the pact with Mussolini. Chancellor Schuschnigg also had resigned and the new premier, Seyss-Inquart, called for German troops and proclaimed union with Germany. Britain and Italy signed a peace and harmony pact in April and, on the 24th, Konrad

Henlein, leader of the Nazis in Sudetenland, proclaimed his eight-point "Karlsbad Program" of demands on the Czechoslovak Government.

I was still engrossed in the perilous situation of the Spanish Loyalists. I received a letter from Dreiser dated April 26, replying to my appeal on behalf of Loyalist Spain.

"Thanks for your letter and I'll do as you say. Don't think I haven't done things for the Loyalists. I've contributed regularly to the Loyalist funds, have written articles and talked long and fiercely on various occasions. I think we'll pay for our indifference if Spain goes fascist. I think Cordell Hull is an enemy of labor and the mass generally. Why does Roosevelt select enemies to his aims and place them in high positions? He is constantly being bitten by once frozen snakes he has chosen to warm at his fireside.

"I'm glad your so rampant. You sound like your real self. I meant to write and say come and bring your friend or call me up when in town. But I had three connecting cases of grippe. Then I moved out here and feel better. If I pass through Bridgeport I'll see you there. Affectionately, T.D."

"P.S. I'm still for Russia but I wish I could know how things really are. They invited me back — all expenses — in 1936 but I was sick. They didn't believe me, I think, but I wanted to go. Illness alone held me back."

When I replied May 10 I was in low spirits:

"The editorial in the *Times* this morning makes me despair that the embargo will be lifted in time to save Loyalist Spain. If the President leaves it up to congress, it may mean a delay long enough for a Franco victory. The British Foreign Office is seeing to it that the embargo continues until their cold-blooded plan has been accomplished."

A prompt reply from TD raised my spirits: "Thanks for the Embargo advice. What an inveterate campaigner you are! You'll die fighting for change — or against it. But don't think that nearly everybody with the campaign against the Spanish Crime is not after me. I get letters, letters, letters. Also letters concerning every other issue in the U.S., and a number from abroad. The rumor is that I am a millionaire. Top for me was 1928, when I had, or thought I had, $600,000. But it soon descended to $200,000. then $100,000. By the fall of 1932 I had this Mt. Kisco place and 50,000 in gold notes which Roosevelt called in and gave greenbacks for. Since then less pay and more income taxes have kept me down to a working norm which tires me. But to all 'issues' I am a millionaire and supposed to contribute liberally. Just the same, I do all I can. Not only that, but all the time, and without my consent, my name is put on all sorts of things as sponsor. I hear of it afterward. But you—well, you can stir me up all you please. I know what a progressive you are. Love, T.D. (P.S.) What has become of Sergei? Not a word in 7 months! He was editor of the Internationale but now his name is off. Are they going to try him? And he's so truly sweet and good."

TD's next letter (June 24) replied to one of mine in which I wrote I was returning to Palo Alto with Jimmie, who would enter the University of California in Berkeley in the fall. Dreiser expected to be in Los Angeles in the summer and would write me from there, he said. "Anyhow, next winter (January and February) I have a West Coast lecture trip and I'll probably see you then. . . . At the time I sent *Direction* to you I meant to send a letter with it. . . . The editor and publisher is Marguerite Harris—a quite interesting woman with a little money. She got the idea and has paid for it herself. She hopes to make Leftist suggestions in such an interesting picture, article and story form as to help bring about a change. She's been looking here and there to find someone to work with her on policy and material and I thought of you."

"I'm here at Noroton—Pratt's Island, until this coming June 30th. I'm living in a Sound side Island cabin which Mrs. Harris leased for the year. . . .

"Yes, I always think of you in Russia—your energy, ideas, enthusiasm. What a fine way to live and how really pleased you must be with it all considering the rusty lives so many people lead. Anyhow, if I don't see you here's luck. And I'll hope to see you in L.A. or S.F. Affectionately, T.D. (P.S.) Not a word from Dinamov."

CHAPTER III

World War II

1. Dreiser's Progressive Activities Increase

We were still so occupied with the tragic course of Loyalist Spain's heroic efforts to save its democratic government that we failed to perceive it was only one of the small countries along the road in the inexorable march of "His Majesty's Government's policy to drive the Nazi menace Eastward."

Hitler Germany was making steady gains in Eastern Europe, with the help of Britain and France. On May 20, 1938, Czech forces mobilized on their frontier. On July 2 the Czech Government rejected the demands made by the Sudeten Nazis, and in August Britain sent a "conciliator" to Prague. By the middle of August, German army maneuvers began. This ominous move prompted the Soviet Government on August 22 to inform the German ambassador that Russia would keep its 1935 promise to support Czechoslovakia in the event of an attack. Ignoring this warning, Hitler warned the Czechs that their "oppression" of the Sudeten Germans must cease. Chamberlain promptly flew to Berchtesgaden to confer with Hitler.

The noose tightened around the necks of the beleagured Czechs when Premier Daladier and Foreign Minister Bonnet of France conferred with the British in London and agreed upon the dismemberment of Czechoslovakia. Since the Czech Government accepted the Anglo-French terms, calling for virtual surrender to Germany, Russia was prevented from aiding her little neighbor.

But the Czechs again mobilized when Chamberlain brought back from his Godesberg meeting with Hitler on September 22 a new list of German demands—even though the mobilization was an impotent gesture in the face of the formidable array of European leaders—Chamberlain, Daladier, Mussolini and Hitler. These gentlemen met at Munich and agreed on terms for partitioning Czechoslovakia. The Soviet Government was summarily excluded from the Munich conference and was helpless to come to the aid of the betrayed Czechs. . . .

By October 10, 1938, German troops and Gestapo agents had completed their occupation of Czech areas ceded by the Munich Pact, going beyond boundaries agreed upon at Munich.

Of course, these historic events were not so clear to us then as they are in perspective. Nor were they clear to Dreiser, except in his shrewd estimation of the role of England. In any case, he made no mention of the latest international developments in his answer from Glendale to my note written during Christmas week, 1938.

He wrote that it was nice to know I was so near and, as he expected to be in San Francisco very soon, he wanted directions for reaching my mother's place.

"I'm here working on a novel. The heat has varied from 85 to 90°, then came a solid week of rain. The winter in New York started so rough that I pulled out—a blizzard at Thanksgiving. But now I'll stay here, I hope, until this book is done. But I'd like to see you. We should have plenty to talk about . . ."

In my reply, I made my first reference to the Munich Pact. I quoted Frank Sullivan's "Greetings, Friends" in the *The New Yorker* (December 24):

> *Kringle, honest, on the level,*
> *You're a piker compared with Neville.*
> *You give trifles such as mittens;*
> *Nev gives everything not Britain's.*
> *The little nations all grow littler*
> *As big-hearted Nev gives them to Hitler.*

> *So let us on this festive date*
> *Arise and re-affirm our hate*
> *For Adolph Hitler, the Nazi thug,*
> *Mussolini, the Fascist mugg,*
> *And each and every moral eunuch*
> *That had a hand in the Pact of Munich.*

> *The rhyme is bad but the Pact is worse —*
> *Neville's plane may be Europe's hearse."*

On December 31 TD wrote that he would be coming up in two weeks and would pick me up at Palo Alto or meet me in San Francisco.

"It's been three years since I was there and just the streets of San Francisco are always exhilarating to me. . . . Yes, I'm sorry about Sergei, and I can't imagine what they could have had against him. He never wrote one word to me that was not in praise of Russia. I always felt he was too silent and cautious. But maybe not. There are a lot of subjects I want to discuss with you. Happy New Year."

The New Year did not promise to be very happy for a large part of the world. On January 25 Franco's troops had taken Barcelona, and over a million refugees entered France as Loyalist troops continued to retreat.

TD wrote me on January 30 that he was speaking in Oakland February 9; then he would come to San Francisco to speak at Town Hall, in the Clift Hotel, at 11 a.m. February 14. He explained that he had been delayed in coming up by two movie conferences — a lot of talking and wasting time from his work.

"Isn't the Loyalist defeat just too sad? I got Roosevelt to send them three million bushels of wheat and some other things but, before he acted it was too late. Just a start. . . ."

In *My Life with Dreiser* (World Publishing, 1951, pp. 260-261) Helen Dreiser enlarges on this casual reference to his efforts to help the Spanish Loyalists. She tells of his participation, on an invitation from the League of American Writers, in the International Peace Conference in Paris, at the time of the Spanish Civil War. Many of the delegates, he felt, were not entirely in sympathy with the Loyalist cause. He was placed toward the end of the long list of speakers, but when people were already leaving in large numbers, Dreiser called out: "Don't go! Don't go! I have something of importance to say!"

As people returned to their seats. Dreiser delivered an impassioned speech in defense of the Spanish Loyalists, and the necessity to cease the bombing of open cities. His speech made the front pages of the evening papers in Paris.

From there he went to Barcelona, and amidst the fascist bombing he observed the suffering of the Spanish people.

On his return, he visited President Roosevelt aboard his yacht, the Potomac and presented his proposals for aid to the Spanish Loyalists. While Roosevelt held to the "neutrality" policy, he promised to do what he could. Later he sent two or three supply ships, for which Dreiser wrote him a personal letter of appreciation:

"That you should have applied the mechanism of the plan suggested, so accurately and effectively, and particularly in the face of the stalemate that any ordinary citizen was certain to encounter, makes still more clear to me the enormous value of a great executive in the Presidential chair . . . most particularly in periods of stress and change."

Dreiser's lecture at the Oakland Forum, entitled "What I Think About Life" was reported in the news items of the San Francisco papers. The only direct report I had was from my son Jimmie, then a freshman at the University of California in Berkeley. After the lecture, he shook hands with the great man (whom he had met in New York in 1928). But there was quite a crowd around him, Jimmie told me, so they exchanged only a few words.

The San Francisco *News* (February 10) carried a two-column article by Neil Hitt, based on an interview after the Oakland lecture. Under the large photograph was the caption: "NO LONGER A ROARING LION." Apparently, TD was in one of his pensive moods when he was apt to make contradictory statements that were open to being misquoted:

"He has come to compromise with destiny," writes his interviewer, evidently unaware that the "roaring lion" had become a roaring crusader against the threat of fascism and war. It is true, he did talk for some time about his altered view of life, due to his studies of science and philosophy:

"My original concept of life was that it was cruel, unjust, a devastating process in which happiness was only an illusion. Perhaps that was because of my early environment. It did not seem right to me that my family should be giving tithes to the Church when we didn't even have potatoes to eat." Then he re-educated himself, he said.

"I am glad, to see however," he added, "that the time is passing when aristocrats can set themselves to one side and look upon other human beings as ants, servants, or slaves. That problem is now on the carpet, and I believe we will have it out." His interviewer suggested: "War?"

"We may yet have Fascism or Communism, though not in this generation. But, unless there is some more generous gesture on the part of the haves toward the have-nots, we may eventually get out in the streets and settle it hand to hand. I would just as leave perish in that fashion as any other," he concluded.

A few days before his scheduled lecture at Town Hall in San Francisco, I came up from Palo Alto to meet him at the Green Street apartment of my brother Heber Epperson and his wife Helen. Very late that evening, when he remarked glumly he guessed he'd have to go back to his hotel, Helen invited him to spend the night.

Years later, after the death of my brother, my sister-in-law mentioned that visit in her letter:

"I will never forget the night Mr. Dreiser spent with us. Heber and I often talked about it, as it just wasn't a thing that happened to everyone. In those days we didn't have too much, and I remember Dreiser had to sleep in sheets that had been used once before. His comment was that he 'had slept under worse conditions many times, so think nothing of it.' That poor guy just didn't want to go back to his hotel room, so what could you do. It always tickled Heber that Dreiser drank a bottle of beer with him before breakfast. Dreiser said he had drunk many things before breakfast, but never beer."

Helen prepared eggs the way he said he liked them — scrambled. After breakfast, my brother asked him what he wanted to see in the city. Without hesitation he replied, "The Golden Gate Bridge."

Heber drove onto the gleaming new bridge. We alighted and walked in the rare sunshine beneath the ruddy spans for some distance toward the Marin side, where the hills were turning a tender green in the early spring. Now and then Dreiser stopped to gaze in rapt silence beyond the Golden Gate to the shining ocean.

After he had taken leave of his hosts, we walked around on the streets, which TD always found exhilarating. One very steep street with wooden steps reminded him of the 200 historic steps in Odessa.

"I remember we walked up and down them several times — and at the top was that marvelous museum of ancient relics from the Greek occupation of the Black Sea Coast!"

And so now we walked up and down the hills of this beautiful city overlooking the broad waters of San Francisco Bay and the Pacific Ocean, talking about those 77 days when we were together all the time. I did not even touch on the dangerous international situation. I did not want to shatter his tenderly nostalgic mood, based on the bond of exotic experiences which was to hold us together till the day of his death.

Inevitably, we wandered down the hills to Chinatown and ate lunch at the Hang Far Low restaurant, whose red and gold balcony hung over the narrow street. After that, we took a cable car down to Powell and Market. At the Greyhound bus station we said goodbye.

Since I could not stay over for the lecture, he wrote me a full report (February 14, 1939):

"I had excellent luck with my crowd today. It was so affectionate and enthusiastic. And poor old Rappaport was so delighted that he paid me for S.F. and Portland in advance. I sent off the share of Briggs, my lecture manager, three hours ago. And now I'm just leaving for Portland. I'll speak on the 16th. Then off to Salt Lake City, where my address is University of Utah, Bureau of Lectures. Why not write me?"

TD went on to describe what happened at his San Francisco lecture:

"I had a big crowd. It really went nuts. Erskine Scott Wood came up with his wife and spoke at the luncheon afterwards. He proposed a $50 million (!) fund in one dollar bills to be contributed to the *Dreiser Democracy Fund* to be used by me or some committee to put the U.S.A. straight! I laughed, but he got a big hand. Then the Jews gathered round wanting to know what they could do, and I suggested a committee of 100 prominent Jews to outline a Democratic Brotherhood Pact, a Pact that would guarantee a fifty-fifty break for all, no undercutting or over-burdening anybody in America. And they swore to try to do it—thus to prove to America that they wanted to meet its democratic ideals and standards. Maybe something will come of it. Anyhow, so it ran. Love T.D."

Harking back to the anti-Semitic scandal, this remark shows how really naively sincere Dreiser was in his conviction that he was not an anti-Semite. He identified as Jews a group of bourgeois intellectuals, who, as such, gathered around him offering help, as they would have done had they been Irish or Italian.

To this letter, TD appended a personal note:

"Dear 'Root' [using the Russian pronounciation], It was so comforting to get your letter today.... After you left I felt depressed. It was so homey to be with you. Just like Odessa, and Mineralni Vodi and Baku, Batum and the Black Sea boat. It's been so long ...

"*P.S.* Thanks to Heber and Helen for letting me stay. They were homey folks, too."

Theodore Dreiser's lecture at Town Hall had caused a stir which was felt for many days around San Francisco Bay. John D. Barry's column "Ways of the World" in the San Francisco *News* (February 21, 1939) was devoted to reminiscences on Dreiser. Here are some extracts:

"His profound sympathy with the disinherited and the blundering of the earth served as his principal driving force. About writing as an art he knew very little, and cared little. We sat at a table with a small group that included a good-humored, talkative celebrity from New York. Silently, Dreiser listened, like a figure of stone ... he had acquired a remarkable faculty, being able to keep still without feeling or causing embarrassment.

"At his lecture he told us more about himself than he realized. Anyone could see that he hadn't carefully prepared. But

he talked out of a full mind, largely about himself and his relation to life. . . . The Catholic Church he mentioned disrespect-
fully, as he had done in his writings. But he perceived enormous power for good there, provided, of course, the Church
were to follow his ideas. One man he praised with enthusiasm — George Fox, founder of the Quakers, 'the greatest
prophet since Jesus Christ.'"

Barry added that at the luncheon which followed they were
told they might ask questions. "So I said, 'If you were boss of
the world what would you do?'

"He assumed I meant to associate him with the Diety, and
made reference to 'the creative forces'. When Miss Julia Robin-
son, the Forum's executive secretary, urged him to be more ex-
plicit, he said he thought what he saw in the Soviet Union
during his visit there in 1927-28 was better than what we had
in the United States."

TD did not write me anything about his lecture in Portland,
Oregon. I am inclined to believe that he did not mention his
Portland lecture because it had a bad reception. His tirade
against England was unfavorably received, according to the
press.

Late in February, TD wrote me from Ogden about his Utah
lectures. After hailing my crusading spirit — "battling constantly, The Unterrified!" he continued:

"Well, anyhow, in a total of six lectures so far — tomorrow
the last — I've managed to stir up arguments galore, not only
in the lecture halls but with the reporters. They never let
me alone. . . . Finally, here in the Mormon area, I'm achieving
editorials. They're beginning to believe that some of the criticisms have weight. Only tomorrow night, I'm through at Pravo,
Utah, and from there head south for Glendale. Just the same,
I hope to see you soon. I may run up. . . .

"I'm glad you liked the day and night in S.F. It's so really
wonderful when two people with related, if not exact, ideas, hit
it off. It makes a day, a month, years — sometimes a life. You
liked the restaurant. Well, you know — I liked the great bridge."

Dreiser sent me a page from the *Herald-Journal* (Logan,
Utah) telling about his lecture in Salt Lake City (February 19)
and repeated in Logan (on the 21st):

"In Salt Lake City Sunday Theodore Dreiser, author of *An American Tragedy,* observed that war involving every nation in the world is inevitable and may come any day. 'The world situation right now is the most treacherous setup I have ever seen. . . . There is no question about war coming.' He then lamented the fact that if war comes America will be in a terrible mess, because Americans think of nothing but swing, attending movies and reading the funny papers. . . . 'Even when America does become involved in a major conflict it will be difficult for our people to realize it, and very painful for them to drag themselves away from their swing sessions and movie palaces and funny papers to defend the country.'"

World events since Munich were confirming Dreiser's anti-British views. On February 28, "peace-in-our-time" Chamberlain smugly announced that Great Britain would recognize the Franco regime as the legal Spanish Government.

The first letter I had from TD after he had returned to Glendale from his lecture tour began with an anxious query because he had not heard from me:

"What's the matter now? Not sick, I hope? Are returned to Bridgeport? Or returned to a former viewpoint? If so — or not so — I'd like to keep in touch with you."

Then followed a far more alarming question:

"I have a very surprising offer, or invitation rather, from a very important country — not Russia. I wonder — I meditate. Would you assume that a sincere, impartial examination of data freely spread before me abroad would lead to (assuming it would run counter to current acceptance here) social ostracism for me — once and for all? Full authority to accept or reject data offered to be left to me *without subsequent charges of bias on the part of the country extending the invitation.*

"Will you let me know — if you feel disposed to comment — what you think of this? At least write. Love, T.D."

I was so upset that I did not even make a copy of my typed reply and so I cannot remember how much I elaborated on the subject — as I did in subsequent letters, of which I did make copies. I shudder even now at the thought of the consequences for him had he accepted that invitation, so obviously from the German Government. At the very time he had received the invitation, Hitler had crushed the Czech Republic as his troops entered Prague. Rumania had signed a trade agreement with Nazi Germany; Lithuania had surrendered Memel to the Nazis. Germany's encirclement of Russia's buffer states was proceeding steadily after Britain's appeasement pact with Hitler had opened the gates.

The Soviet Government was reacting to the Munich Pact in a manner which showed their growing fear of attack. In this light, Stalin's purges of military and government leaders might reasonably be attributed to paranoia — perhaps incited by a traitor or traitors who had his confidence. But Dreiser at this point — a stubbornly independent thinker — seemed to blame Britain more than Germany for the *Drang nach Osten*.

I answered Dreiser's request for comment on his invitation at once and without equivocation: "DON'T DO IT!" His response on April 11 was ambiguous but to me a satisfactory statement:

"Well, thanks. And I feel much more comfortable. Are you going back East without seeing me? Why not take the bus down for a day or two. There's plenty to entertain you, and if we don't do anything else we can discuss the dear English."

This he proceeded to do on the next page.

"I am sure our American financiers, trust and corporation magnates are in league with all others of that ilk in England, Japan and elsewhere. Observe Dr. J.P. Morgan sculling the retroactive fascist Archbishop of Canterbury around in his yacht, the 'Corsair'. Morgan and Co. are English-American bankers, not American bankers. J.P. Morgan before 1929 had organized America, Inc. — 167 corporations — which was to control the U.S. and appoint Dwight Morrow to be its first secretary, acting as the President in Washington. Congress exposed all this. Roosevelt suppressed general advertising of the fact. Why? The argument was it would cause the rank and file of Americans to lose faith in their government. Write any radical congressman for the data. Pascalli, now Pope, was in on this. He came over to see Morgan, Morrow, *et al*."

Dreiser's Anglophobia confused and antagonized some of his friends when the book on which he was now working, *Is*

America Worth Saving? was published. "It is the policy of His Majesty's Government to drive the Nazi menace Eastward" was, however, the declaration published in the *London Times* much earlier, which other friends had not forgotten.

In the midst of all this confusion and anxious speculation about the state of the world, I received something from Theodore Dreiser refreshingly removed from the grim reality of the world situation and more in the mood of our San Francisco walk. It was his latest book, just off the press: *The Living Thoughts of Thoreau, Presented by Theodore Dreiser* (Longmans, Green, 1939). He had written across the title page:

> "To Ruth (Kennell)
> with admiration and affection
> from T.D.
> Glendale, March 31, 1939."

Turning the pages, I felt the presence of the Dreiser who had stood on the Golden Gate Bridge gazing out across the ocean to infinity. In his introduction, he explains that Thoreau's thoughts "are scattered higgledy-piggledy through fourteen volumes of notes that he left. They also include 'Walden', and his letters and essays of the twenty-two years of his writing life. Still, if you are interested, you can piece them together for yourself, as I have done . . . in this volume. . . . For Thoreau, poet-wise, and having at the same time the intense energy of the seeker and dreamer, was forever knocking at the door of the mystery through all the days of his time-restricted life (he died at the age of 45). Indeed, although he can only hint at the probable evolution of some of its marvels (he wrote before Darwin), nearly all that he has to say comes to you as a song, a song of a mystic force, embodying itself through beauty."

2. Confusions and Clarities

Twelve years after the "incorrigible individualist" set sail for the unknown shores of the vast Russian continent, he had become a zealous pamphleteer. Enclosed with a letter (September, 1939) from Hollywood, was a four-page carbon copy of his article, "Civilization — Where? What?"

He explained in the letter: "I was asked by a weekly here, the *Hollywood Tribune*, which has just failed, to say whether Civilization is about to pass! I haven't sent it elsewhere, but since you say I should be expressing myself, I am sending it. An earlier punch went on request to *Common Sense*. They plan to publish that. More later. Can't write at once. I'm always doing for Russia as this shows. You may distribute this thing as you choose. TD."

His article was written after German Foreign Minister von Ribbentrop flew to Moscow to sign a ten-year non-aggression pact with the Soviet Union (August 22, 1939). This event was the natural climax to successive acts of aggression on the part of Nazi Germany after Munich. The Polish Government, backed by Britain, had refused to agree to Soviet troops coming to their aid on Polish soil. In the ensuing crisis, Foreign Minister Litvinov resigned and was replaced by Molotov. At this warning sign that the Russians were preparing to stop Hitler at the Curzon Line, Chamberlain made a show of seeking Soviet collaboration against Nazi Germany. He sent a fourthrate diplomat, William Strang, and an inferior military mission without credentials or instructions to Moscow to start negotiations. (Note that it was Chamberlain himself who had gone by plane to Berchtesgaden to confer with Hitler.) But what really broke down the months of fruitless talks was the revelation (in *New York Times* front-page headlines, July 24, 1939) that the Hudson-Wohlthat negotiations between the British and Hitler for a billion-pound sterling appeasement loan to the German Government were in progress at the same time.

Yet when the Russians signed the nonaggression and trade

agreement with the Nazis on August 22, the British and American press were loud in their denunciation of the "betrayal" by the Russians. Many liberal friends of Soviet Russia were disillusioned and joined the chorus of bitter reproach; some members of the Communist party resigned in protest.

In a countermove to the Nazi-Soviet pact, the British and Poles signed a mutual assistance pact in London. Hitler had refused to negotiate with Poland, insisting that Danzig and the Polish Corridor must be returned to the Third Reich. On September 1, German troops invaded Poland. Forced to take some action, the British and French ambassadors announced that they would fulfill their obligations to aid Poland if the troops were not withdrawn. Following a two-hour ultimatum to Germany, on September 3, 1939 Britain and France declared war. This was the beginning of the "phony war." Winston Churchhill joined the cabinet as First Lord of the Admiralty and Anthony Eden became Secretary of State. . . .

This was the international situation when Dreiser sent me a copy of his article, "Civilization — Where? What?"

I was aware that he did not wholly agree with my point of view on current world affairs. His strong anti-British attitude, based on his study of the history of British duplicity, inclined him toward a sympathetic view of Germany's position as a world power. He had a more optimistic interpretation of the aims of the Third Reich than most liberals could tolerate.

Actually, his approving reference to conditions in Germany in his article, "Civilization — Where? What?" was based entirely on his last visit there in 1928. At that time, a liberal government was in power. The German Communist Party was the largest, next to the Russian, in the Communist International, whose official language was German. He did not seem to understand that this was the compelling reason for the rise of a counter-revolutionary force resulting, in the early 1930's in seizure of power by the National Socialist Party (Nazis). In fact, German Communists and their sympathizers were the first to be arrested, imprisoned, tortured and executed. Meanwhile, the trade unions were smashed and the extermination of the Jewish population began.

At the same time, he never wavered in his support of the new Soviet society. He heartily approved of the Soviet-Nazi Pact as beleaguered Russia's urgent defensive measure. Thus, his "pro-German" leaning was not only engendered by his hatred of British imperialism, but perhaps even more by his illusion that New Russia's collaboration with "New" Germany would be mutually beneficial, especially in checkmating the treacherous machination of the Western democracies.

Although shocked and distressed at the confused idea TD had expressed in the article regarding the possibility of collaboration between Socialist Russia and National Socialist Germany under Hitler, I did not find time to reply until October 26. I told him I was glad to have his article, and then hastened to tell him I disagreed with him on one point. "And it's fundamental," I declared. "This is your failure to discriminate sharply between Nazi Germany and Socialist Russia. It seems to me that such a point of view is quite as dangerous as those of Westbrook Pegler and Congressman Martin Dies, who say nazism and communism are similar ideologies.

"Hitler's Germany is indeed, to my mind, uncivilized, not because the German people are uncivilized, but because when Hitler came to power he became the leader and the tool of a fascist dictatorship, a powerful financial oligarchy. . . . which is the essence of fascism . . . fascism is capitalism at bay . . ."

I went on, almost matching in length Dreiser's article which I was answering, to explain that Russia was cooperating with Nazi Germany in order to have time to strengthen its defenses. "Where you get the idea," I concluded, "that there is anything socialistic about Nazi Germany is beyond me. . . ."

TD did not wait long to reply. "Yours is a discouraged letter," he wrote on October 31 from Hollywood. "And I myself do not know what to make of the European situation. It is seemingly too complicated to follow. My personal deduction, at *first*, was that Hitler had truly split with England and France and that Russia had come to some workable understanding with Hitler that would permit of both going ahead on a social-democratic basis. But when I heard that Poland would not allow the Russian Army to aid the Poles, I began to doubt. I had not forgotten Hitler's share in the destruction of democratic Spain, nor England's nor France's, nor Italy's. . . . We would not accept a democratic Spain and so threw the country to Mussolini and Hitler — or Franco and the Catholics!

"Just the same," Dreiser concluded, still clinging to his pro-German position, "if Russia is not to sweep Europe soon, I would prefer to see a strong German state to the rotten finan-dictatorship now holding in France, England, Hungary and the Balkans, and elsewhere. . . .

"Anyhow, I wrote 'The Dawn Is in the East' in good faith and sent a copy to Russia. Apletin cabled me afterward that it was published in full in *Pravda.* That means with the personal approval of Stalin. If he objected to the comments on Germany he did not order them cut. . . .

"*Your article is excellent (The Nation,* November 4, 1939). I intend to send it on to others, but it will not make them happy — not if England, France and Germany are to combine against Russia. But if so why did they let Russia take a part of Poland, and then to offset that, tie up with Turkey! It seems lunatic — or maybe it is just too ably crafty for me to grasp. . . . I will have to wait and try to sense what really is afoot, if anything good is afoot. . . .

"Out here there appears to be a real fear that Ham and Eggs will win. I don't know, but I would vote for it as a protest. This state — the money crowd — is so savagely fascist. It would like a money dictator. Their cruelty to labor and [the] poverty is really infuriating. Because of it, I have taken up with all radical protests and speak to the CIO, Newspaper Guild and other groups whenever asked. I have even devised a technical worker-leader procedure which might help labor defeat capital. It has already been endorsed by the local Newspaper Guild. . . .

"Not strange to say I can't learn to like Los Angeles. It is too luxury conscious; too greedy for a petty little measure of social precedence. Its so-called radicals are soft and lazy. I'll get out presently and go back to Manhattan Island, or Connecticut, near Stamford, or maybe Old Bedford. I like it there. Love and good luck, T.D."

During November of 1939, correspondence between us continued to be frequent and lengthy.

"Yours was a grand letter," I began in my answer (November
13), "encouraging to me, for it shows how earnestly you are trying to see through the fog of censorship and propaganda and
piece fragments of facts together. As for your article, 'Dawn is
in the East', you did not send it to me — unless 'Civilization.
Where? What?' is the same one. If it is a different one, I wish I
might see a copy of the one published in *Pravda*—that's great . . .

"At present I feel pretty gloomy about the state of our own
democracy. In less than three months, we have almost completely lost freedom of the press and radio, and free speech is in
a precarious condition."

"I'm so glad you sent me that UP dispatch about the Dean of
Canterbury. Good for the Dean — and in Westminster Abbey,
too! The British press is not as venomous against Russia as
ours. . . . When are you coming East? I'll be going to California
Jan. 1st — I'm so proud of all your help to the oppressed there."

I mailed another letter to TD the very next day. I had just received one from Franklin Folsom, Executive Secretary of the
League of American Writers. I wrote: "It seems there is a bitter
fight on policy now going on in the League, centering around
the Soviet-Nazi Pact. Mr. Folsom had an unofficial suggestion
to make that you write a letter addressed to American writers
and send it to Folsom, he thinks the National Board would like
to print it in the Bulletin. He is not authorized to solicit con-
tributions. Perhaps one letter to American writers could be
sent to the *N.Y. Times,* or the *New Republic,* or *Nation*; then
the League could reprint it in their Bulletin. It's all for the
Cause," I concluded.

I did not have a direct reply to my two letters, but TD wrote
(December 19, 1939):

"I have been intending to write and thank you for all the
light you gave me but I have been busy working locally for the
Cause, speaking, as well as doing my own work. These militant social equities certainly do drive one hard — and I don't
mind. I wish to do it. But it crowds one." Dreiser went on in
fervent language, "Just now the world is truly depressing to

me. The vast volume of lies! The corporation plotting for a dictatorship! The inhuman cruelty to labor! The war and death involved! I talk all the time — violently — and write. But one voice! One person! The leisure classes the world over seem to have banded together to saddle themselves on the backs of slaves. Roosevelt looks to me like a willing tool. And except for a very few there are no forthright writers. Even the late Heywood Broun is sneered at in the obituaries an an 'unsound' one, at best favoring the 'Communist slavery'.

"I hope your all right. I know how you feel! Are you here on the Coast or in Bridgeport? Let me know. I'd like to see you a lot. Love. T.D."

Dreiser was continuing his lecture tours late in 1939 and into 1940. He lectured in Washington D.C. for the Committee for American Friendship and in New York for the American Peace Mobilization (APM), to which I belonged. Besides, he was talking on radio networks.

In *My Life with Dreiser* (p. 271), Helen tells how he replied to the literary critics who belittled his propagandistic pamphleteering and soap-box lecturing, and reproached him for not producing another novel since *The American Tragedy*.

"How can one more novel mean anything," he demanded, "in this catastrophic period through which the world is passing? No, I must write on economics."

It was then that he began work on his book, *America Is Worth Saving*.

The confusion about Dreiser's two articles, "Civilization" and "Dawn Is in the East" was cleared up when I received the latter. "Dawn" is missing from my files (perhaps I had to return it to TD). However, my letter to him acknowledging it (November 26) gives some inkling of its contents:

"I was glad to get your article, 'Dawn Is in the East.' I see that it is quite different from and much better than 'Civilization.' You said some very good things and I don't wonder that *Pravda* printed it in full. Mentioning all the practical accomplishments of the Soviet Union, which the capitalist countries are so silent about, was very effective. So also the reference to Winston Churchill's prediction of its early collapse."

I went on to write about the incidents on the Soviet-Finnish border, and the encouragement given the Finns by the British and American governments.

"The truth is," I wrote, having done my homework and prepared an article for the *Nation* with the title, "Reunion in Finland" (this time flatly rejected), "that Finland is the one remaining possibility as a base for military operations against the Soviet Union. Russia has destroyed the other bases in the Balkans and Baltic States. The Mannerheim Line was built with British capital. A bitterly anti-Soviet regime had been maintained in Finland since 1918 . . .

"It is not 'little Finland' that 'big Russia' fears," I went on to explain, rather fatuously fearing that Dreiser might not be aware of this, "but other big powers which might use the Mannerheim Line as a base of attack. They seem to agree on one thing – that the real enemy is communism, and they are rehearsing now for a war to crush it."

On November 28 the Soviet Union denounced the nonaggression pact with Finland, and two days later Soviet troops invaded Finland and Soviet planes bombed Finnish cities. Meanwhile, letters between TD and me were few, but Theodore Dreiser was not idle. On January 9, 1940, he sent me a copy of his reply to a telegram he had received on January 8 from Fred Smith, Finnish Relief Fund, Inc., asking him, at the request of Herbert Hoover, to write an article on the Finnish situation for distribution to 1200 cooperating newspapers.

Dreiser's reply was sent the next day:

> Dear Mr. Smith: As is generally known, I hope, I am not just another American propaganda sucker. Relief for the Finns might be well enough in its way providing there had been any relief for the bombed and starved *democratic* Spaniards in 1934-35. Did Mr. Hoover speak for them then? Or for the Mussolini-murdered Abyssinians in 1934-35? And American money and supplies for them then or for the Chinese . . . consecutively murdered and still being murdered by the Japanese since 1933 and on? On the contrary, we continue to arm Japan – not the Chinese – and no propaganda about that.
>
> As bad as anything I recall is the fact that in 1932 when the American Veterans of the World War invaded Washington to de-

mand financial relief for themselves, their wives and children (that was the worst year of the Depression) it was Mr. Hoover who turned out the army with tanks and machine guns to dislodge them! And since then, I have not heard him nor any of his political and economic associates pleading for financial equity for the millions of jobless and starving Americans.... On the contrary, the cry now is: (1) for economic if not military relief for the poor Finns; (2) economic and financial relief for our financiers and industrialists—their banks, corporations, families (lower taxes, that is), but by implication more taxation for the masses.... As for taxing the labor machines which throw out men and women workers, and so pour constantly increasing profits into the pockets of the owners—taxing them so much per man power according to the number of human workers they displace (a tax I have advocated for some time)—not a word from anyone. Yet the justice of it is obvious. And far more important than pouring more American millions into more European wars the while Americans starve....

In view of this," Dreiser concluded, "I beg leave to suggest adding one more slogan to our already very large collection: AMERICAN RELIEF FOR AMERICANS FIRST. It will aid ten or fifteen millions Americans as opposed to a possible million Finns. For certainly the entire 3½ million population cannot be down and out already. If our papers do not lie, and of course they never lie, it is the Russians who seem to need help against the Finns. *Signed* Theodore Dreiser.

Two weeks later, this blossoming pamphleteer sent me a copy of a letter he had received from Adelaide Bean, secretary of the Theater Arts Committee in New York City (January 19, 1940), welcoming his "brilliant reply" to the Hoover Committee and informing him that "We plan to reprint and distribute 5,000 copies for the benefit of our co-workers in the entertainment field who have been deprived by the newspapers of the privilege of reading it." Enclosed was a copy of the Committee's statement to the press, in the name of 2500 professionals in the entertainment industries. Dreiser was asked to lend his name to a committee for the restoration of the Federal Theater.

Dreiser replied January 22, 1940:

Dear Miss Bean: Certainly print the 5000. If you have any left I would be glad to have fifty of them... As regards lending my name to your committee, yes, you may use my name. However, I have never agreed with the original plan for control and direction of this movement for the restoration of the Federal Theater. My idea is ... to create, as a part of the Presidential Cabinet, a Secretary of the Arts. So many phases of the art necessities of the country could in that way be reached and encouraged ... than certainly can be assured by state, regional or local adminstration. In the first place, a Cabinet Secretary for the Arts would be nationally observed. . . . His word would have weight. To such a secretary one could look rightly for the establishment of grand opera in every city of regional import in the country. He could ... bring about endowments and maintenance of Federal opera houses ... as well as Federal theaters and schools for acting, singing. . . . Certainly, he could bring into existence in regions which cannot now afford them, circulating art and literary exhibits, which would aesthetically educate and entertain millions who are not now reached in this way.

"Best of all, as I see it, such an office would tend to offset ... the social and economic aggressiveness of trade and commerce – the Big Business standard of money and what it should be used for by Government; its present-day insistence on its private right to the collection and control and distribution by *it* of our national economy and all its objectives ... I should like to see your Federation endorse this idea ... Yours very truly, Theodore Dreiser.

Letters between us were less frequent during this confusing period of the phony war, when Theodore Dreiser was turning out crusading literature by the bushel, and I too was not idle.

On January 26, 1940, Russian troops began to crack the Mannerheim Line.

TD's letter on February 3 explained why he had not written a personal message for some time. "Since your letter came and longer, I've spent 10 days in bed with a cold. Only today I'm up. . . . Things are moving fast and badly toward war, I think, and U.S. as the treasury from which the money will be drawn. . . . I do all I can but our Christian Americans and the Catholic Church and the Plunder Bund will get us in. I never doubt it for a minute. I'm off Roosevelt for life. This country is splitting into well-outlined camps and I'm for the underdog.

"By the way, do you read *The People's World?* If not, do so. Its published in S. F. and also here. It's the best workers' paper, or let us say equity paper, I ever read. It's amazingly informed, sane, vigorous, and fights as such a paper should fight today.

You will be delighted with it and you may be working for it soon. I'm so grateful for it, and I'm so tired of namby-pamby liberals. They give me a headache. I sent a copy of my Hoover letter to the Federal Theater group. . . . It has been re-printed by a dozen papers. I'm enclosing a letter they wrote me and my suggestion for a National Secretary of the Arts. Tell me if you agree with that."

A letter from Helen (dated February 15), confused me concerning the period in which he was alleged to have been confined to his bed: "Mr. Dreiser just dictated the enclosed from his bed where he has been confined for three weeks. The doctors say he will be able to regain his health again, but, they say, he will have to be very careful for a while."

I worried about his illness and was relieved to receive a letter from him (February 27):

"Up and working for a while today," the letter ran. "Sorry I couldn't write before. Wanted to send this $5 so you could buy stamps for your pamphlet. If I make some real money out here I'll collect a small staff of researchers and fighting writers and do a little propagandizing on my own. . . ."

"Recently," he continued, "I suggested, financed and am going to sponsor a collection of items which will run under the head of England and Democracy. It begins with England under the Romans and comes right down to Bermuda. . . . It includes about 16 or 18 brief summaries – England and the French Revolution, England and the Boers, England and India, England and Africa, China, U.S., etc. When I get copies I'll send one. . . .

"Am getting better," TD went on cheerily. "May be out and around in 10 days, I hope. Write me. . . . I intend to come up to S.F. and will see you – if I may. I love your 'Dear Comrade' – Remember the *Tovarish* waiters fighting in the Rostov restaurant? I am delighted to see the Russians pounding the Finns. . . . They'll take Finland (I hope) and maybe hang Baron Mannerheim (I hope)."

On March 12, 1940, Russia and Finland signed an armistice which ceded eastern Finland to the Soviet Union in exchange for Karelia.

In his next letter, Dreiser enclosed a telegram from Jessica Smith, editor of *Soviet Russia Today*, dated March 15, asking him to "join a number of leading Americans in writing several hundred words for publication in answer to the question 'do you believe the cause of international peace has been furthered and the possibility of spreading the world war reduced by the outcome of the Soviet-Finnish conflict?'"

A leaflet containing his answer was enclosed with the telegram. It was far more than "several hundred words." However, I give only a few excerpts:

CONCERNING DIVES AND LAZARUS

No, I do not believe so – not as long as England can get any additional sucker countries or enslaved colonies to do her fighting for her . . . The poor Finns undoubtedly thought they were once more saving the world for Democracy when they allowed England, France and Germany . . . to build and furnish her Mannerheim Line for her. But she was mistaken. This kind of service on the part of England was another little trick to use Finland as a corridor through which England (and her European allies) could attack Russia, and at the same time bring the U.S. running.

Poor little Finland! Enormous, horrible, imperialist Russia! The only country that has given the working class – not the loafing class – a break. And the ignorant Finns, led by a bought and paid for governing group, had to die for that. The building of the Mannerheim Line by small Finland – population 3,400,000 – is not to be explained by either the fears or the resources of such a population. . . . Belgium allowed England to build one for her in 1912 to keep the Germans out and spent four years under Germany's heel for her pains.

But why should England wish to attack Russia?. . . In the Russian Soviet system, England, for the first time in her history, has met a new power which she really fears and wishes to destroy . . . and to that end she has already sacrificed Democratic Spain, Socialist Austria, Democratic Czechoslovakia, Capitalist Poland and Democratic Finland – all under the guise of saving democracy. . . .

By April 1940 Dreiser was apparently himself again. This was still the period of the phony war which had followed the invasion of Poland. England had declared war on Germany in fulfillment of her obligation to Poland, but had taken no military action against the Nazis. Instead, during the Finnish War, both Britain and France had shown their hostility to the Soviet Union by helping Finland with arms and volunteers and by causing Soviet Russia to be expelled from the League of Nations.

Only after German troops had invaded Holland, Belgium and Luxembourg did the British army march. Chamberlain's appeasement policy collapsed and Winston Churchill formed a new cabinet. Heroic English troops were evacuated from Dunkirk. The treasonable French leaders allowed German troops to occupy Paris in June, without a struggle. Finally, in August, the bombing of London became a horrible reality for Western Europe.

3. *Crusader against War and the British Empire*

During the period from September 1939 to a year later, Dreiser's crusading on behalf of the Soviet Union rose to a fever pitch, as his frequent letters and enclosures to me indicated. He saw things in plain black and white, at once naive and realistic. He was so convinced of the treachery of "perfidious Albion" during the Chamberlain regime that he saw Hitler as a counterweight to Britain's double-dealing. He believed the Soviet-Nazi Pact was the ultimate defensive move against the Munich Pact which had given Czechoslovakia to Hitler. He still clung to the hope that the pact, which had delayed the German attack, would save Russia from a Nazi invasion.

On April 3, TD wrote me about his return to active duties, but he did not feel sure he would be strong enough to fill a speaking engagement on the 20th. "I was in bed six weeks and seem to be pulling back not so fast—although up and around. I write well enough at a desk, but walking out is not the stimulating thing it was. . . .

"I'm so glad you like the Dives and Lazarus thing. It will be in this month's *Soviet Russia Today*. But I've had calls for it here and there—for fifty's and twenty-five's. Just today the Book of the Day Shop, a sort of Left of Center book store, called

for 1000, and 500 of this thing on World War I I'm enclosing.
The shop is paying the printer for them! The manager of the
place said he hung up a copy of Dives and Lazarus and there
was such a crowd around it all the time, he decided to give it
away and have its readers go outside. The newspapers are so
completely closed to any but the corporation side that the
public has no place to go to learn what they want to know. If
only I had one or two hundred such left-center book stores or
meeting places throughout the country I might win a large
number of people to our way of thinking. If you know of any
names of places to send any and will furnish me the list, I'll
send them, or I'll furnish copies and money for stamps and
envelopes, and you send them.

"This war is such a trying affair. It has so many people
stirred up and worrying. And now the capitalist gangsters are
taking over the KKK, turning it loose on the so-called Reds.
Next comes a good beating or burning for some of us. But here's
luck. And that we don't go under.

"And Roosevelt! And his promising to bring this country
into the war on the Allied side! Well, love and best wishes. TD."

His April 19 letter was in the same vein. He had sent me the
hundred copies of his leaflet, "War," but was so pushed by work
that he couldn't write. "Besides my own stuff I have any number of requests for statements from all sorts of organizations —
to help China, Spain, the Poles, the Finns, the Red Cross — to
say nothing of Birth Control, cancer victims, lepers, consump-
tives, the Negro and share croppers. . . . It is really more than
one person can do. . . . Above all, it makes clear the mental and
emotional turmoil holding all over the world and the enormous
suffering and need. Just now I am asked to say, 'How can libraries and librarians best help to keep America out of war and
preserve American Democracy?' But I'm sure I don't know. Do
you? I wish I did. . . . I'm so sorry you have to go back in
May. . . . If I feel strong enough, I hope to run up. But will
I . . . ? *P.S.* Cablegram from Russia today. Pravda wanting an
article on Unemployment here."

The leaflet "War" was not lengthy by Theodore Dreiser's
standards. Every word is as true today as it was in April 1940.
It might well have been written by him today had he lived to

speak out against the Vietnam War—substituting the United States for the Third Reich—or had he lived to speak out militantly against the intolerable conditions of the blacks and the poor whites at home. Dreiser wrote:

> This war business is very like the sword that, up to the arrival of gunpowder, it wielded. Personally, I still believe in self-defense which is obviously the proper answer to Predatory war. But I also believe in the defense of others against inequity either by themselves or by the social and legal forces which they erect in order to see that they (the victims of inequity) are legally and honestly defended. Hence, I believe in Constitutions, Bills of Rights, and their fulfillment by just laws, honest representative bodies, honest courts, honest juries and an honest and decent police system designed to protect all the people in their constitutional rights—not in any sense to misuse or prey on them. And I have always felt that these things are worth fighting for.
>
> I also believe that it is not only human and natural for the strong... to come to the rescue of the weak when and where they feel them to be the victims of predatory crooks, robbers and murderers. And where the strong are either absent or indifferent to the sufferings of the weak I believe it to be the proper wisdom as well as duty of those who are weak individually to combine in order to be able to drive off their powerful and predatory enemies....
>
> Life is and ever must be an equation or balance between all sorts of contending forces.... Neither chemically nor physically, socially nor financially can it be workably run off into unbalance. In chemistry and physics explosions follow—disastrous and frightful to behold. And of humanity... assembled under forms of government, the same is true. Where... a few, because of extorted wealth, set themselves apart and above the many... you have (1) revolution and so a restoration of balance, or (2) where equity is defeated and inequity prevails you have the death of that nation. If you do not believe this, consider Rome that declined and fell with the arrival of the Caesars; Italy that plundered up to the days of Mussolini; monarchical France that ended with the French Revolution; autocratic Russia that ended with the Russian Revolution... autocratic China that ended with the Boxer Rebellion.... Wars spring from the greed and inequity of individuals, and the oppression and resulting enforced ignorance and weakness of the masses. Yet the greedy and subtle individuals who, lacking wisdom, set themselves apart from the welfare, education and comfort of the masses, do nothing more than bring about the misery and inefficiency of the masses, and so most certainly their own national and individual decay and death....

And wars—I mean predatory wars—are never anything more than brigand adventures. Where they succeed for a time... they bring about nothing more than rival brigandage on the part of others who are fools enough to believe that stolen goods are better than earned goods.... They have not brains enough to know that it has never worked. The government that truly succeeds and lives is an orderly and equitable one....

Again, on June 8, he wrote that it was nice to hear from me but was sorry I had escaped East—"which excludes the Evangeline-Gabriel arrangement..." (Our little joke, since we were always missing one another in our trips back and forth across the continent. I had not seen him since our meeting in San Francisco in Feburary 1939.)

"There is so much pro-ally and anti-labor uproar around here," he went on, "that I scarcely know what to think. I speak my mind rather freely, but I'm beginning to receive caustic letters from former liberals who now see the presence of a 5th column here. Also that the Communists are a menace to our noble form of democracy. You can guess how bad it is here when I tell you that the city has recalled the red-baiter, Hines, to deal with the communist and subversive labor menace! I may not be in for any personal trouble but I wonder. I once exchanged a number of hard words with Hines face to face in San Francisco....

"How are you getting along with your writing.... I always feel that you have a realistic novel or two in your keeping that you could write if you would, but that you do not like to deal realistically with life. Am I wrong? Anyhow, it's nice to hear from you and between your social reform labors you should crowd in a letter to me. Love, T.D."

In a letter from Hollywood dated July 20, TD wrote that while he would remain in the Los Angeles area that summer and winter, he expected to take a trip to New York to pack and ship some furniture and books. "Also to store some library material with the University of Pennsylvania. I won't stay very long, I'll get in touch with you....

"Here's one more Social Snack—and in case you want more copies to mail I enclose 6 more.... You could write several swell realistic novels if you would. But if your going to worry over 'what people will say' – well, goodbye. Realism isn't turned out with conventionalism in mind. If you doubt it read Shakespeare. Yes, I'm 'hactive'. Spoke Thursday night here. Again Sunday night. Love, T.D."

The "social snack" which he enclosed in several copies was a printed leaflet containing a copy of the appeal he had received from Boys Brotherhood of New York, Inc. for Aid for Slum Children, dated July 10, 1940:

"Dear Mr. Dreiser: Mister, can I have some fresh air? Lady, will you treat me to some sunshine for a few weeks? It will be only $1. a day because I do lots of the camp work myself. . . . A little green grass – a few trees – maybe a swim and a game of baseball without dodging cars. . . . It doesn't cost much to send these kids to camp – Will you help by returning the enclosed folder with your check?"

Below the appeal on the leaflet was TD's reply (July 16, 1940):

S. Bayard Colgate
Chairman of the Board
Dear Mr. Colgate: Your letter requesting money to aid the children of the N.Y. slums to get a two weeks' vacation in the country is, of course, moving and worthy of a national response – particularly since the conditions you describe are not confined to New York alone. . . . Like you I have known about them all my life in New York and elsewhere in America – "the dirty crowded streets – the cramped tenements – the heat in the city – humidity – baking – sweltering. Kids playing in the gutters, chasing balls under trucks, swimming in the garbage-laden Hudson or East River, panting on fire escapes on sultry nights. . . ."

However, since all of this is so general, I am moved to ask you why you do not approach Mr. Roosevelt in connection with this problem. I suggest this because Mr. Roosevelt is planning to spend 14 billion dollars to build battleships and aeroplanes and to organize an army of young Americans to defend this country against all its possible anti-democratic enemies of the future – strong, healthy, patriotic and brave young Americans. So the kids of your slums will be those soldiers of tomorrow. Yet here you are appealing to individual Americans to shoulder this burden. Rather it is the business of the National Government to do this. . . . Anyhow, why not ask Congress to tax me and you and Mr. and Mrs. Roosevelt and all others, including our sixty families, in order to raise money to abolish these conditions *now*. Theodore Dreiser.

Apparently, TD was in one of his retrospective moods when he wrote me October 11, 1940:

"Sometimes I wonder if all of us are not being distracted and blown out of our true courses by this economic dog fight which is all that it is. Wealth fighting poverty first and then, once successful, turning to fight rival wealth. But all are agreed to maintain the scarcity-plenty arrangement. . . . What a filthy set-up. And when, what I really want to do is to write a novel. . . ."

I could understand that sense of loss a writer feels when he is impelled to leave his unfinished manuscript to join a social crusade. With a sigh for the neglected literary work, he returned to his crusading:

"Believe it or not," he continued, "I have just completed and am now reading the proofs of a social battle book, which I have entitled, 'Is Democracy Worth Saving?', 90,000 words. Veritas Press, N.Y. $2. for clothbound, $1.50, paper bound. However, large quantities are to be sold to the American Peace Mobilization and other organizations for $1, and are to be distributed at that price. Of course I will send you one as a gift. You will have to read it to get its import. . . . I've thought of you a lot but thought also that you could not find time for me. But how glad I'd be to see you. As always, T.D."

Early the following year, the same book was published by Modern Age Books under the title *American Is Worth Saving*. In a review by William German in the San Francisco *Chronicle* (February 9, 1941), the final paragraph read:

"Using the novel as his medium, Theodore Dreiser has long been obsessed with the cruelties of life. Now, forsaking the novel for the soap box, he is still obsessed with the same cruelties. He did better with the novel."

"Poor Dreiser," torn between the novel and the crusade, sent me an "autographed" copy of the script in advance of a speech to be broadcast over the Mutual Network (Los Angeles Station KHJ, November 1, 1940), introducing the Communist presidential candidate, Earl Browder. (In presenting

Dreiser, the announcer stated that "Mr. Dreiser speaks as an independent voter and guest of the Communist party.)

I am here because like millions of other Americans I am frustrated by the political set-up which denies me the right to vote as I choose — that is, to keep us out of war. I happen to know that in this particular election we are being robbed of that freedom of choice... by the corporations and the men who own and control the industries of the country.... The people are concerned about conscription, about the determination of our rulers to defend the British Empire in every quarter of the globe — that's what they have a right to vote on. But what do we find? We find that the two major political parties have agreed not to disagree on that matter. They have agreed not to argue or differ on the question of foreign policy.... So we are deprived of the right of choice, the right of free debate, the right of a decision in the most important crisis of the nation.... Our American lords of big business.... are using every means to bar minority parties from the ballot. I am not a Communist, and I don't agree with the entire program of the Communist Party. But I can read; and I know that here in America the Communist Party has come out against the war ... that they attempt to face the problems of our own people, of how to put our people back to work, how to wipe out hunger amid plenty, of how to spread some of the vast wealth among the people who produce it. As a result, the Communist Party is being gagged; I think it's outrageous to tell you or me we can't vote for the Communist, or any other candidates we want to vote for ... the only way is to vote a protest vote. In twenty-four states there is no anti-war party to vote for. So in those states strike out the names of candidates on the ticket and write the names of candidates you do favor. That will register your protest until such time as we independents here in America can organize a party strong enough to force itself on the ballot.... I know the Communist candidate. He is an honest and able man, and I consider it a privilege to introduce him.

> (*Signed*) Theodore Dreiser His X mark.

TD wrote jestingly that he had signed the important document so that I could auction it off in fund-raising for the "Cause."

I answered promptly (October 26, 1940), thanking him for the signed "document" and assuring him it had brought a pretty penny at the fund-raising party in Bridgeport for the American Peace Mobilization.

I added that the full-page ad in the *New York Times* by the Committee on Election Rights was heartening. "There was your name, big as life. . . . I'm enclosing the page in case you did not see it. Keep it if you'd like a copy for your files. If not, I'd appreciate your signature on it to auction. . . . I also have a signed copy of your letter to the Finnish Relief Committee. . . . Now that should be worth something.

"Then if you'd send me a signed copy of your recent letter to *Editor and Publisher* on a free press, I'd auction all three. I know you have many admirers around here, and many expressed enthusiasm for that letter on freedom of the press. . . .

"Ruth McKenney will be present and I thought we could make the auction amusing and exciting, with some of the signed papers. . . . In any case, I'd like some copies of that *Free Press* letter. Yes, you sent me the letter about the slums. . . ."

I closed with, "The question is not do I have time for you, but how, in the midst of your varied and active life you find time for me. I am grateful for your letters. As ever, lovingly,"

"To me the meaning of the USSR in the world today seems so obvious that I wonder how anyone with a little social wisdom or sense of equity can miss its import."

Thirteen years after his Russian tour, these were the opening words of Theodore Dreiser's article in the November 1940 issue of *Soviet Russia Today,* hailing the Soviet Union on its 23rd anniversary:

"Then to what can one attribute the vast amount of misunderstanding and consequential opposition?" he asked. "The answer is ignorance of the masses, who, subsequent to the ten days that shook the world, have been treated to an uninterrupted barrage of lies by those who were and still are in the seats of the mighty in other lands; but who were in 1917 shaken to their finger and toe nails by the spectacle of the Russian royalty . . . crashing from their thrones . . . and this, praise God, finally came to pass . . . in 1917 . . . in the face of a world of imperialist plotting . . . a constant defamatory propaganda on the part of the agents, and hired liars of wealth. . . . Today you have a never-ending downpour of lies and misrepresentations concerning this vast program — now no longer an experiment, but a proved success affecting the health, education and social welfare . . . of 200 million people, who no longer face enforced ignorance, hunger, and social degradation, but the marvelous privilege of working one for all and all for one."

"And," continued Theodore Dreiser, who, 13 years before had loyally defended the free-enterprise system in the offices of Soviet political and industrial leaders, "it is the implication of this fact, written large over one-sixth of the earth, that has evoked the screams of fear and hate that today fill the capitalistic and imperialist world press. . . . For they now know that the day of artificial scarcity is over. Science and invention have established the certainty of that. Also, that however much they seek to hold, not only the necessities but the comforts of life from the millions in order that they, these miserable defective few, may shine as lords of money and privileges — they cannot prevail. . . . Not much longer will hundreds of millions of pounds of coffee, meat, fruit, cotton, wheat, corn, be either destroyed or held back from the markets of the world in order that these few may stuff themselves with food while the rest starve. Not much longer."

At the end of 1940, TD was occupied with moving from Mt. Kisco, New York. He had bought a house on King's Road in Hollywood and spent some time in moving furniture and effects from Iroki and placing them in the new home. He also landscaped the garden. It seems this was his last and his most loved home.

Early in 1941, I saw him in New York at a meeting of the League of American Writers. My husband and another couple were with me. Surprised to see me there, he came over to us and met Frank for the first time. He sat beside us for the rest of the evening. Afterward, he took me to meet Marguerite Tjader Harris. Much earlier, he had tried to arrange a meeting between us. Greeting her at last, I regretted the lost opportunity to work with her as our mutual friend had suggested.

Dreiser's book *America Is Worth Saving*, documenting the reasons for his bitter condemnation of Great Britain's imperialism was published at this time. Among the unenthusiastic reviews, most of them bemoaning the great American novelist's "forsaking the novel for the soapbox," the two-column comment by Granville Hicks (*Saturday Review*, February 22, 1941) was relatively objective. This, in spite of his being one of the liberals who turned against the Soviet Union after the pact with Nazi Germany. He admitted that while the book "adds nothing to Dreiser's stature, it does, however, break a ten-years' silence."

Mr. Hicks meant, of course, as did the other critics, that social tracts are not "literature." In fact, they had ignored the same material published by a left-wing press and sponsored by a peace organization, under the title, *Is Democracy Worth Saving?* Considering the large number of his published pamphlets, leaflets, articles and a critical study of Thoreau, the "ten-years' silence" was clamorous, to say the least.

But Mr. Hicks went on to concede that, "With much of the book many persons will agree . . . that capitalism has demonstrated its inefficiency, that poverty in an age of abundance is ridiculous and criminal, that democracy must solve the problem of full production and equitable distribution . . . Dreiser dislikes capitalism, but there is something he hates more— England . . . 'this black spider of the nations' . . . Moreover, his account of the role of British—and American—capitalism in contributing to the rise of fascism is substantially accurate. No one serves democracy by ignoring these facts."

Hicks' reference in the review to the "Soviet Union, of which he (Dreiser) thinks well" is a gross understatement of Dreiser's regard for the first socialist society. After what he saw there, he had come to believe that socialism was the ultimate solution to imperialist crimes and starvation in the midst of plenty. His hatred of England, on the other hand, was not just blind hatred of a government. He was beginning to perceive the pattern of imperialism as defined by Lenin—an apparatus for sucking wealth out of the underdeveloped countries in the name of religion and democracy.

One of the few favorable reviews of *America Is Worth Saving* was by Richard Ramsey in the *New Dealer* (May 1, 1941):

" 'Stay out of this imperialist war!' " Dreiser cries. "Without slandering the people of England, he gives chapter and verse of the brutal, undemocratic, arrogant history of the British ruling class ... Nor does Dreiser spare Hitler, nor the Fascists of France, nor the enemies of the people everywhere. They're all in this book, named by name ... the ... parasitic millionaires."

THEODORE DREISER
116 W. 11ᵗʰ St
N.Y.C

Jan 24 - 38

Dear Ruth:

I know you think I don't give you many thoughts or I'd write oftener - at least answer your letters promptly. But its not true. your - I think of you much - year in and year out - because of your vivid, restless, searching, brooding temperament. For me your mind

[wavy line]

I hope you are ok. Write me when you can. Love.

T.D.

A letter from TD to the author.

CHAPTER IV:

Hitler Invades the Soviet Union

1. Dreiser Modifies His Views on Germany

A few months after our meeting in New York, the German Wehrmacht, the mightiest army in history — unscathed by the "phony war" — invaded the Soviet Union. Securely intrenched in Czechoslovakia's Bohemia (thanks to Munich), they struck through Poland. For Theodore Dreiser the collapse of the Soviet-Nazi Pact was a bitter disillusionment. His courage and honesty in admitting that he had been mistaken about Germany's intentions compare favorably with the light rebukes liberal critics aimed at Chamberlain at the time of the Munich deal. To liberals, Chamberlain's pact with Hitler was a personal act of "appeasement," but they were not disillusioned about the nature of the British government. On the other hand, Russia's countermove a year later turned liberals like Granville Hicks against the Soviet government for life.

Granville Hicks recently wrote a very favorable review of Swanberg's biography of Dreiser, under the heading, "A Liar in Search of the Truth" (*Saturday Review,* April 24, 1965). Agreeing with Swanberg's derisive reference to Dreiser's support of the Soviet Union, Hicks wrote:

"As Swanberg says, and others have said before him, Dreiser's interest in Communism was religious in character, reflecting both his political blindness and his humanitarian aspirations. Liar that he was, in his serious work he was always fumbling his way toward the truth."

It is true that "fumbling his way toward the truth" through the lies and treachery of Britain and France, Theodore Dreiser saw the "phony war" and later the delay in opening a second front as a strategy to destroy the Soviet power and at the same time weaken the military strength of their common foe. Although he suffered "various unpleasantnesses," Dreiser never retreated from his heretical views on the Soviet Union.

Theodore Dreiser was the first of the distinguished American writers who cabled best wishes to the Red Army after the Nazi attack. The 50th anniversary issue of the Moscow journal *Foreign Literature* (May 1967) published the text of several of these cablegrams. This is my translation of the Russian text of Dreiser's greeting:

> To the Union of Soviet Writers, July 1941: Nothing in the history of mankind, not the insane adventurism in search of power and glory; not the terrible mass extermination of the people and their enslavement by Darius, Alexander, Caesar, Attila, Genghis Khan, Tamerlane, Napoleon—can equal by their senseless, barbaric devastation and massacre the unprovoked aggression of Hitler against Soviet Russia since the Soviet Union is the one country which, at last, has set up a just and generally progressive form of government.
>
> I consider the aggression of Hitler a monstrous wrong—in the fullest sense of the word—against a great power. This is a cold-blooded and criminal effort to destroy the freedom of mankind—and what is more serious—spiritual and social justice in the family of nations, such as no other people, no other race anywhere, any time, has dreamed of.
>
> These crimes must be cut short and their initiators and perpetrators must be conquered and punished in public for their crimes. We see how England, for her own self-preservation, comes to the aid of Russia. As for America, I together with millions of other Americans will call upon our government not only to defend the road to peace by aiding Russia now but also for a better understanding of this great democracy which has done more for its millions of progressive people during this brief period of its existence than America has done for its people.

Among the writers whose telegrams appeared in this issue of *Foreign Literature* were Ernest Hemingway, Upton Sinclair, Lion Feuchtwanger and Hewlett Johnson.

The Dean of Canterbury wrote: "I grieve for your great sacrifice. Deeply admire the wonderful manhood and strength of the great Russian people carrying the banner of civilization in the struggle against fascism. Complete confidence in your certain victory and your unfailing effort to the end."

Hemingway expressed "100% solidarity with the Soviet Union in their fight to defend all peoples against fascist enslavement."

In the anxious months following the Nazi invasion, my correspondence with Theodore Dreiser was neglected. I was too busy writing stories for young people about Russia, which now found a ready market. I also took time off to argue with liberals who expected, along with American and British imperialists that the mightiest army in the world would cut through Russia "like a knife through butter" — and secretly or subconsciously hoped they would.

When I did write from my brother's home in Amarillo, Texas, where my aging mother was now living, a reply from TD (December 3, 1941) came promptly. The blue letterhead indicated a change of address to 1015 N. King's Road, Hollywood:

"It's nice to get the latest news to date concerning you. I have assumed that you were in Bridgeport. You looked and spoke so well at the Writers League meeting that I assumed everything was going well at least. I have been supporting Russia so earnestly that I have attracted the personal attention of Mr. Dies. Just the other day, because Prof. F. V. Harper of the Indiana University Law School chose to introduce me at Indianapolis, his committee announced it would investigate him and seek his removal. I think he is the Dean of the school. I think Dies has given up on me because I always emphasize our Free Press, Radio, Movies. Also Mr. Dies' right to have his say so, whether paid for by the corporations or not...."

2. Japanese Attack Pearl Harbor

Suddenly, after what was obviously a lapse of a few days, TD started a new paragraph with: "As I write this I am pausing to listen to Roosevelt's address to the American people calling for war against Japan. Only yesterday came the news of the bombardment of Pearl Harbor and the death of 5000 Americans. I can imagine your reactions and you can imagine mine...."

"I think they expect to drive us out of the Philippines, and Asia and the South Seas," Dreiser's letter continued, "but I hope we pay them out and so help Russia and China." TD added, "Anyhow, I'm in a troubled and contentious frame of mind. So I won't see you this winter. Sorry! Better luck next time. I always recall our days in Russia together with so much pleasure. Write me when you are moved to do so. . . ."

After the United States entered the war, correspondence between us lapsed for a time. I had little time for letter writing. But it did not occur to me that Dreiser's silence might be my fault until, in reply to my belated letter, he gently reproached me for not writing.

After the collapse of his hopes for Soviet-Nazi collaboration in a constructive program, he did feel personally betrayed by Germany's breaking the pact. Then, after Pearl Harbor, when the United States joined the other Western democracies and declared war against the Axis powers, he saw that American public opinion and U.S. war efforts were directed mainly at the Asian member of the Axis, which had so savagely attacked our navy at Pearl Harbor. He himself, always a truly patriotic American, reacted spontaneously to this direct attack.

In any case, I feared that the common cause which had bound us together—devotion to Communist Russia and hatred of its deadly enemy, fascism—might no longer be paramount.

But I was wrong. At this time he saw more clearly than many of us how tenuous was this American-Soviet friendship, how cynically based on self-interest were the oratorical utterances of Church on the night of June 22, after the German invasion, to which I myself had listened with tearful gratitude:

"No one has been a more consistent opponent of communism than I have in the last twenty-five years. I will unsay no word that I have spoken . . . But," Churchill had said, "I see the Russian soldiers standing on the threshold of their native land . . . I see them guarding their homes . . . I see the ten thousand villages where the means of existence is wrung so hardly from the soil, but . . . where maidens laugh and children play. I see advancing on all this in hideous onslaught the Nazi war machine. . . like a swarm of crawling locusts. I see the German

bombers in the sky, still smarting from many a British whipping, delighted to find what they believe is an easier and safer
prey. . . . "

Churchill went on to promise that Britain would support
Russia: "Hitler wishes to destroy the Russian power because
he hopes that if he succeeds in this, he will be able to bring
back the main strength of his Army and Air Force from the
East and hurl it upon this Island. . . ."

Even this revealing statement did not cloud my trust in
Britain's support. Yet Theodore Dreiser, in his telegram to
the Union of Soviet Writers, had commented scornfully: "We
see how England, for her own self-preservation, comes to the
aid of Russia."

As anxious months grew into years without the promised
second front, Dreiser's distrust of the British hardened. The
sneers of his old friend H. L. Mencken seemed more and more
fatuous, although the break with Mencken saddened him.

It was in this mood that he went to Toronto in September
1942 to speak at the Town Forum. As soon as he arrived in
Canada, he was interviewed and his remarks were misquoted
by the reporters. Bitterly attacked as pro-Nazi by the Writers
War Board, he was barred from speaking in Canada and expelled from the country, although he denied that he had said,
as they charged, that he wanted Hitler to "defeat and rule the
English people."

Upon his return to the United States, he made a statement
in Indianapolis (*My Life with Dreiser*, p 282):

> . . . On the basis of this report (in the newspapers) the supposed
> Dept. of Justice of Canada ordered my banishment. . . . The Writers'
> War Board . . . without taking the trouble to inquire of me what I
> had actually said . . . flew into print with the denunciation of me
> implying that I had become an ally of Hitler. . . . Ordinarily, I would
> have dismissed this for its servility to British Toryism were it not
> for two important facts: First, the great danger to our relations
> with the only peoples who have thus far thwarted the Nazis in their
> effort to conquer the world; the other, the denunciation by you,
> Pearl Buck, who also signed the Writers' War Board statement
> after you had traveled through the Far East and . . . graphically
> reported the results of our policy of business as usual. By that I

mean the bombs and gasoline we have furnished to the Japanese for over four years which have enabled them to burn the cities of China and murder their women and children. You also have seen and truthfully reported the brutal rule by the British Tories of the colonial people of the East.

How does it happen that you would sign your name to a document of this kind without inquiring as to what was actually said by me? Instead, you join the chorus that we need unity in our war effort. Unity around what? Unity around the whipping post? . . . . What essential difference is there between Hitler's firing squad in the conquered countries and Churchill's whipping post in India? . . . But you will say that we are at war and cannot offend our allies. What allies? The British Tories, who were more responsible than anyone else for bringing this holocaust on the world; or the great masses of India, Russia, China and the common people of England who heroically fought against Munich and are today giving their lives by the millions on the altar of freedom? . . . I yield to no one in my love of our country and of humanity. My record in the struggle against Nazism is too clear to need repeating, but I see in our continual tagging along behind the British policy of business as usual the ultimate defeat of our country. . . .

As I see it, there is only one way we can win this war and freedom and peace for everyone and that is by joining forces quickly with the people of Russia, India and China . . . the time has come when we must speak boldly against injustice and perfidy. . . . Why did all mention of India suddenly disappear from American newspapers the moment the American people became sincerely interested in its freedom as an honest and sensible interpretation of the Atlantic Charter, and their conception of what we are fighting for – the Four Freedoms of all peoples of the world?

As to the Churchill interpretation of his agreement with Stalin regarding a Second Front, I do not know of any American record when our country has welshed on an agreement, or explained it away by an interpretation such as that made by Churchill – to the effect that an understanding reached between Russia and England looking toward the opening of a Second Front in 1942 *did not mean that at all.* . . .

George Bernard Shaw was at his Shavian best when he came to the defense of Theodore Dreiser (*PM*, September 27, 1942):

"George Bernard Shaw said Saturday in London that the press reports he had seen concerning Theodore Dreiser's remark that he would prefer to see Germans in Britain rather than the 'horse-riding snobs' who are here now were insufficient for comment, but he added:

"'To say that Dreiser's comments regarding the war are furiously inaccurate is only to say that they are like everyone else's comments regarding the war.

"'In England we denounce crimes of the German Reich because we do not know that our British Empire has committed so many of these crimes itself that it does not become us to give ourselves moral airs unless we sincerely repent our past, a change of heart whereof we have given the world no assurance whatever. Although the English do not know their own history, Americans know it, the Irish know it, the Indians know it to their cost. There is no reason to suppose the Germans do not know it. Dreiser evidently knows it and reacts explosively when we pose as Herrenvolk exactly as Hitler does.

"'There's nothing to fuss about,' Shaw concluded cheerily. 'If Dreiser is soundly determined to see Adolph Hitler damned first, he can say what he likes about wicked old England. We can take care of ourselves with America's help, or even without it, at a pinch.'"

According to Helen (*My Life with Dreiser,* p. 285), TD was delighted at Shaw's blast at the Canadian critics. He scribbled a reply on October 10 thanking Shaw "for the kindly lifeline to the presumably drowning critic of dear old England. . . . I think it would do the dear mother-land a lot of good if we followed your hint and allowed her to save herself in just one pinch. . . . This 'hands across the sea' stuff—our hands, for instance—constantly conveying supplies eastward to the motherland, well, you know. Even children occasionally turn on an over-exacting parent. The Irish ought to know. . . . With unchanging admiration and affection, Theodore Dreiser."

3. Dreiser Concentrates on His Novels

After the very upsetting Canadian interlude, Dreiser had returned home, determined to finish *The Bulwark*. It was some time after this that I must have written him, for I have his letter (dated December 16, 1943):

"Dear Ruth: It's nice to hear from you and I hope all goes well. But your inquiry after two years of silence as to why I haven't written to you in two years rather answers itself, doesn't it, particularly since I saw and greeted you in New York two years ago and rather expected a word after that. However, no hard feelings for I felt then that you were engaged elsewhere.

"But," he added, as though to make amends for that peevish remark, "I always remember that tour that, truly apart from the delight of it with you, taught me plenty. Later I made inquiry by mail as to the whereabout of Dinamov but never learned anything. So I have troubled over the thought that some harm might have come to him and I still do. His was such a pleasing personality.

"As for me I have worked on my novel — not yet finished — and a philosophy which I will put out one of these days. I am not so hot for Los Angeles these days. It is getting too large, the distances too great and the public too movie-minded to suit me. So I stick close to my desk, read and work. And physically I appear to be alright. So.

"Write me when you feel moved to do so and I'll answer with what news I have. Incidentally, Merry Xmas and all my best wishes. T.D. Hows the boy?"

After years of feverish cooperation with peace groups to prevent the United States and the Soviet Union from becoming involved in the war with the Axis powers, he now could relax his crusading and do what he really wanted to do — write a novel. Moreover, he had never fully regained his health and former vigor after the long illness.

Some time in 1944 I evidently had written him a long letter, and when he did not reply, had followed it up with another. For he wrote me November 28, 1944, from King's Road, Hollywood:

"Thanks for your affectionate and informative letter and I note that you are still as industrious in this matter of making right triumph over wrong, good over evil, wisdom over ignorance, liberality over greed, etc., as usual. You'll never change, you have an eye single to perfection and you'll die working at the business of bringing them into being.

"As for myself, while I fight for the cause of a better world, still I take occasional time off to brood over the possibility or impossibility of it. At the same time I contribute to the Red Cross, the 6th War Loan, Russian Aid Society, save old papers, old clothes, shirts, shoes. Incidentally, I preach and fight for the cause of Russia year in and year out, to say nothing of the enslaved nations of Europe, the minor lands of which I saw so much. But I'm a poor second to you, I know that, for I have always been able to *feel* your active and enduring humanity and will die witnessing same I am sure.

"As for that long and very sweet letter you say you wrote me," TD continued, to my dismay, "nothing doing — it never arrived. Look on the upper shelf in the cupboard and you'll find it there. Meanwhile, I know that you like me (care a little) and always will. But that goes double, for I think of you plenty, not only as working for a better day for everybody in Bridgeport — but, as once upon a time, guiding and aiding me in Russia. Remember the night we left Moscow (laughing) for Kharkov leaving poor Dinamov to stare after us? . . . Well, life will be as it will be and so I enter no complaints. I'd rather try to help where I can. By the way, I have your article, The Immortal Railroad, here beside me and will read it as soon as I finish this letter. . . .

"Meanwhile, this letter is drawing to a close. I have a bundle of mail — mostly, believe it or not — papers, magazines, documents from Russia. Fortunately, I have several pro-Russian friends who read Russian and I unload all this data on them. If you were here I'd turn it over to you. Anyhow, here's long life and better days and the wish that you show up here, if for no more than a vacation. And so — with all good wishes, and the most pleasant of memories, Affectionately, T.D. By the way, whatever became of Dinamov? I addressed several letters to him but never received a reply." Again, he repeated that question to which I, sad at heart, had no reply: "Is he dead, or in prison, or what? T.D."

Dreiser's December 1944 Christmas card was in a roguish vein—a painting of a snow-banked farmhouse and barn. Inside, he wrote: "With all best wishes for 1945. This is from my winter quarters in Hollywood. I work in the barn. T.D."

TD again mentioned Sergey Dinamov, whose disappearance had long preyed on his mind, in a letter from King's Road (January 16, 1945):

"Thanks for such news as you had of Dynamov. I always liked Dynamov although I knew nothing of his private life and never imagined that you were very much drawn to him although I did feel he was very much attached to you. Now that you tell me of his exile and his probably later compulsory army service, I feel sorry for him. . . . Besides, one thing that touched me was his story of his poverty as a child. It was very sad and I have always worried over him and his fate. . . ."

This long letter ended on a cheerful note.

"Out here its warm and bright. The driving holidays are over except for an annoying cough and my annual income tax I'm doing as well as can be expected—almost better, really. and here's wishing you the same and many of them—ThD. *P.S.* I always recall with laughter (*now*) how much that woman doctor who went along with our party to look after my *health* hated me. . . . Good luck and best wishes."

Now our long correspondence was drawing to a close. On February 10, 1945, he wrote me from King's Road:

"Dear Ruth—Thanks for your letter and the story. I like the latter very much. It is so human and illuminative I don't wonder at its being bought for publication. You ought to be able to turn out a number—with your interesting life to draw from.

"I'm not feeling so well—rather run down for some reason—too little exercise, I fancy. But I'm hoping to feel better and then get my novel done. I'm glad you've decided to ignore—. He has become a bore, writing to whoever heard of me in any way. . . . Meantime, I'm hoping that some day I'll be able to meet up with you again. I'd so much like to get your present point of view. *The world seems such a mess.* [Emphasis his.]

Love and all good wishes, T.D. I may go East in May. If I do I'll get a stop-over for Bridgeport just to have another look at and talk with you."

In reply, I mentioned the great importance of the Yalta Conference decisions for the postwar world. I knew he was absorbed in finishing his books and was not following events as closely as usual. I enclosed a copy of a letter to *The Nation* on which I was working. American liberals were unhappy, of course, I commented to TD, about the "Danger" that Yalta would unconditionally restore to the USSR White Russia and part of the Ukraine, which were within the Curzon Line—the legal boundary set by the League of Nations. Polish troops had seized this territory while participating in the Civil War against the Bolshevik Revolution. In the pact with Nazi Germany, the Russians had reclaimed it. . . .

I did not receive a direct reply to this letter, but I could not reproach him. I was fully aware that after his return from the ill-fated journey to Ottawa in the fall of 1942 he was determined to finish the two novels. Helen quoted him as declaring, "Damn it all, I am going to work on a novel, and I would like to see anyone take me away from it."

The novel, *The Bulwark,* was at that time two-thirds completed. It told the story of a Quaker family and it required much careful research, understanding and imagination. There had been a great amount of work yet to finish. I did not realize, as I do now, that I should have continued sending letters and material to him without waiting for replies. He might have found a letter from me now and then helpful. During this period Helen was dragging him off to all kinds of churches and cults, because she really believed it was good for him.

Thus, world-shaking events passed without any exchange of comments between us: April 12, 1945, the death of President Roosevelt; May 8th, V.E. Day; July 17, the Potsdam Conference —and the most earth-shaking event of all—which presaged a nightmarish era in the planet's history, reducing all the strategies of national power struggles to a stultifying balance of terror—the atom bomb dropped on Hiroshima on August 6, 1945, and a second, on Nagasaki, August 9. These events were not even mentioned in Dreiser's letter of August 13!

It was at this crucial period in history that Theodore Dreiser withdrew from active participation in mass protest movements to finish two novels, the rough drafts of which had been prepared long before he became a crusading pamphleteer. He realized that time was running out for him. His last letter to me (August 13, 1945) from King's Road, Hollywood, reflects his preoccupation with literary work:

"It's a long time between letters or rather letters between us but I'm always cheered when I get one from you ... your 'so disciplined and positive,' as well as active in your social labors — so much so that I always think of you as writing and slaving on behalf of the underprivileged. Yet whether I live by your standards or not I always wish that you lived nearer — or nearest to me so that I might see and talk with you. Failing that as I do, I take it out in thinking nice things of you and our so pleasant and informative trip through Russia.

"Alas, I didn't get to N.Y. this last year or I would have called on you at Bridgeport. The reason is that I've been so busy first finishing a long contemplated novel — *The Bulwark* — and second working on a second novel — *The Stoic* which is not wholly finished but so near it that it will be done in a few weeks — maybe two or three. Meantime I've had one ill and another, an attack of rheumatism for one thing, which is now gone — also a touch of arthritis — but I'm fairly ok now.

"Meanwhile — well I attend meetings betimes — write statements for this publication or that and try my hand at a short story. I have put over two movies — *Sister Carrie,* although bought and paid for by RKO has been shelved — why God only knows. It is a natural for the movies but there appears to be some moral or social ill in it which causes the buyers to store it in an iron safe and then forget it. So — well such is the news. More than that I can only wish to see you again. Affectionately, TD. Here's luck to your work."

Literary critics have had much to say about these last two books Theodore Dreiser worked so hard to finish before his death. *The Bulwark,* some like to believe, indicated that he turned to religion at the end of his life. Actually, he turned to writing *about* religion. His respect for the Quakers as a religious group, especially for their founder George Fox, whom he called "the greatest prophet since Jesus Christ," moved him to write a novel about a Quaker family. He wrote, as always in his fiction, not about his personal views but about those of his characters.

His old friend and literary secretary, Marguerite Tjader Harris, together with Helen, helped him finish *The Bulwark.* In an interview about her own book, *Theodore Dreiser: a New Dimension,* (Bridgeport *Sunday Post,* September 26, 1965), Mrs. Harris praised *The Bulwark* as containing "the essence of a wonderful movie. It seems to me that it has a typical American theme." She was then at work editing Dreiser's *Notes on Life.* She told the interviewer that "chiefly as a result of her work with Dreiser on these notes on religion and philosophy she developed a personal interest in religion which led her to become a Catholic."

Dreiser was violently against Catholicism as a religious institution. Not until he was 13 was he permitted to go to a public instead of a Catholic school. So it is hard to believe that his notes on religion led Mrs. Harris to become a Catholic.

Replying to my "Dutch unklish" criticisms of the proofs of *Dreiser Looks at Russia,* he had made a clear distinction:

"Philosophically and practically there is a vast difference between *religion* and *dogmatic religion.* There is, for instance, the religion which is a response to as well as an awe or reverence before the beauty and wisdom of creative energy. Many people – free of dogma – enjoy it. . . ."

I believe this more accurately reflects his attitude toward religion than the trite assertions of literary critics about Dreiser's "turning to religion" toward the end of his life.

John Lydenberg writes in his essay on Dreiser, "Ishmael in the Jungle" (*American Radicals,* Monthly Review Press, 1957):

"The mysticism that had always lurked behind his materialism came increasingly to the fore. . . . He sought restlessly for an absolute of his own. The outcome of his search appears in his posthumous books. . . . *The Stoic* ends with the heroine's rather soggy conversion to Yoga. *The Bulwark* much more convincingly depicts a Quaker's doubts and his ultimate reconciliation to religion. . . . On Good Friday Dreiser took Communion in a Congregational Church. In the fall he joined the Communist Party. . . . If, toward the end, he found some peace in the mysticisms of Eastern religions, or the mystery of sharing of Christ's body and blood, or the symbolism of world brotherhood in Communism, this did not mean he had fallen into acceptance of his father's puritan moralism or Russia's totalitarianism."

As to the soggy ending of *The Stoic*: On the day before his death on December 28, Dreiser was working with Helen on the next to the last chapter. She finished the book after his death. It was Helen who was studying the cults such as Yoga and Rosicrucianism. It was Helen who, in all kindness, was dragging him off to Protestant churches such as the Congregational and Christian Scientist. She sincerely wanted to find spiritual peace in religion not only for herself (and living with Dreiser she needed it) but also for him.

As for Dreiser's finding any peace in the "mystery of sharing Christ's body and blood," I think he would say, "That's the bunk." I myself was reared in a Protestant Church, and I believe that most of the congregation like myself, quietly conformed to this ritual without that gruesome thought disturbing our peace of mind.

The "moralism" of Dreiser's father was not "puritan" but German Catholic. As for Dreiser's finding "symbolism" in communism, he would have said, "What rot! Communism isn't a religion. It's a scientific plan for a socialist society in which no man can exploit the labor of another for private profit. And," he might have added, "a government which enforces that law for the welfare of all the people is the opposite of totalitarian."

Zeal for a cause is not religion. The Standard Dictionary defines religion as "recognition by man of a controlling superhuman power entitled to obedience, reverence and worship."

Toward the end of her book, Helen wrote: "During the month of June (1945) Dreiser was considering the possibility of applying for membership in the Communist Party. Up to that time, he had always said he would never join any party. But he was convinced that they would succeed in stamping out Fascism throughout the world. As he said: 'Theirs were the first and clearest voices raised against the march of aggression in China, Ethiopia and Spain.'" His application was dated July 20, 1945.

The Daily Worker (December 31, 1945) published the text of Dreiser's letter applying for membership. It is such a clear statement of his views that I'm sure he needed little help from Marxist ghost-writers, as some critics suggest:

"... In the United States, I feel that the Communists have helped to deepen the understanding of the heritage of American freedom as a guide to action in the present. During the years when fascism was preparing for its projected conquest of the world, American Communists fought to rally the American people against fascism. They saw the danger and they proposed the remedy. ...

"These historic years have deepened my conviction that widespread membership in the Communist movement will greatly strengthen the American people, together with the anti-fascist forces throughout the world, in completely stamping out fascism and achieving new heights of world democracy, economic progress and free culture. Belief in the greatness and dignity of man has been the guiding principle of my life and work. The logic of my life and work therefore leads me to apply for membership in the Communist Party of America."

In this same frame of reference, I view his Christmas message to me. At that time, patriotic Americans trusted Stalin as the glorified leader of an ally whose heroic efforts and sacrifices were the decisive factor in our common victory.

Our Christmas tree was still up. Some presents were still under its branches. Greeting cards were on display in a gay array — one in particular which had come the day before Christmas depicting an old-fashioned winter scene was (postmarked Los Angeles, December 20, 1945):

"Dear Ruth: From this alleged summer in winter climate Christmas wishes to you. It's bright and warm today but yesterday 7 degrees above zero. Yet Stalin having returned to his job I'm cheerful again. Here's all my best thoughts for the New Year. TD."

I was at the typewriter in my cubbyhole off the hall. My tall son, Jimmie, stood in the doorway, on his face a look of grave concern. In his hand was *The New York Times,* taken from the doorstep.

"Mamma," he said gently. "Dreiser is dead."

I sat frozen in my chair for a moment. Then I rose and walked past him into the front bedroom and stood staring at the traffic on the old King's Highway to Boston. Even Jimmie could not share my sense of loss, although, in a small way, he had been a part of this strange friendship. It had been born in the new era and nurtured in its social upheavals and wars for 18 years. Now it was ended on this earth. But what we had accomplished together remained and is recorded in this book.

Theodore Dreiser   *Drawing by Hugo Gellert*

Burning of the Veils, Baku　　　　　　　*Engraving by A. Krabichezika*

APPENDIX

APPENDIX

1. Statement on Workers' Dwellings in Leningrad

Housing conditions in the different countries naturally follow the line of the cultural development of the people of a country. In Russia I find the people essentially communal in temperament, more than any other nation or race with which I have come in contact. Not only do they seem willing because of the present Soviet system to share their social necessities, according to the material limitations of the country, but temperamentally in the majority of cases they appear to prefer this manner of living.

Considering this fact, I think the new housing plan for workers and their families in Russia amply meets the present demand. Externally the houses are as attractive and as well built and well placed as the middle-class apartment houses in the best American cities. On the interior, not only because of the present housing conditions in Russia, but because of the temperament of the people themselves, the arrangement follows a line that, to the American at least, seems backward. Too many people occupy one room, too many single rooms are joined in one flat with a single toilet and a communal kitchen. To the Westerner, this would appear as unnecessary and socially injurious congestion. But as for light, air, sanitation, conveniences, it seems that they offer quite all that a modern apartment in Russia required, and obviously it is a really tremendous and splendid advance over the past.

Nov. 28, 1927   *(Signed)* THEODORE DREISER
Leningrad, U.S.S.R.

2. Statement on Leaving the Soviet Union

After a two months' visit in Soviet Russia, I should like before I leave for the United States to give to the Russian public the first statement of my general impressions:

As a westerner, accustomed to the comparatively mild climate of the United States, I can only look upon Russia as a boreal world that would try any save those born of its very soil. Russians ought to be hardy because they survive so much that people of milder climes could not endure. To me, at times and in places, it seems to possess a kind of harsh beauty born of biting winds and vast places. That man should find it necessary to conquer it at all seems almost pitiful.

311

Yet dotted as it is with so huge a population, hitherto restrained by such untutored conditions, it seems not a little astounding that it should be the scene of the latest experiment in human government. Personally, I am an individualist and shall die one. In all this communistic welter, I have seen nothing that dissuades me in the least from my earliest perceptions of the necessities of man. One of these is the individual dream of self-advancement, and I cannot feel that even here communism has altered that in the least. On the other hand, after the crushing weight of czarism and the unbridled capitalism that one sees in places, I can sympathize with the emotions of those who swung from oppression of the mass to their unlimited emanicipation and authority. It is so plain that just now not the individual in general but the individual in particular, as an artisan and little more, comes first. Everything is to be done for him; the intellectual — assuming that the laborer has the mentality so to do — is to be used by him, as a servant of his mass needs. Naturally, as an individualist this makes me smile, for I see only the most individualistic political leaders of Europe trying to guide him to an understanding of what this means, that even now he grasps or fully believes it, I doubt. More likely it is the shimmering array of material benefits dangled before him that interests and enthralls him and what he actually believes is that great and powerful individuals are now kind enough to aid him in his struggle for a better life. And he is grateful to them for that. And so am I. But that the right of the superior brain to the superior directing and ruling positions has been done away with I question. Really I do not believe it. In Russia as elsewhere I am sure you will find the sly and the self-interested as well as the kind and the wise slipping into the positions of authority, executing for the rank and file the necessary program which guarantees their comfort. And as time goes on, if not now, with a much larger return for their services. It is a survival which I for one am sure will never be completely abrogated.

Now as for what this superior group of idealists have done for Russia so far I have only praise. For one thing, and to my immense delight, they have swept dogmatic and brain-stultifying religion from its position of authority and cast it into the background of importance where it belongs. Furthermore, they have given to the collective mentality of Russia freedom to expand, and while perhaps this expansion is a little too much colored by the new dogmas of communism, I do not really object, for exact communism is not by any means in force here now and I doubt if it will be much so in the future. For unless I miss my guess, the Russian mind is at bottom a realistic mind and it will see life for what it is — a struggle not to be too much handicapped by the incurably incompetent any more than it is to be too dogmatically ruled by the self-seeking and indifferent materialist.

I am pleased by the enormous housing program and the material evidence of its fulfillment in every part of the Union. It is wonderful to see the new factories, the new schools, hospitals, clubs and scientific institutions which are now already dotting the land. I sincerely hope that this vast enthusiasm for the modernization of Russia and the introduction of western facilities of every kind will not slacken until the land is the paradise which this most amazing group of idealists wish it to be. It certainly is a land that needs and deserves a brighter day and a gayer spirit. And I for one would do nothing anywhere to counteract the fulfillment of this program. On the other hand, there are certain obvious defects in either the Russian temperament, or the fulfillment of this program, or both, which I think should be attended to now. One of these is the immediate care of the thousands of homeless children whom one encounters in every part of Russia. It is useless to say as many do that the government as yet lacks either the means or the facilities for their assumption and care. The trade unions, I notice, do not lack means for their new homes and their new clubs and new theaters. But they had better suspend action on some of these material comforts for themselves until they have done the needful thing for these children, and it is a shame and an outrage, a commentary on the Russian temperament itself, too dark to be endured for one minute if the nation has that dignity and self-respect which it so consistently claims.

Another thing that strikes me as not only irritating but discreditable is the national indifference to proper sanitation. One hears so much of what is to be in the future, but there is so much that could be done right now with a little more than the will of the people to be cleaner than they are. The Russian house, the Russian yard, the Russian street, the Russian toilet, the Russian hotel, the individual Russian's attitude toward his own personal appearance, are items which convey to the westerner (and particularly to a traveler from America) a sense of something neither creditable or wholesome and which cannot possibly be excused on the ground of poverty. There are as poor people in Holland, Germany, France, and England as there are in Russia, but you would never find them tolerating the conditions which in Russia seem to be accepted as a matter of course. Cleanliness is not a matter of national law or fiat, or even prosperity, public or private, but of the very essence of the individual himself. Either he loves and responds to cleanliness or he does not. If he does, he will make untold sacrifices to keep himself free of disorder and filth; if he does not, no law this side of a bayonet will aid him. And it seems to me that the Russians whom I have seen, from the Baltic to the Caspian, are far more indifferent to the first essentials of sanitation than any of the more progressive nations of whom they now claim to be one. It will not do, as some insist, to say that all this is a matter of prosperity and equipment; it is not, I insist it is not. And unless the international slur in regard to this is to remain, the Russian, individually and not nationally, will have to bestir himself and purify as well as decorate his immediate physical surroundings.

Your hotels, trains, railway stations and restaurants are too dirty and too poorly equipped. You do not wash your windows often enough. You do not let in enough air. You either overheat or underheat the chambers which you occupy. You live too many in one room and are even lunatic enough to identify it with a communistic spirit. I rise to complain. And I suggest in this connection that more individualism and less communism would be to the great advantage of this mighty country.

Now as to the future of this great program, I think that it will succeed providing first, that the program which the government now has of introducing the latest labor-saving devices in every phase of the national life is fulfilled, and second, that the discrepancy between the cost of manufacture and the wages of the worker is bridged. For as I see it, as yet there is too much effort to make the laborer socially comfortable and too little to make him thoroughly efficient. Really there should be no talk of the seven-hour day until the workers are earning enough to pay for the latest type of machinery which would make such a day possible.

In the next place, one of the staggering problems which confronts this government is that of the peasant and the land—one hundred and twenty million peasants, the enlightening of whom in regard to modern agricultural methods is still incipient. It is true that there are a large number of what in America would be known as agricultural stations, with all the latest information and machinery in regard to farming and stock-raising. But it is one thing to take this information to the peasant and another to make him accept it. Mostly, unless I am maliciously informed, he desires nothing so much as to be let alone, to be allowed to go along in the way he had hither-to gone. The problem of interesting him has barely been touched and I see that his indifference is one of your severest trials.

Now my solution would be for the government to divide the land into departments and according to its peculiar potentialities, that it place at the head of each department an agriculturist or board of agriculturists whose business would be to develop it quite as any commercial or financial prospect anywhere would be developed. The government should provide machinery and whatever other equipment might be necessary and then employ farmers quite as a factory employs hands. They should be organized in unions, paid so much a day, limited to so many hours of work and allowed to look after their own welfare quite as trade unionists now look after theirs. By this method, their efficiency might be standardized; farm schools could be operated at the source of the crop supply. The literature, the equipment and the practical methods would all be at the door of the farmer-unionist and by that method the entire possibilities of the enormous agricultural area of Russia be brought into full force. If this could be done, most certainly Russia would leap into the forefront of nations, economically stable and powerful. Also she would be the first to solve this disconcerting and depressing problem which now faces every nation, capitalist or otherwise, the world over.

In spite of many difficulties connected with this trip, I have appreciated the opportunity given me by the Soviet Government of witnessing the details of this great experiment and I have only the kindest thoughts of and the best wishes for its eventual success.

Odessa, Jan. 13th, 1928   THEODORE DREISER

3. Dorothy Dudley's Comment on Dreiser

Commentaries after Theodore Dreiser's death tended to picture him as a great American writer who retired during the last years of his life. In my chronological account of his activities after his return from the Russian tour in 1928, I believe I have presented evidence of the most dedicated social and literary works of his entire life in the period from 1928 to December 28, 1945.

In support of my evaluation, I can present no more convincing statement than that of Dorothy Dudley, his old friend and biographer in her reply to a news article and editorial which had appeared in the New York Herald Tribune *(December 30, 1945):*

To the New York *Herald Tribune:*
As one of the biographers of Theodore Dreiser, allow me to correct the impression given by your article and editorial of last Sunday. You say that "Mr. Dreiser had lived in semi-retirement since establishing his home in Hollywood ten years ago," and that except for the two novels, *The Bulwark* and *The Stoic,* finished shortly before his death, he had "done little writing in recent years." . . .

To my knowledge in the last fifteen years Dreiser has not only completed the novels you mention, of Dreiserian scope, but had gone far toward working out a system of philosophy . . . in reference to which, according to your editorial, "he felt he had to coin a word to describe himself precisely — equitist."

When one considers these three projects alone . . . "little writing" appears to me a frivolous comment on so great a man. Dreiser's publisher told me that Dreiser did something unprecedented in 1943 — paid back his advance on these books in order to have liberty to finish

them without pressure. After the publication of *An American Tragedy*
Dreiser put out in the next seven years five books: *Moods, A Gallery
of Women, Dawn, Dreiser Looks at Russia, Tragic America*. It was a
period of transition in the life of this giant.

During the decade of the '30s and well into the '40s, Dreiser was
turning away from his initial premise: "Writing about life as he saw
it"—and turning more and more passionately toward rebuilding the
very structure of society.

In defense of his proposals and hopes, far from retiring, he wrote
a wealth of articles and delivered in person many addresses throughout the Americas and Europe. He worked actively for Republican
Spain, Socialist-Communist France, Soviet Russia, the radical labor
movement here, organized labor everywhere. More and more he
pinned his faith to the pattern of Soviet Russia. Often he worked on
the danger line of class and racial wars. At the same time he wrote
and spoke constantly for a Secretaryship of Art in the Cabinet, for a
national theater and many other art projects. To him culture and good
government should be inseparable. In contrast to his earlier years as a
creative writer, Dreiser entered indefatigably the political forum of
the Left. He proclaimed himself more and more openly an enemy of
privileged English aristocracy and American capitalism. In a word,
he did not withdraw; he was ostracized by the ruling classes by virtual exclusion from their press....

Are these years the record of a man in semi-retirement? No, Theodore Dreiser died in action.

New York, January 1, 1946   DOROTHY DUDLEY

INDEX